THE PHILOSOPHY OF
SCHOPENHAUER

THE PHILOSOPHY OF

SCHOPENHAUER

Edited, with an introduction by I R W I N E D M A N

THE

MODERN LIBRARY

NEW YORK

68- 7699

INTRODUCTION

THE popularity of Schopenhauer with a large un-
academic public is easily explained. Part of the explanation
is to be found in the extraordinarily vivacious and luxurious
discourse that was his medium. He is one of the great
German prose writers, and even in translation there is the
tang of sense, the pungency of realistic observation in his
pages. But there is something more. He seems to the reflective layman to have hit upon the inner essence and
divined the essential tragedy of human existence. His
philosophy is not the closet dialectic of the schools, though
even in the dialectical branches of thought he is nobody's
fool; it is philosophy in the old and appealing meaning of
wisdom of life. The plain man here recognises something he has long felt and never articulated. This philosophy is the alert, half-sad, half-cynical harvest of a candid
eye. That is why lawyers and men of the world, ac-
quainted with the disillusioned realms of experience, why
adolescents just waking up from their own dreams, have
found in Schopenhauer a philosophy they could feel at
home with. Schopenhauer's philosophy is the Pathétique
Symphony of nineteenth-century thought. Like that popular piece of musical *Weltshmerz*, it has its limitations.
These any technical student of philosophy is free to point
out, as is also any classical critic of the romantic temperament. There is at once in these pages a high hand with
the philosophical respectabilities and a soft luxuriance with
grief that are the despair of the sober technician in philosophy and the reposeful classicists in literature. But below

the carelessness of technique and the irony and pity there is a high, impeccable and irrefutable insight. The Western world has nowhere found a more complete exposition of the essence of things as it appears to those who live by impulse, and the tragedy of things for those who know that impulse must always be partially frustrated, and the life that generates impulse ultimately doomed. Instead of trying, as so many philosophers have tried, to resolve the discords of experience into a smooth and illusory coherence, Schopenhauer faced those discords and built his philosophy upon them. This disillusioning feat of picturesque honesty has impressed those who have found most other philosophies systems of obscure optimism.

The biography of a philosopher is, under the aspect of eternity, irrelevant to his life. What a man says and what that saying signifies is the sole just preoccupation of a philosophical critic. It is, in a profound sense, none of his business why a thinker came to say the things he did or why he chose to say them in the particular fashion for which he is famous. Yet in the case of Schopenhauer, if ever, the life illuminates the doctrine and the philosophy is an expression of the man. The pessimism, the ill-temper, the sallies of poetic insight and of realistic perception, the obsession with the obsession of sex, the fulminations against academic philosophers and the failure to exemplify their virtues, all seem to be functions of the life Schopenhauer led and the man he was. Born at Danzig, on February 22, 1788, he was brought up in the family of a wealthy merchant. A streak of insanity ran in the paternal side of the family, and the death of Schopenhauer's father in a canal at Hamburg seemed to be a suicide. In his life, Schopenhauer was moody, high strung, and so great a lover of liberty that when the free city of Danzig lost its independence to Poland, in 1793, he moved to Hamburg. Schopenhauer's mother, one of the popular novelists of her day, on her husband's death moved to Weimar, where her salon became the center of the intellectual and literary colony gathered there. Schopenhauer and his mother could not bear each other's company, and after a definite quarrel during which the mother pushed her son downstairs, he left Weimar, never to see his mother again.

Schopenhauer, on his father's death, took a course in the Gymnasium; later, on an allowance from his mother, a university course. During this intellectual education, he lived the life of a worldling and a man about town. He was almost influenced by Fichte to join a war of liberation against Napoleon, but he himself thought that "Napoleon only gave untrammelled and concentrated utterance to that self-assertion and lust for more life which weaker mortals feel, but most perforce disguise."

Schopenhauer won his doctor's degree by his dissertation on the fourfold root of sufficient reason, published in 1833, which turned out to be the cornerstone of his system. This book is the intellectual foundation of his major work, "The World as Will and Idea." It is a clear analysis of the principle of causation, in its physical, logical, and metaphysical senses. The first edition of Schopenhauer's masterpiece attracted comparatively no attention. In 1836 "The Will in Nature" was published, in 1844 the enlarged edition of "The World as Will and Idea." His final two works were the "Ground Problem of Ethics," published in 1841, and two substantial volumes of "Parerga et Paridipomena," translated into English as the "Essays."

Schopenhauer had a brief, inglorious adventure into academic life. In 1822 he was invited to lecture at the University of Berlin as Privat Docent. Choosing the same hours as Hegel, then the reigning lord in philosophy, he found his classrooms empty of students. He resigned in disgust, and, a little later, fleeing the cholera epidemic in Berlin, went to Frankfort, where he settled down for the remainder of his life. He died there at seventy-two. He lived modestly on an income from an interest in his father's firm, travelled a little in Italy, but for the most part lived out his life in a boarding house, having for his sole friend and companion a dog. Despite the fact that the universities ignored him, his philosophy gained fame, and what is more, an ardent personal following among men of affairs and men of the world. Praise came to him from Wagner for his philosophy of music and from Nietzsche for his philosophy of will. At seventy, he was a world figure. At seventy-two he died alone, on September 21, 1860.

There is little in his life to stir one to personal admiration. It is that of a rather sharp, vain recluse, haunted in his earlier years by sex, in his later ones by the lust for fame and an embittered contempt of his academic contemporaries. His fears of poison and of violence, his ungoverned fury about women, his cynical underscoring of all the seamy sides of human conduct, the absence in his life of every tie of affection, do not make an amiable figure. But on the credit side must be placed a genuine metaphysical zeal, a fanatic devotion to his conception of truth, and the passion of a romantic poet.

The philosophy of Schopenhauer takes its cue, almost borrows its technique, from Kant. The latter had instituted "A Copernican revolution" in philosophy by declaring that the apparent structure of nature was truly a structure of appearance: the forms of understanding constituted the apparent order of things. Schopenhauer agreed with Kant, on this general point, and gave the point his own formulation. "All the furniture of Heaven and earth was an appearance whose constitution was determined by the principle of sufficient reason, that fourfold form of those connections by which the understanding understood," and in understanding which it constituted the phenomenal world. The whole apparently so solid world of matter is simply the nexus of things in time and space, a nexus which is simply another name for the law of causation, itself an unescapable form of the understanding. It is unnecessary to follow Schopenhauer in his detailed analysis of the forms of the principle of sufficient reason, those orders of physical, logical, mathematical, and moral determinants which regulate our knowledge of, which constitute and guarantee the nature of, the world of phenomena. It is unnecessarily superfluous for the understanding of his position to trace his analysis of perception and conception and the relation between them. The whole of Book I, which is concerned with these, is done with engaging lucidity, though its analysis of mathematics is questionable. But the whole of it is aimed to make just one fundamental point. It is the logical prelude to a discussion of the realm of the real. It is an analysis of that intellectual schema of the mind which confines knowledge always to knowledge of appearances.

It is a critique of the world that knowledge reveals. The objective world which seems indeed so objective is indeed truly so. It is object for a subject, and the nature of its objectivity is determined by the nature of that knowledge which the subject may have. The whole of that cosmos which the materialist boasts to be matter, is matter surely enough. But matter is itself simply another name for causation; causation is the union of space and time; space and time are forms of understanding; save that they are the subject's avenues of knowledge, there would be no matter. The world, for each individual, is his "idea" of it. It is not in that "world as idea" that reality is to be found. Reality in the ordinary sense is unknowable, since what is knowable is only the order of appearances. This whole external world is simply a construction of the intellect, and the intellect is simply the instrument that arises in the service of that inner reality which each of us experiences as the desire which he is aware of in his own body, in his physical tensions, in his unconscious strivings, in his will. That Will, which alone is immediately known to us, is recognised, too, in Nature. From the pull of gravitation and the tendency of crystals to form a pattern, from the movements of the stars to the consciously directed volitions of man, the inner nature of things is not that world which the intellect knows, but that Will which the individual experiences in his own blind impulses and which he finds exemplified and repeated on a cosmic scale in the inner processes of Nature.

Kant had found the Reality in an Unknowable that was posited as an act of practical reason or Faith. For Schopenhauer, the Unknowable Reality is that Will in the interests of which Knowledge arises, that Will which is a blind striving, in whose service the slavish intellect constructs a practical and illusive world. It is a will toward no rational end. It is a blind will to live. In human beings it cloaks itself with sophistries of intellect and rational excuses. In brute and in unconscious nature, it operates with naked blindness.

"Spinoza says that if a stone which has been projected through the air, had consciousness, it would believe that it was moving of its own free will. I add this only, that the stone would be right. The impulse given it is for the stone what the motive is for me, and what in the case of the stone appears as cohesion, gravitation, rigidity, is in its inner nature the same as that which I recognise in myself as will, and what the stone also, if knowledge were given to it, would recognise as will."

Schopenhauer recognises several important facts as pointing toward the universal and unified reality that is the Will. One is inner teleology, the harmonious connivances of organs to the fulfillment of an end; another is the recognisable types and unities in all the multifarious variety of transient individuals that to knowledge constitute the picture of Nature. Individuals vary in time and space; they are variables and temporal instances of those invariant eternal grades of

objectification in which the unitary and universal Will mani‑
fests itself.

Schopenhauer finds two grounds for pessimism in the fact
that the blind striving will is the inner reality of nature
and the essence of life. Those two grounds for pessimism
lie first in the fact that the will is doomed to privation. It is
striving because it is unfulfilled. Secondly, where it does
find fulfillment, that fulfillment turns out to be illusion.
Schopenhauer sings a long dirge of sadness, a long lugubrious
description of the way in which the human will oscillates
between suffering and boredom. Half of life is the stinging
pain of frustration, the other half the dull pain of boredom.
Schopenhauer is the apotheosis of romantic irony expressing
a romantic disgust over a world that does not meet the needs
of the assertive will, and the irony of that will which finds
the emptiness of what it thought it needed.

There is nothing for Schopenhauer, then, but to seek some
method of salvation and escape. Happiness is impossible since
where one thought one was going to obtain it, one finds
nothing but unhappiness. The most that one can hope for is
a Quietistic redemption. That is possible for brief moments
in the world of Art, for the world of Art as Schopenhauer
describes it in his Book III is the world as Platonic idea. In
the quite momentary contemplation of Art and in the pro‑
ductions of genius the human will recognises those eternal
grades of the will, its changeless essences which outlive the
vicissitudes of change itself, and are shining and implacable
archetypes in which the will may escape change and time,
suffering and disillusion. In the rapt contemplation of the
sculptured essence of man, men may escape the restless striv‑
ing of their own souls and the restless and innumerable tem‑
poral vanities of individual men. In the experience of the
eternal types and patterns of love in lyric poetry men may
escape the pains and frustrations of their own transient loves
and tragedies of life. And in the flow and movement of

music the will recognises in the intimate and poignant stream of sound its own intimate and poignant life. If the plastic and the literary arts reveal the eternal forms of the world, it is in music that the will itself is immediately rendered. And so for Schopenhauer music is the most perfect and successful of the arts since it reveals the will with immediacy and urgency to itself.

But the arts provide only moments of escape. From the changing and distracting world of time they permit brief flights into the timeless and will-less perception of artistic contemplation. Scientific and practical knowledge are bounded by the provincial demands, personal cravings, the temporal distractions of the will. In the arts one escapes at once the world of illusion that is the world of knowledge, the world of pain and disillusion, that is the world as will. But one escapes for moments only, one returns with increased bitterness with the world of things in time and space to the rude pressure of desire. There must if one is to attain this, if not happiness, be a more radical way of escape. That is provided in Schopenhauer's analysis not by the momentary escape of the æsthete, but by the eternal escape of the ascetic. Since the world out of which all pain and ennui flow is itself an objectification of the will, if one denies the will, one denies the world. To become profoundly and radically ascetic is the way to peace and to Nirvana. By a radical denial of the world, one escapes the world, for with the denial of the will the world is destroyed. That radical denial is possible through the discovery that Buddha, from whom Schopenhauer learned so much, made so long ago. When through the insight of sympathy it is recognised that one's own sufferings are part of that universal suffering which is the penalty of the assertion of a blind will doomed to frustration, then the futility of one's own will against that of others, then the misery involved in the assertion of will at all becomes evident. Insight produces sympathy and sympathy produces saintliness. The artist and the ascetic escape from the world into a momentary and paradisial vision of the eternal quietudes of the arts. A saint escapes by reducing the world to nothingness, the denial of his own imperious and blind and indubitably frustrative will. To become a saint by abnegation is to be at peace. Suicide which might seem a more easy and immediate escape is for Schopenhauer no escape at all, for suicide is simply a more emphatic and petulant assertion of the will. It is a distraction of the body which is simply one instance of the will; it is not the denial of that universal blind striving will which is the source of all suffering. Schopenhauer offers us the choice of two ways out of the sufferings and disillusions of life. One, the amiable transient way of the fine arts; two, the sanctified and eternal way of the saint.

"The World as Will and Idea" is of course Schopenhauer's masterpiece, but his "Essays," too, have had a singular power of suasion, illumination and charm to innumerable readers whom the ordinary academic philosopher can neither persuade, illuminate nor charm. Some of his essays are famous for a kind of obstreperous cynicism such as his essay on women; some are notable for their sudden incisive light on intellectual method or conception as in his essay on history. But it is his major work that will always remain of the chiefest interest. For all of its extravagance or perhaps because of it he will remain the urbane spokesman of all those who remain throughout life at once wistful and disillusioned, and recognise the facts of experience and wish that they were not so. His rank as a metaphysician has never been very high, his idealism is both second hand and largely borrowed from Kant, and for all its parade of logical apparatus, it is none too consistent or convincing. His delineation of the characteristic dilemma of the romantic will which can never get what it wants and can never love what it gets is unsurpassed in the history of thought. His pages on the insight of genius and the quality of æsthetic perception, his luminous suggestions on the art of music, his dramatic and vivid rendering of that pity and that negation which constitute the life of saintliness will give him a permanent place.

He was the first one, too, in the history of thought emphatically to insist on the primacy of will over intellect, on the instrumental character of mind in life and in philosophy. He started a movement to which James, Bergson, and Dewey owe not a little. And he combines in his writings the elements of three usually distinct and disparate personalities, a man of the world, a man of thought, and a man of letters. The net result in his case was one of the unparalleled works of art in the history of philosophy; "The World as Will and Idea" remains a piece of speculative literature by a writer with the imagination of a poet and the precision of an observing realist. It was his imagination that, borrowing its materials from Kantian idealism, constructed a highly romantic metaphysical world; it was his realism that gave him a sense of the suffering, injustices, and disillusions of life. It is this combination that has made him appeal at once to the perpetual adolescence of life and to hard-headed middle-aged realists. He remains one of the very great second-raters in the history of European thought, and a permanent exposition of that mood which beginning with the self frets at an unsatisfactory cosmos, and in the midst of which it does not seek what seems impossible happiness, but from which it tries to escape to a heaven of quietude and peace. It is a quaint irony that Schopenhauer, at heart a cynical epicurean, should have become the *vade mecum* of the æsthete and the spiritual ascetic. In whatever quarrels one may find with his philosophy, his prose will always remain immitigably convincing.

NEW YORK
May, 1928

IRWIN EDMAN

First Book

THE WORLD AS IDEA

———

FIRST ASPECT

THE IDEA SUBORDINATED TO THE PRINCIPLE OF SUF-
FICIENT REASON: THE OBJECT OF EXPERIENCE
AND SCIENCE

Sors de l'enfance, ami réveille toi!
—Jean Jacques Rousseau.

THE PHILOSOPHY OF SCHOPENHAUER

I

§ 1. "THE world is my idea":—this is a truth which holds good for everything that lives and knows, though man alone can bring it into reflective and abstract consciousness. If he really does this, he has attained to philosophical wisdom. It then becomes clear and certain to him that what he knows is not a sun and an earth, but only an eye that sees a sun, a hand that feels an earth; that the world which surrounds him is there only as idea, *i.e.*, only in relation to something else, the consciousness, which is himself. If any truth can be asserted *a priori*, it is this: for it is the expression of the most general form of all possible and thinkable experience: a form which is more general than time, or space, or causality, for they all presuppose it; and each of these, which we have seen to be just so many modes of the principle of sufficient reason, is valid only for a particular class of ideas; whereas the antithesis of object and subject is the common form of all these classes, is that form under which alone any idea of whatever kind it may be, abstract or intuitive, pure or empirical, is possible and thinkable. No truth therefore is more certain, more independent of all others, and less in need of proof than this, that all that exists for knowledge, and therefore this whole world, is only object in relation to subject, perception of a perceiver, in a word, idea. This is obviously true of the past

3

and the future, as well as of the present, of what is farthest
off, as of what is near; for it is true of time and space themselves, in which alone these distinctions arise. All that in
any way belongs or can belong to the world is inevitably
thus conditioned through the subject, and exists only for the
subject. The world is idea.

This truth is by no means new. It was implicitly involved in the sceptical reflections from which Descartes
started. Berkeley, however, was the first who distinctly
enunciated it, and by this he has rendered a permanent
service to philosophy, even though the rest of his teaching
should not endure. Kant's primary mistake was the neglect
of this principle, as is shown in the appendix. How early
again this truth was recognised by the wise men of India,
appearing indeed as the fundamental tenet of the Vedânta
philosophy ascribed to Vyasa, is pointed out by Sir William
Jones in the last of his essays: "On the philosophy of the
Asiatics" (Asiatic Researches, vol. iv., p. 164), where he
says, "The fundamental tenet of the Vedânta school consisted not in denying the existence of matter, that is, of
solidity, impenetrability, and extended figure (to deny which
would be lunacy), but in correcting the popular notion of
it, and in contending that it has no essence independent of
mental perception; that existence and perceptibility are
convertible terms." These words adequately express the
compatibility of empirical reality and transcendental ideality.

In this first book, then, we consider the world only from
this side, only so far as it is idea. The inward reluctance
with which any one accepts the world as merely his idea,
warns him that this view of it, however true it may be, is
nevertheless one-sided, adopted in consequence of some
arbitrary abstraction. And yet it is a conception from which
he can never free himself. The defectiveness of this view
will be corrected in the next book by means of a truth which
is not so immediately certain as that from which we start

here; a truth at which we can arrive only by deeper research and more severe abstraction, by the separation of what is different and the union of what is identical. This truth, which must be very serious and impressive if not awful to every one, is that a man can also say and must say, "the world is my will."

In this book, however, we must consider separately that aspect of the world from which we start, its aspect as knowable, and therefore, in the meantime, we must, without reserve, regard all presented objects, even our own bodies (as we shall presently show more fully), merely as ideas, and call them merely ideas. By so doing we always abstract from will (as we hope to make clear to every one further on), which by itself constitutes the other aspect of the world. For as the world is in one aspect entirely *idea*, so in another it is entirely *will*. A reality which is neither of these two, but an object in itself (into which the thing in itself has unfortunately dwindled in the hands of Kant), is the phantom of a dream, and its acceptance is an *ignis fatuus* in philosophy.

§ 2. That which knows all things and is known by none is the subject. Thus it is the supporter of the world, that condition of all phenomena, of all objects which is always presupposed throughout experience; for all that exists, exists only for the subject. Every one finds himself to be subject, yet only in so far as he knows, not in so far as he is an object of knowledge. But his body is object, and therefore from this point of view we call it idea. For the body is an object among objects, and is conditioned by the laws of objects, although it is an immediate object. Like all objects of perception, it lies within the universal forms of knowledge, time and space, which are the conditions of multiplicity. The subject, on the contrary, which is always the knower, never the known, does not come under these forms, but is presupposed by them; it has therefore neither multiplicity nor its opposite unity. We never know it, but it is always the knower wherever there is knowledge.

So then the world as idea, the only aspect in which we consider it at present, has two fundamental, necessary, and inseparable halves. The one half is the object, the forms of which are space and time, and through these multiplicity. The other half is the subject, which is not in space and time, for it is present, entire and undivided, in every percipient being. So that any one percipient being, with the object, constitutes the whole world as idea just as fully as the existing millions could do; but if this one were to disappear, then the whole world as idea would cease to be. These halves are therefore inseparable even for thought, for each of the two has meaning and existence only through and for the other, each appears with the other and vanishes with it. They limit each other immediately; where the object begins the subject ends. The universality of this limitation is shown by the fact that the essential and hence universal forms of all objects, space, time, and causality, may, without knowledge of the object, be discovered and fully known from a consideration of the subject, *i.e.*, in Kantian language, they lie *a priori* in our consciousness. That he discovered this is one of Kant's principal merits, and it is a great one. I however go beyond this, and maintain that the principle of sufficient reason is the general expression for all these forms of the object of which we are *a priori* conscious; and that therefore all that we know purely *a priori* is merely the content of that principle and what follows from it; in it all our certain *a priori* knowledge is expressed. In my essay on the principle of sufficient reason I have shown in detail how every possible object comes under it; that is, stands in a necessary relation to other objects, on the one side as determined, on the other side as determining: this is of such wide application, that the whole existence of all objects, so far as they are objects, ideas and nothing more, may be entirely traced to this their necessary relation to each other, rests only in it, is in fact merely relative; but of this more presently. I have further shown, that the necessary relation which the principle of sufficient reason expresses generally, appears in other forms corresponding to the classes into which objects are divided, according to their possibility; and again that by these forms the proper division of the classes is tested. I take it for granted that what I said in this earlier essay is known and present to the reader, for if it had not been already said it would necessarily find its place here.

§ 3. The chief distinction among our ideas is that between ideas of perception and abstract ideas. The latter form just one class of ideas, namely concepts, and these are the possession of man alone of all creatures upon earth. The capacity for these, which distinguishes him from all the lower animals, has always been called reason.[1] We shall consider these abstract ideas by themselves later, but, in the first place, we shall speak exclusively of the *ideas of perception*. These comprehend the whole visible world, or the sum total of experience, with the conditions of its possibility. We have already observed that it is a highly important discovery of Kant's, that these very conditions, these forms of the visible world, *i.e.*, the absolutely universal element in its perception, the common property of all its phenomena, space and time, even when taken by themselves and apart from their content, can, not only be thought in the abstract, but also be directly perceived; and that this perception or intuition is not some kind of phantasm arising from constant recurrence in experience, but is so entirely independent of experience that we must rather regard the

[1] Kant is the only writer who has confused this idea of reason, and in this connection I refer the reader to the Appendix, and also to my "Grundprobleme der Ethik": Grundl. dd. Moral. § 6, pp 148-154, first and second editions.

latter as dependent on it, inasmuch as the qualities of space and time, as they are known in *a priori* perception or intuition, are valid for all possible experience, as rules to which it must invariably conform. Accordingly, in my essay on the principle of sufficient reason, I have treated space and time, because they are perceived as pure and empty of content, as a special and independent class of ideas. This quality of the universal forms of intuition, which was discovered by Kant, that they may be perceived in themselves and apart from experience, and that they may be known as exhibiting those laws on which is founded the infallible science of mathematics, is certainly very important. Not less worthy of remark, however, is this other quality of time and space, that the principle of sufficient reason, which conditions experience as the law of causation and of motive, and thought as the law of the basis of judgment, appears here in quite a special form, to which I have given the name of the ground of being. In time, this is the succession of its moments, and in space the position of its parts, which reciprocally determine each other *ad infinitum*.

Any one who has fully understood from the introductory essay the complete identity of the content of the principle of sufficient reason in all its different forms, must also be convinced of the importance of the knowledge of the simplest of these forms, as affording him insight into his own inmost nature. This simplest form of the principle we have found to be time. In it each instant is, only in so far as it has effaced the preceding one, its generator, to be itself in turn as quickly effaced. The past and the future (considered apart from the consequences of their content) are empty as a dream, and the present is only the indivisible and unenduring boundary between them. And in all the other forms of the principle of sufficient reason, we shall find the same emptiness, and shall see that not time only but also space, and the whole content of both of them, *i.e.*, all that proceeds from causes and motives, has a merely relative existence, is only through and for another like to itself, *i.e.*, not more enduring. The substance of this doctrine is old: it appears in Heraclitus when he laments the eternal flux of things; in Plato when he degrades the object to that which is ever becoming, but never being; in Spinoza as the doctrine of the mere accidents of the one substance which is and endures. Kant opposes what is thus known as the mere phenomenon to the thing in itself. Lastly, the ancient wisdom of the Indian philosophers declares, "It is Mâyâ, the veil of deception, which blinds the eyes of mortals, and makes them behold a world of which they cannot say either that it is or that it is not: for it is like a dream; it is like the sunshine on the sand which the traveller takes from afar for water, or the stray piece of rope he mistakes for a snake." (These similes are repeated in innumerable passages of the Vedas and the Puranas.) But what all these mean, and that of which they all speak, is nothing more than what we have just considered—the world as idea subject to the principle of sufficient reason.

§ 4. Whoever has recognised the form of the principle of sufficient reason, which appears in pure time as such, and on which all counting and arithmetical calculation rests, has completely mastered the nature of time. Time is nothing more than that form of the principle of sufficient reason, and has no further significance. Succession is the form of the principle of sufficient reason in time, and succession is the whole nature of time. Further, whoever has recognised the principle of sufficient reason as it appears in the presentation of pure space, has exhausted the whole nature of space, which is absolutely nothing more than that possibility of the reciprocal determination of its parts by each other, which is called position. The detailed treatment of this, and the formulation in abstract conceptions of the results which flow from it, so that they may be more conveniently used, is the subject of the science of geometry. Thus also, whoever has recognised the law of causation, the aspect of the principle of sufficient reason which appears in what fills these forms (space and time) as objects of perception, that is to say, matter, has completely mastered the nature of matter as such, for matter is nothing more than causation, as any one will see at once if he reflects. Its true being is its action, nor can we possibly conceive it as having any other meaning. Only as action does it fill space and time; its action upon the immediate objects (which is itself matter) determines that perception in which alone it exists. The consequence of the action of any material object upon any other, is known only in so far as the latter acts upon the immediate object in a different way from that in which it acted before; it consists only of this. Cause and effect thus constitute the whole nature of matter; its true being is its action. (A fuller treatment of this will be found in the essay on the Principle of Sufficient Reason, § 21, p. 77.) The nature of all material things is therefore very appropriately called in German *Wirklichkeit*,[1] a word which is far more expressive than *Realität*. Again, that which is acted upon is always matter, and thus the whole being and essence of matter consists in the orderly change, which one part of it brings about in another part. The existence of matter is therefore entirely relative, according to a relation which is valid only within its limits, as in the case of time and space.

But time and space, each for itself, can be mentally presented apart from matter, whereas matter cannot be so presented apart from time and space. The form which is inseparable from it presupposes space, and the action in which its very existence consists, always imports some change, in other words a determination in time. But space

---

[1] Mira in quibusdam rebus verborum proprietas est, et consuetudo sermonis antiqui quædam efficacissimis notis signat. *Seneca,* epist. 81.

and time are not only, each for itself, presupposed by matter, but a union of the two constitutes its essence, for this, as we have seen, consists in action, *i.e.*, in causation. All the innumerable conceivable phenomena and conditions of things, might be co-existent in boundless space, without limiting each other, or might be successive in endless time without interfering with each other: thus a necessary relation of these phenomena to each other, and a law which should regulate them according to such a relation, is by no means needful, would not, indeed, be applicable: it therefore follows that in the case of all co-existence in space and change in time, so long as each of these forms preserves for itself its condition and its course without any connection with the other, there can be no causation, and since causation constitutes the essential nature of matter, there can be no matter. But the law of causation receives its meaning and necessity only from this, that the essence of change does not consist simply in the mere variation of things, but rather in the fact that at the *same part of space* there is now *one thing* and then *another*, and at *one* and the same point of time there is *here* one thing and *there* another: only this reciprocal limitation of space and time by each other gives meaning, and at the same time necessity, to a law, according to which change must take place. What is determined by the law of causality is therefore not merely a succession of things in time, but this succession with reference to a definite space, and not merely existence of things in a particular place, but in this place at a different point of time. Change, *i.e.*, variation which takes place according to the law of causality, implies always a determined part of space and a determined part of time together and in union. Thus causality unites space with time. But we found that the whole essence of matter consisted in action, *i.e.*, in causation, consequently space and time must also be united in matter, that is to say, matter must take to itself at once the distinguishing qualities both of space and time, however much these may be opposed to each other, and must unite in itself what is impossible for each of these independently, that is, the fleeting course of time, with the rigid unchangeable perduration of space: infinite divisibility it receives from both. It is for this reason that we find that co-existence, which could neither be in time alone, for time has no contiguity, nor in space alone, for space has no before, after, or now, is first established through matter. But the co-existence of many things constitutes, in fact, the essence of reality, for through it permanence first becomes possible; for permanence is only knowable in the change of something which is present along with what is permanent, while on the other hand it is only because something permanent is present along with what changes, that the latter gains the special character of change, i.e., the mutation of quality and form in the permanence of substance, that is to say, in matter.[1] If the world were in space alone, it would be rigid and immovable, without succession, without change, without action; but we know that with action, the idea of matter first appears. Again, if the world were in time alone, all would be fleeting, without persistence, without contiguity, hence without co-existence, and consequently without permanence; so that in this case also there would be no matter. Only through the union of space and time do we reach matter, and matter is the possibility of co-existence, and, through that, of permanence; through permanence again matter is the possibility of the persistence of substance in the change of its states.[2] As matter consists in the union of space and time, it bears throughout the stamp of both. It manifests its origin in

---

[1] It is shown in the Appendix that matter and substance are one.
[2] This shows the ground of the Kantian explanation of matter, that it is "that which is movable in space," for motion consists simply in the union of space and time.

space, partly through the form which is inseparable from it, but especially through its persistence (substance), the *a priori* certainty of which is therefore wholly deducible from that of space [1] (for variation belongs to time alone, but in it alone and for itself nothing is persistent). Matter shows that it springs from time by quality (accidents), without which it never exists, and which is plainly always causality, action upon other matter, and therefore change (a time concept). The law of this action, however, always depends upon space and time together, and only thus obtains meaning. The regulative function of causality is confined entirely to the determination of what must occupy *this time and this space*. The fact that we know *a priori* the unalterable characteristics of matter, depends upon this derivation of its essential nature from the forms of our knowledge of which we are conscious *a priori*.

But as the object in general is only for the subject, as its idea, so every special class of ideas is only for an equally special quality in the subject, which is called a faculty of perception. This subjective correlative of time and space, in themselves as empty forms, has been named by Kant pure sensibility; and we may retain this expression, as Kant was the first to treat of the subject, though it is not exact, for sensibility presupposes matter. The subjective correlative of matter or of causation, for these two are the same, is understanding, which is nothing more than this. To know causality is its one function, its only power; and it is a great one, embracing much, of manifold application, yet of unmistakable identity in all its manifestations. Conversely all causation, that is to say, all matter, or the whole of reality, is only for the understanding, through the understanding, and in the understanding. The first, simplest, and ever-present example of understanding is the perception of

[1] Not, as Kant holds, from the knowledge of time, as will be explained in the Appendix.

the actual world. This is throughout knowledge of the cause from the effect, and therefore all perception is intellectual. The understanding could never arrive at this perception, however, if some effect did not become known immediately, and thus serve as a starting-point. But this is the affection of the animal body. So far, then, the animal body is the *immediate object* of the subject; the perception of all other objects becomes possible through it. The changes which every animal body experiences, are immediately known, that is, felt; and as these effects are at once referred to their causes, the perception of the latter as *objects* arises. This relation is no conclusion in abstract conceptions; it does not arise from reflection, nor is it arbitrary, but immediate, necessary, and certain. It is the method of knowing of the pure understanding, without which there could be no perception; there would only remain a dull plant-like consciousness of the changes of the immediate object, which would succeed each other in an utterly unmeaning way, except in so far as they might have a meaning for the will either as pain or pleasure. But as with the rising of the sun the visible world appears, so at one stroke, the understanding, by means of its one simple function, changes the dull, meaningless sensation into perception. What the eye, the ear, or the hand feels, is not perception; it is merely its data. By the understanding passing from the effect to the cause, the world first appears as perception extended in space, varying in respect of form, persistent through all time in respect of matter; for the understanding unites space and time in the idea of matter, that is, causal action. As the world as idea exists only through the understanding, so also it exists only for the understanding.

§ 5. It is needful to guard against the grave error of supposing that because perception arises through the knowledge of causality, the relation of subject and object is that of cause and effect. For this relation subsists only between

the immediate object and objects known indirectly, thus
always between objects alone. It is this false supposition
that has given rise to the foolish controversy about the
reality of the outer world; a controversy in which dogmatism and scepticism oppose each other, and the former
appears, now as realism, now as idealism. Realism treats the
object as cause, and the subject as its effect. The idealism
of Fichte reduces the object to the effect of the subject.
Since however, and this cannot be too much emphasised,
there is absolutely no relation according to the principle of
sufficient reason between subject and object, neither of
these views could be proved, and therefore scepticism
attacked them both with success. Now, just as the law of
causality precedes perception and experience as their condition, and therefore cannot (as Hume thought) be derived
from them, so object and subject precede all knowledge,
and hence the principle of sufficient reason in general, as
its first condition; for this principle is merely the form of
all objects, the whole nature and possibility of their
existence as phenomena: but the object always presupposes
the subject; and therefore between these two there can be
no relation of reason and consequent. My essay on the
principle of sufficient reason accomplishes just this: it explains the content of that principle as the essential form
of every object—that is to say, as the universal nature of
all objective existence, as something which pertains to the
object as such; but the object as such always presupposes
the subject as its necessary correlative; and therefore the
subject remains always outside the province in which the
principle of sufficient reason is valid. The controversy as to
the reality of the outer world rests upon this false extension
of the validity of the principle of sufficient reason to the
subject also, and starting with this mistake it can never
understand itself. On the one side realistic dogmatism,
looking upon the idea as the effect of the object, desires to

separate these two, idea and object, which are really one, and to assume a cause quite different from the idea, an object in itself, independent of the subject, a thing which is quite inconceivable; for even as object it presupposes subject, and so remains its idea. Opposed to this doctrine is scepticism, which makes the same false presupposition that in the idea we have only the effect, never the cause, therefore never real being; that we always know merely the action of the object. But this object, it supposes, may perhaps have no resemblance whatever to its effect, may indeed have been quite erroneously received as the cause, for the law of causality is first to be gathered from experience, and the reality of experience is then made to rest upon it. Thus both of these views are open to the correction, firstly, that object and idea are the same; secondly, that the true being of the object of perception is its action, that the reality of the thing consists in this, and the demand for an existence of the object outside the idea of the subject, and also for an essence of the actual thing different from its action, has absolutely no meaning, and is a contradiction: and that the knowledge of the nature of the effect of any perceived object, exhausts such an object itself, so far as it is object, *i.e.*, idea, for beyond this there is nothing more to be known. So far then, the perceived world in space and time, which makes itself known as causation alone, is entirely real, and is throughout simply what it appears to be, and it appears wholly and without reserve as idea, bound together according to the law of causality. This is its empirical reality. On the other hand, all causality is in the understanding alone, and for the understanding. The whole actual, that is, active world is determined as such through the understanding, and apart from it is nothing. This, however, is not the only reason for altogether denying such a reality of the outer world as is taught by the dogmatist, who explains its reality as its independence of the subject. We also deny it, because no object apart from a subject can be conceived without contradition. The whole world of objects is and remains idea, and therefore wholly and for ever determined by the subject; that is to say, it has transcendental ideality. But it is not therefore illusion or mere appearance; it presents itself as that which it is, idea, and indeed as a series of ideas of which the common bond is the principle of sufficient reason. It is according to its inmost meaning quite comprehensible to the healthy under-standing, and speaks a language quite intelligible to it. To dispute about its reality can only occur to a mind per-verted by over-subtilty, and such discussion always arises from a false application of the principle of sufficient reason, which binds all ideas together of whatever kind they may be, but by no means connects them with the subject, nor yet with a something which is neither subject nor object, but only the ground of the object; an absurdity, for only objects can be and always are the ground of objects. If we examine more closely the source of this question as to the reality of the outer world, we find that besides the false application of the principle of sufficient reason generally to what lies beyond its province, a special confusion of its forms is also involved; for that form which it has only in reference to concepts or abstract ideas, is applied to per-ceived ideas, real objects; and a ground of knowing is demanded of objects, whereas they can have nothing but a ground of being. Among the abstract ideas, the concepts united in the judgment, the principle of sufficient reason appears in such a way that each of these has its worth, its validity, and its whole existence, here called *truth*, simply and solely through the relation of the judgment to some-thing outside of it, its ground of knowledge, to which there must consequently always be a return. Among real objects, ideas of perception, on the other hand, the principle of sufficient reason appears not as the principle of the ground

of *knowing*, but of *being*, as the law of causality: every real
object has paid its debt to it, inasmuch as it has come to be,
i.e., has appeared as the effect of a cause. The demand for
a ground of knowing has therefore here no application and
no meaning, but belongs to quite another class of things.
Thus the world of perception raises in the observer no question or doubt so long as he remains in contact with it: there
is here neither error nor truth, for these are confined to the
province of the abstract—the province of reflection. But
here the world lies open for sense and understanding;
presents itself with naïve truth as that which it really is—
ideas of perception which develop themselves according to
the law of causality.

§ 6. For the present, however, in this first book we
consider everything merely as idea, as object for the subject. And our own body, which is the starting-point for each
of us in our perception of the world, we consider, like all
other real objects, from the side of its knowableness, and
in this regard it is simply an idea. Now the consciousness of
every one is in general opposed to the explanation of objects as mere ideas, and more especially to the explanation
of our bodies as such; for the thing in itself is known to
each of us immediately in so far as it appears as our own
body; but in so far as it objectifies itself in the other
objects of perception, it is known only indirectly. But this
abstraction, this one-sided treatment, this forcible separation
of what is essentially and necessarily united, is only adopted
to meet the demands of our argument; and therefore the
disinclination to it must, in the meantime, be suppressed and
silenced by the expectation that the subsequent treatment
will correct the one-sidedness of the present one, and complete our knowledge of the nature of the world.

At present therefore the body is for us immediate object;
that is to say, that idea which forms the starting-point of the
subject's knowledge; because the body, with its immediately

known changes, precedes the application of the law of causality, and thus supplies it with its first data. The whole nature of matter consists, as we have seen, in its causal action. But cause and effect exist only for the understanding, which is nothing but their subjective correlative. The understanding, however, could never come into operation if there were not something else from which it starts. This is simple sensation—the immediate consciousness of the changes of the body, by virtue of which it is immediate object. Thus the possibility of knowing the world of perception depends upon two conditions; the first, *objectively expressed*, is the power of material things to act upon each other, to produce changes in each other, without which common quality of all bodies no perception would be possible, even by means of the sensibility of the animal body. And if we wish to express this condition *subjectively* we say: The understanding first makes perception possible; for the law of causality, the possibility of effect and cause, springs only from the understanding, and is valid only for it, and therefore the world of perception exists only through and for it. The second condition is the sensibility of animal bodies, or the quality of being immediate objects of the subject which certain bodies possess. The mere modification which the organs of sense sustain from without through their specific affections, may here be called ideas, so far as these affections produce neither pain nor pleasure, that is, have no immediate significance for the will, and are yet perceived, exist therefore only for *knowledge*. Thus far, then, I say that the body is immediately *known*, is *immediate object*. But the conception of object is not to be taken here in its fullest sense, for through this immediate knowledge of the body, which precedes the operation of the understanding, and is mere sensation, our own body does not exist specifically as *object*, but first the material things which affect it: for all knowledge of an object proper, of an idea perceived in space, exists only through and for the understanding; therefore not before, but only subsequently to its operation. Therefore the body as object proper, that is, an idea perceived in space, is first known indirectly, like all other objects, through the application of the law of causality to the action of one of its parts upon another, as, for example, when the eye sees the body or the hand touches it. Consequently the form of our body does not become known to us through mere feeling, but only through knowledge, only in idea; that is to say, only in the brain does our own body first come to appear as extended, articulate, organic. A man born blind receives this idea only little by little from the data afforded by touch. A blind man without hands could never come to know his own form; or at the most could infer and construct it little by little from the effects of other bodies upon him. If, then, we call the body an immediate object, we are to be understood with these reservations.

In other respects, then, according to what has been said, all animal bodies are immediate objects; that is, starting-points for the subject which always knows and therefore is never known in its perception of the world. Thus the distinctive characteristic of animal life is knowledge, with movement following on motives, which are determined by knowledge, just as movement following on stimuli is the distinctive characteristic of plant-life. Unorganised matter, however, has no movement except such as is produced by causes properly so called, using the term in its narrowest sense. All this I have thoroughly discussed in my essay on the principle of sufficient reason, § 20, in the "Ethics," first essay, iii., and in my work on Sight and Colour, § 1, to which I therefore refer.

It follows from what has been said, that all animals, even the least developed, have understanding; for they all know objects, and this knowledge determines their movements

as motive. Understanding is the same in all animals and in
all men; it has everywhere the same simple form; knowledge of causality, transition from effect to cause, and from
cause to effect, nothing more; but the degree of its acute-
ness, and the extension of the sphere of its knowledge varies
enormously, with innumerable gradations from the lowest
form, which is only conscious of the causal connection between the immediate object and objects affecting it—that is
to say, perceives a cause as an object in space by passing to
it from the affection which the body feels, to the higher
grades of knowledge of the causal connection among objects
known indirectly, which extends to the understanding of the
most complicated system of cause and effect in nature. For
even this high degree of knowledge is still the work of
the understanding, not of the reason. The abstract concepts
of the reason can only serve to take up the objective connections which are immediately known by the understanding, to make them permanent for thought, and to relate
them to each other; but reason never gives us immediate
knowledge. Every force and law of nature, every example
of such forces and laws, must first be immediately known
by the understanding, must be apprehended through perception before it can pass into abstract consciousness for
reason. Hooke's discovery of the law of gravitation, and
the reference of so many important phenomena to this
one law, was the work of immediate apprehension by the understanding; and such also was the proof of Newton's
calculations, and Lavoisier's discovery of acids and their
important function in nature, and also Goethe's discovery
of the origin of physical colours. All these discoveries are
nothing more than a correct immediate passage from the
effect to the cause, which is at once followed by the recognition of the ideality of the force of nature which expresses
itself in all causes of the same kind; and this complete insight is just an example of that single function of the

understanding, by which an animal perceives as an object in space the cause which affects its body, and differs from such a perception only in degree. Every one of these great discoveries is therefore, just like perception, an operation of the understanding, an immediate intuition, and as such the work of an instant, an *apperçu*, a flash of insight.

§ 7. With reference to our exposition up to this point, it must be observed that we did not start either from the object or the subject, but from the idea, which contains and presupposes them both; for the antithesis of object and subject is its primary, universal and essential form. We have therefore first considered this form as such; then (though in this respect reference has for the most part been made to the introductory essay) the subordinate forms of time, space and causality. The latter belong exclusively to the *object*, and yet, as they are essential to the object *as such*, and as the object again is essential to the subject *as such*, they may be discovered from the subject, *i.e.*, they may be known *a priori*, and so far they are to be regarded as the common limits of both. But all these forms may be referred to one general expression, the principle of sufficient reason, as we have explained in the introductory essay.

This procedure distinguishes our philosophical method from that of all former systems. For they all start either from the object or from the subject, and therefore seek to explain the one from the other, and this according to the principle of sufficient reason. We, on the contrary, deny the validity of this principle with reference to the relation of subject and object, and confine it to the object. It may be thought that the philosophy of identity, which has appeared and become generally known in our own day, does not come under either of the alternatives we have named, for it does not start either from the subject or from the object, but from the absolute, known through "intellectual intuition," which is neither object nor subject, but the identity of the two. I will not venture to speak of this revered identity, and this absolute, for I find myself entirely devoid of all "intellectual intuition." But as I take my stand merely on those manifestoes of the "intellectual intuiter" which are open to all, even to profane persons like myself, I must yet observe that this philosophy is not to be excepted from the alternative errors mentioned above. For it does not escape these two opposite errors in spite of its identity of subject and object, which is not thinkable, but only "intellectually intuitable," or to be experienced by a losing of oneself in it. On the contrary, it combines them both in itself; for it is divided into two parts, firstly, transcendental idealism, which is just Fichte's doctrine of the *ego*, and therefore teaches that the object is produced by the subject, or evolved out of it in accordance with the principle of sufficient reason; secondly, the philosophy of nature, which teaches that the subject is produced little by little from the object, by means of a method called construction, about which I understand very little, yet enough to know that it is a process according to various forms of the principle of sufficient reason. The deep wisdom itself which that construction contains, I renounce; for as I entirely lack "intellectual intuition," all those expositions which presuppose it must for me remain as a book sealed with seven seals. This is so truly the case that, strange to say, I have always been unable to find anything at all in this doctrine of profound wisdom but atrocious and wearisome bombast.

The systems starting from the object had always the whole world of perception and its constitution as their problem; yet the object which they take as their starting-point is not always this whole world of perception, nor its fundamental element, matter. On the contrary, a division of these systems may be made, based on the four classes of possible objects set forth in the introductory essay. Thus Thales and the Ionic school, Democritus, Epicurus, Giordano Bruno,

and the French materialists, may be said to have started from
the first class of objects, the real world: Spinoza (on account
of his conception of substance, which is purely abstract, and
exists only in his definition) and, earlier, the Eleatics, from
the second class, the abstract conception: the Pythagoreans
and Chinese philosophy in Y-King, from the third class,
time, and consequently number: and, lastly, the schoolmen,
who teach a creation out of nothing by the act of will of an
extra-mundane personal being, started from the fourth class
of objects, the act of will directed by knowledge.

Of all systems of philosophy which start from the object,
the most consistent, and that which may be carried furthest,
is simple materialism. It regards matter, and with it time and
space, as existing absolutely, and ignores the relation to the
subject in which alone all this really exists. It then lays hold
of the law of causality as a guiding principle or clue, regarding it as a self-existent order (or arrangement) of things,
veritas æterna, and so fails to take account of the understanding, in which and for which alone causality is. It seeks
the primary and most simple state of matter, and then tries
to develop all the others from it; ascending from mere
mechanism, to chemism, to polarity, to the vegetable and
to the animal kingdom. And if we suppose this to have been
done, the last link in the chain would be animal sensibility—
that is, knowledge—which would consequently now appear
as a mere modification or state of matter produced by
causality. Now if we had followed materialism thus far
with clear ideas, when we reached its highest point we would
suddenly be seized with a fit of the inextinguishable laughter
of the Olympians. As if waking from a dream, we would
all at once become aware that its final result—knowledge,
which it reached so laboriously, was presupposed as the indispensable condition of its very starting-point, mere matter; and when we imagined that we thought matter, we
really thought only the subject that perceives matter: the

eye that sees it, the hand that feels it, the understanding that knows it. Thus the tremendous *petitio principii* reveals itself unexpectedly; for suddenly the last link is seen to be the starting-point, the chain a circle, and the materialist is like Baron Münchausen who, when swimming in water on horseback, drew the horse into the air with his legs, and himself also by his cue. The fundamental absurdity of materialism is that it starts from the *objective*, and takes as the ultimate ground of explanation something *objective*, whether it be matter in the abstract, simply as it is *thought*, or after it has taken form, is empirically given—that is to say, is *substance*, the chemical element with its primary relations. Some such thing it takes, as existing absolutely and in itself, in order that it may evolve organic nature and finally the knowing subject from it, and explain them adequately by means of it; whereas in truth all that is objective is already determined as such in manifold ways by the knowing subject through its forms of knowing, and presupposes them; and consequently it entirely disappears if we think the subject away. Thus materialism is the attempt to explain what is immediately given us by what is given us indirectly. All that is objective, extended, active—that is to say, all that is material—is regarded by materialism as affording so solid a basis for its explanation, that a reduction of everything to this can leave nothing to be desired (especially if in ultimate analysis this reduction should resolve itself into action and reaction). But we have shown that all this is given indirectly and in the highest degree determined, and is therefore merely a relatively present object, for it has passed through the machinery and manufactory of the brain, and has thus come under the forms of space, time and causality, by means of which it is first presented to us as extended in space and ever active in time. From such an indirectly given object, materialism seeks to explain what is immediately given, the idea (in which alone the object that materialism starts with exists), and finally even the will from which all those fundamental forces, that manifest themselves, under the guidance of causes, and therefore according to law, are in truth to be explained. To the assertion that thought is a modification of matter we may always, with equal right, oppose the contrary assertion that all matter is merely the modification of the knowing subject, as its idea. Yet the aim and ideal of all natural science is at bottom a consistent materialism. The recognition here of the obvious impossibility of such a system establishes another truth which will appear in the course of our exposition, the truth that all science properly so called, by which I understand systematic knowledge under the guidance of the principle of sufficient reason, can never reach its final goal, nor give a complete and adequate explanation: for it is not concerned with the inmost nature of the world, it cannot get beyond the idea; indeed, it really teaches nothing more than the relation of one idea to another.

"No object without a subject," is the principle which renders all materialism for ever impossible. Suns and planets without an eye that sees them, and an understanding that knows them, may indeed be spoken of in words, but for the idea, these words are absolutely meaningless. On the other hand, the law of causality and the treatment and investigation of nature which is based upon it, lead us necessarily to the conclusion that, in time, each more highly organised state of matter has succeeded a cruder state: so that the lower animals existed before men, fishes before land animals, plants before fishes, and the unorganised before all that is organised; that, consequently, the original mass had to pass through a long series of changes before the first eye could be opened. And yet, the existence of this whole world remains ever dependent upon the first eye that opened, even if it were that of an insect. For such an eye is a necessary condition of the possibility of knowledge, and the whole world exists only in and for knowledge, and without it is not even thinkable. The world is entirely idea, and as such demands the knowing subject as the supporter of its existence This long course of time itself, filled with innumerable changes, through which matter rose from form to form till at last the first percipient creature appeared,—this whole time itself is only thinkable in the identity of a consciousness whose succession of ideas, whose form of knowing it is, and apart from which, it loses all meaning and is nothing at all. Thus we see, on the one hand, the existence of the whole world necessarily dependent upon the first conscious being, however undeveloped it may be; on the other hand, this conscious being just as necessarily entirely dependent upon a long chain of causes and effects which have preceded it, and in which it itself appears as a small link. These two contradictory points of view, to each of which we are led with the same necessity, we might again call an *antinomy* in our faculty of knowledge, and set it up as the counterpart of that which we found in the first extreme of natural science. The objective world, the world as idea, is not the only side of the world, but merely its outward side; and it has an entirely different side—the side of its inmost nature—its kernel—the thing-in-itself. This we shall consider in the second book, calling it after the most immediate of its objective manifestations—will. But the world as idea, with which alone we are here concerned, only appears with the opening of the first eye. Without this medium of knowledge it cannot be, and therefore it was not before it. But without that eye, that is to say, outside of knowledge, there was also no before, no time. Thus time has no beginning, but all beginning is in time. Since, however, it is the most universal form of the knowable, in which all phenomena are united together through causality, time, with its infinity of past and future, is present in the beginning of knowledge. The phenomenon which fills the first present must at once be known as causally bound up with and dependent upon a sequence of phenomena which stretches infinitely into the past, and this past itself is just as truly conditioned by this first present, as conversely the present is by the past. Accordingly the past out of which the first present arises, is, like it, dependent upon the knowing subject, without which it is nothing. It necessarily happens, however, that this first present does not manifest itself as the first, that is, as having no past for its parent, but as being the beginning of time. It manifests itself rather as the consequence of the past, according to the principle of existence in time. In the same way, the phenomena which fill this first present appear as the effects of earlier phenomena which filled the past, in accordance with the law of causality. Those who like mythological interpretations may take the birth of Kronos (χρονος), the youngest of the Titans, as a symbol of the moment here referred to at which time appears, though indeed it has no beginning; for with him, since he ate his father, the crude productions of heaven and earth cease, and the races of gods and men appear upon the scene.

This explanation at which we have arrived by following the most consistent of the philosophical systems which start from the object, materialism, has brought out clearly the inseparable and reciprocal dependence of subject and object, and at the same time the inevitable antithesis between them. And this knowledge leads us to seek for the inner nature of the world, the thing-in-itself, not in either of the two elements of the idea, but in something quite distinct from it, and which is not encumbered with such a fundamental and insoluble antithesis.

Opposed to the system we have explained, which starts from the object in order to derive the subject from it, is the system which starts from the subject and tries to derive the object from it. The first of these has been of frequent and common occurrence throughout the history of philoso-

phy, but of the second we find only one example, and that
a very recent one; the "philosophy of appearance" of J. G.
Fichte. In this respect, therefore, it must be considered;
little real worth or inner meaning as the doctrine itself had.
It was indeed for the most part merely a delusion, but it
was delivered with an air of the deepest earnestness, with
sustained loftiness of tone and zealous ardour, and was defended with eloquent polemic against weak opponents, so
that it was able to present a brilliant exterior and seemed
to be something. But the genuine earnestness which keeps
truth always steadfastly before it as its goal, and is unaffected by any external influences, was entirely wanting to
Fichte, as it is to all philosophers who, like him, concern
themselves with questions of the day. In his case, indeed, it
could not have been otherwise. A man becomes a philosopher
by reason of a certain perplexity, from which he seeks to
free himself. This is Plato's ϑαυμαξειν, which he calls a
μαλα Φιλοσοφικον παδος. But what distinguishes the false
philosopher from the true is this: the perplexity of the latter
arises from the contemplation of the world itself, while
that of the former results from some book, some system of
philosophy which is before him. Now Fichte belongs to the
class of the false philosophers. He was made a philosopher
by Kant's doctrine of the thing-in-itself, and if it had not
been for this he would probably have pursued entirely different ends, with far better results, for he certainly possessed remarkable rhetorical talent. If he had only penetrated
somewhat deeply into the meaning of the book that made
him a philosopher, "The Critique of Pure Reason," he
would have understood that its principal teaching about mind
is this. The principle of sufficient reason is not, as all scholastic philosophy maintains, a *veritas æterna*—that is to say, it
does not possess an unconditioned validity before, outside of,
and above the world. It is relative and conditioned, and valid

only in the sphere of phenomena, and thus it may appear as the necessary nexus of space and time, or as the law of causality, or as the law of the ground of knowledge. The inner nature of the world, the thing-in-itself can never be found by the guidance of this principle, for all that it leads to will be found to be dependent and relative and merely phenomenal, not the thing-in-itself. Further, it does not concern the subject, but is only the form of objects, which are therefore not things-in-themselves. The subject must exist along with the object, and the object along with the subject, so that it is impossible that subject and object can stand to each other in a relation of reason and consequent. But Fichte did not take up the smallest fragment of all this. All that interested him about the matter was that the system started from the subject. Now Kant had chosen this procedure in order to show the fallacy of the prevalent systems, which started from the object, and through which the object had come to be regarded as a thing-in-itself. Fichte, however, took this departure from the subject for the really important matter, and like all imitators, he imagined that in going further than Kant he was surpassing him. This philosophy of Fichte, otherwise not worth mentioning, is interesting to us only as the tardy expression of the converse of the old materialism. For materialism was the most consistent system starting from the object, as this is the most consistent system starting from the subject. Materialism overlooked the fact that, with the simplest object, it assumed the subject also; and Fichte overlooked the fact that with the subject (whatever he may call it) he assumed the object also, for no subject is thinkable without an object. Besides this he forgot that all *a priori* deduction, indeed all demonstration in general, must rest upon some necessity, and that all necessity is based on the principle of sufficient reason, because to be necessary, and to follow from given grounds are convertible conceptions.[1] But the principle of sufficient reason is just the universal form of the object as such. Thus it is in the object, but is not valid before and outside of it; it first produces the object and makes it appear in conformity with its regulative principle. We see then that the system which starts from the subject contains the same fallacy as the system, explained above, which starts from the object; it begins by assuming what it proposes to deduce, the necessary correlative of its starting-point.

The method of our own system is *toto genere* distinct from these two opposite misconceptions, for we start neither from the object nor from the subject, but from the *idea*, as the first fact of consciousness. Its first essential, fundamental form, is the antithesis of subject and object. The form of the object again is the principle of sufficient reason in its various forms. Each of these reigns so absolutely in its own class of ideas that, as we have seen, when the special form of the principle of sufficient reason which governs any class of ideas is known, the nature of the whole class is known also; for the whole class, as idea, is no more than this form of the principle of sufficient reason itself; so that time itself is nothing but the principle of existence in it, *i.e.*, succession; space is nothing but the principle of existence in it, *i.e.*, position; matter is nothing but causality; the concept (as will appear immediately) is nothing but relation to a ground of knowledge. This thorough and consistent relativity of the world as idea, both according to its universal form (subject and object) and according to the form which is subordinate to this (the principle of sufficient reason) warns us, as we said before, to seek the inner nature of the world in an aspect of it which is *quite different and quite distinct from the idea;* and in the next book we shall find this in a fact which is just as immediate to every living being as the idea.

[1] On this see "The Fourfold Root of the Principle of Sufficient Reason," § 49.

But we must first consider that class of ideas which belongs to man alone. The matter of these is the concept, and the subjective correlative is reason, just as the subjective correlative of the ideas we have already considered was understanding and sensibility, which are also to be attributed to all the lower animals.[1]

§ 8. As from the direct light of the sun to the borrowed light of the moon, we pass from the immediate idea of perception, which stands by itself and is its own warrant, to reflection, to the abstract, discursive concepts of the reason, which obtain their whole content from knowledge of perception, and in relation to it. As long as we continue simply to perceive, all is clear, firm, and certain. There are neither questions nor doubts nor errors; we desire to go no further, can go no further; we find rest in perceiving, and satisfaction in the present. Perception suffices for itself, and therefore what springs purely from it, and remains true to it, for example, a genuine work of art, can never be false, nor can it be discredited through the lapse of time, for it does not present an opinion but the thing itself. But with abstract knowledge, with reason, doubt and error appear in the theoretical, care and sorrow in the practical. In the idea of perception, illusion may at moments take the place of the real; but in the sphere of abstract thought, error may reign for a thousand years, impose its yoke upon whole nations, extend to the noblest impulses of humanity, and, by the help of its slaves and its dupes, may chain and fetter those whom it cannot deceive. It is the enemy against which the wisest men of all times have waged unequal war, and only what they have won from it has become the possession of mankind. Therefore it is well to draw attention to it at once, as we already tread the ground to which its province belongs. It has often been said that we ought to follow truth

[1] The first four chapters of the first of the supplementary books belong to these seven paragraphs.

even although no utility can be seen in it, because it may
have indirect utility which may appear when it is least expected; and I would add to this, that we ought to be just
as anxious to discover and to root out all error even when
no harm is anticipated from it, because its mischief may be
very indirect, and may suddenly appear when we do not
expect it, for all error has poison at its heart. If it is mind,
if it is knowledge, that makes man the lord of creation,
there can be no such thing as harmless error, still less
venerable and holy error. And for the consolation of those
who in any way and at any time may have devoted strength
and life to the noble and hard battle against error, I cannot
refrain from adding that, so long as truth is absent, error
will have free play, as owls and bats in the night; but sooner
would we expect to see the owls and the bats drive back the
sun in the eastern heavens, than that any truth which has
once been known and distinctly and fully expressed, can
ever again be so utterly vanquished and overcome that the
old error shall once more reign undisturbed over its wide
kingdom. This is the power of truth; its conquest is slow
and laborious, but if once the victory be gained it can never
be wrested back again.

Besides the ideas we have as yet considered, which, according to their construction, could be referred to time, space,
and matter, if we consider them with reference to the
object, or to pure sensibility and understanding (*i.e.,* knowledge of causality), if we consider them with reference to the
subject, another faculty of knowledge has appeared in man
alone of all earthly creatures, an entirely new consciousness,
which, with very appropriate and significant exactness, is
called *reflection.* For it is in fact derived from the knowledge of perception, and is a reflected appearance of it. But
it has assumed a nature fundamentally different. The forms
of perception do not affect it, and even the principle of
sufficient reason which reigns over all objects has an entirely

different aspect with regard to it. It is just this new, more highly endowed, consciousness, this abstract reflex of all that belongs to perception in that conception of the reason which has nothing to do with perception, that gives to man that thoughtfulness which distinguishes his consciousness so entirely from that of the lower animals, and through which his whole behaviour upon earth is so different from that of his irrational fellow-creatures. He far surpasses them in power and also in suffering. They live in the present alone, he lives also in the future and the past. They satisfy the needs of the moment, he provides by the most ingenious preparations for the future, yea for days that he shall never see. They are entirely dependent on the impression of the moment, on the effect of the perceptible motive; he is determined by abstract conceptions independent of the present. Therefore he follows predetermined plans, he acts from maxims, without reference to his surroundings or the accidental impression of the moment. Thus, for example, he can make with composure deliberate preparations for his own death, he can dissemble past finding out, and can carry his secret with him to the grave; lastly, he has an actual choice between several motives; for only in the abstract can such motives, present together in consciousness, afford the knowledge with regard to themselves, that the one excludes the other, and can thus measure themselves against each other with reference to their power over the will. The motive that overcomes, in that it decides the question at issue, is the deliberate determinant of the will, and is a sure indication of its character. The brute, on the other hand, is determined by the present impression; only the fear of present compulsion can constrain its desires, until at last this fear has become custom, and as such continues to determine it; this is called training. The brute feels and perceives; man, in addition to this, *thinks* and *knows*: both *will*. The brute expresses its feelings and dispositions by gestures and sounds;

man communicates his thought to others, or, if he wishes, he conceals it, by means of speech. Speech is the first production, and also the necessary organ of his reason. Therefore in Greek and Italian, speech and reason are expressed by the same word; ὸ λογος, *il discorso. Vernunft* is derived from *vernehmen,* which not a synonym for the verb to hear, but signifies the consciousness of the meaning of thoughts communicated in words. It is by the help of language alone that reason accomplishes its most important achievements,—the united action of several individuals, the planned co-operation of many thousands, civilisation, the state; also science, the storing up of experience, the uniting of common properties in one concept, the communication of truth, the spread of error, thoughts and poems, dogmas and superstitions. The brute first knows death when it dies, but man draws consciously nearer to it every hour that he lives; and this makes life at times a questionable good even to him who has not recognised this character of constant annihilation in the whole of life. Principally on this account man has philosophies and religions, though it is uncertain whether the qualities we admire most in his conduct, voluntary rectitude and nobility of feeling, were ever the fruit of either of them. As results which certainly belong only to them, and as productions of reason in this sphere, we may refer to the marvellous and monstrous opinions of philosophers of various schools, and the extraordinary and sometimes cruel customs of the priests of different religions.

It is the universal opinion of all times and of all nations that these manifold and far-reaching achievements spring from a common principle, from that peculiar intellectual power which belongs distinctively to man and which has been called reason, ὸ λογος, το λογιστικον, το λογιμον, *ratio.* Besides this, no one finds any difficulty in recognising the manifestations of this faculty, and in saying what is rational and what is irrational, where reason appears as distinguished from the other faculties and qualities of man, or lastly, in pointing out what, on account of the want of reason, we must never expect even from the most sensible brute. The philosophers of all ages may be said to be on the whole at one about this general knowledge of reason, and they have also given prominence to several very important manifestations of it; such as, the control of the emotions and passions, the capacity for drawing conclusions and formulating general principles, even such as are true prior to all experience, and so forth.

The understanding has only one function—immediate knowledge of the relation of cause and effect. Yet the perception of the real world, and all common sense, sagacity, and inventiveness, however multifarious their applications may be, are quite clearly seen to be nothing more than manifestations of that one function. So also the reason has one function; and from it all the manifestations of reason we have mentioned, which distinguish the life of man from that of the brutes, may easily be explained. The application or the non-application of this function is all that is meant by what men have everywhere and always called rational and irrational.[1]

Although concepts are fundamentally different from ideas of perception, they stand in a necessary relation to them, without which they would be nothing. This relation therefore constitutes the whole nature and existence of concepts. Reflection is the necessary copy or repetition of the originally presented world of perception, but it is a special kind of copy in an entirely different material. Thus concepts may quite properly be called ideas of ideas. The principle of sufficient reason has here also a special form. Now we have seen that the form under which the principle of sufficient reason appears in a class of ideas always constitutes

[1] Compare with this paragraph §§ 26 and 27 of the third edition of the essay on the principle of sufficient reason.

and exhausts the whole nature of the class, so far as it consists of ideas, so that time is throughout succession, and
nothing more; space is throughout position, and nothing
more; matter is throughout causation, and nothing more.
In the same way the whole nature of concepts, or the class
of abstract ideas, consists simply in the relation which the
principle of sufficient reason expresses in them; and as this
is the relation to the ground of knowledge, the whole nature
of the abstract idea is simply and solely its relation to another
idea, which is its ground of knowledge. This, indeed, may,
in the first instance, be a concept, an abstract idea, and this
again may have only a similar abstract ground of knowledge; but the chain of grounds of knowledge does not extend *ad infinitum;* it must end at last in a concept which has
its ground in knowledge of perception; for the whole world
of reflection rests on the world of perception as its ground
of knowledge. Hence the class of abstract ideas is in this
respect distinguished from other classes; in the latter the
principle of sufficient reason always demands merely a relation to another idea of the *same* class, but in the case of
abstract ideas, it at last demands a relation to an idea of
another class.

Those concepts which, as has just been pointed out, are
not immediately related to the world of perception, but only
through the medium of one, or it may be several other concepts, have been called by preference *abstracta,* and those
which have their ground immediately in the world of perception have been called *concreta.* But this last name is only
loosely applicable to the concepts denoted by it, for they are
always merely *abstracta,* and not ideas of perception. These
names, which have originated in a very dim consciousness of
the distinctions they imply, may yet, with this explanation,
be retained. As examples of the first kind of concepts, *i.e.,*
abstracta in the fullest sense, we may take "relation," "virtue," "investigation," "beginning," and so on.   As examples

of the second kind, loosely called *concreta*, we may take such concepts as "man," "stone," "horse," &c. If it were not a somewhat too pictorial and therefore absurd simile, we might very appropriately call the latter the ground floor, and the former the upper stories of the building of reflection.[1]

Reason is feminine in nature; it can only give after it has received. Of itself it has nothing but the empty forms of its operation. There is no absolutely pure rational knowledge except the four principles to which I have attributed meta-logical truth; the principles of identity, contradiction, ex-cluded middle, and sufficient reason of knowledge. For even the rest of logic is not absolutely pure rational knowledge. It presupposes the relations and the combinations of the spheres of concepts. But concepts in general only exist after experience of ideas of perception, and as their whole nature consists in their relation to these, it is clear that they pre-suppose them. No special content, however, is presupposed, but merely the existence of a content generally, and so logic as a whole may fairly pass for pure rational science. In all other sciences reason has received its content from ideas of perception; in mathematics from the relations of space and time, presented in intuition or perception prior to all ex-perience; in pure natural science, that is, in what we know of the course of nature prior to any experience, the content of the science proceeds from the pure understanding, *i.e.*, from the *a priori* knowledge of the law of causality and its connection with those pure intuitions or perceptions of space and time. In all other sciences everything that is not derived from the sources we have just referred to belongs to ex-perience. Speaking generally, *to know rationally* (*wissen*) means to have in the power of the mind, and capable of being reproduced at will, such judgments as have their suf-ficient ground of knowledge in something outside them-selves, *i.e.*, are true. Thus only abstract cognition is *rational*

[1] Cf. Ch. 5 and 6 of the Supplement.

knowledge (*wissen*), which is therefore the result of reason, so that we cannot accurately say of the lower animals that they *rationally know* (*wissen*) anything, although they have apprehension of what is presented in perception, and memory of this, and consequently imagination, which is further proved by the circumstance that they dream. We attribute consciousness to them, and therefore although the word (*bewusstsein*) is derived from the verb to know rationally (*wissen*), the conception of consciousness corresponds generally with that of idea of whatever kind it may be. Thus we attribute life to plants, but not consciousness. *Rational knowledge* (*wissen*) is therefore abstract consciousness, the permanent possession in concepts of the reason, of what has become known in another way.

§ 12. *Rational knowledge* (*wissen*) is then all abstract knowledge,—that is, the knowledge which is peculiar to the reason as distinguished from the understanding. Now, as reason only reproduces, for knowledge, what has been received in another way, it does not actually extend our knowledge, but only gives it another form. It enables us to know in the abstract and generally, what first became known in sense-perception, in the concrete. But this is much more important than it appears at first sight when so expressed. For it depends entirely upon the fact that knowledge has become rational or abstract knowledge (*wissen*), that it can be safely preserved, that it is communicable and susceptible of certain and wide-reaching application to practice. Knowledge in the form of sense-perception is valid only of the particular case, extends only to what is nearest, and ends with it, for sensibility and understanding can only comprehend one object at a time. Every enduring, arranged, and planned activity must therefore proceed from principles,—that is, from abstract knowledge, and it must be conducted in accordance with them. Thus, for example, the knowledge of the relation of cause and effect arrived at by the understanding, is in itself far completer, deeper and more exhaustive than anything that can be thought about it in the abstract; the understanding alone knows in perception directly and completely the nature of the effect of a lever, of a pulley, or a cog-wheel, the stability of an arch, and so forth. But on account of the peculiarity of the knowledge of perception just referred to, that it only extends to what is immediately present, the mere understanding can never enable us to construct machines and buildings. Here reason must come in; it must substitute abstract concepts for ideas of perception, and take them as the guide of action; and if they are right, the anticipated result will happen. In the same way we have perfect knowledge in pure perception of the nature and constitution of the parabola, hyperbola, and spiral; but if we are to make trustworthy application of this knowledge to the real, it must first become abstract knowledge, and by this it certainly loses its character of intuition or perception, but on the other hand it gains the certainty and preciseness of abstract knowledge. The differential calculus does not really extend our knowledge of the curve, it contains nothing that was not already in the mere pure perception of the curve; but it alters the kind of knowledge, it changes the intuitive into an abstract knowledge, which is so valuable for application.

This quality of concepts by which they resemble the stones of a mosaic, and on account of which perception always remains their asymptote, is the reason why nothing good is produced in art by their means. If the singer or the virtuoso attempts to guide his execution by reflection he remains silent. And this is equally true of the composer, the painter, and the poet. The concept always remains unfruitful in art; it can only direct the technical part of it, its sphere is science. We shall consider more fully in the third book, why all true art proceeds from sensuous knowl-

edge, never from the concept. Indeed, with regard to behaviour also, and personal agreeableness in society, the
concept has only a negative value in restraining the grosser
manifestations of egotism and brutality; so that a polished
manner is its commendable production. But all that is attractive, gracious, charming in behaviour, all affectionate-
ness and friendliness, must not proceed from the concepts,
for if it does, "we feel intention, and are put out of tune."
All dissimulation is the work of reflection; but it cannot
be maintained constantly and without interruption: *"nemo
potest personam diu ferre fictum,"* says Seneca in his book
de clementia; and so it is generally found out and loses
its effect. Reason is needed in the full stress of life, where
quick conclusions, bold action, rapid and sure comprehension
are required, but it may easily spoil all if it gains the upper
hand, and by perplexing hinders the intuitive, direct discovery, and grasp of the right by simple understanding, and
thus induces irresolution.

Lastly, virtue and holiness do not proceed from reflection,
but from the inner depths of the will, and its relation to
knowledge. The exposition of this belongs to another part
of our work; this, however, I may remark here, that the
dogmas relating to ethics may be the same in the reason of
whole nations, but the action of every individual different;
and the converse also holds good; action, we say, is guided
by *feelings,*—that is, simply not by concepts, but as a matter
of fact by the ethical character. Dogmas occupy the idle
reason; but action in the end pursues its own course independently of them, generally not according to abstract
rules, but according to unspoken maxims, the expression of
which is the whole man himself. Therefore, however different the religious dogmas of nations may be, yet in the
case of all of them, a good action is accompanied by unspeakable satisfaction, and a bad action by endless remorse.
No mockery can shake the former; no priest's absolution can

deliver from the latter. Notwithstanding this, we must allow, that for the pursuit of a virtuous life, the application of reason is needful; only it is not its source, but has the subordinate function of preserving resolutions which have been made, of providing maxims to withstand the weakness of the moment, and give consistency to action. It plays the same part ultimately in art also, where it has just as little to do with the essential matter, but assists in carrying it out, for genius is not always at call, and yet the work must be completed in all its parts and rounded off to a whole.[1]

As regards the *content* of the sciences generally, it is, in fact, always the relation of the phenomena of the world to each other, according to the principle of sufficient reason, under the guidance of the *why*, which has validity and meaning only through this principle. *Explanation* is the establishment of this relation. Therefore explanation can never go further than to show two ideas standing to each other in the relation peculiar to that form of the principle of sufficient reason which reigns in the class to which they belong. If this is done we cannot further be asked the question, *why*: for the relation proved is that one which absolutely cannot be imagined as other than it is, *i.e.*, it is the form of all knowledge. Therefore we do not ask why $2 + 2 = 4$; or why the equality of the angles of a triangle determines the equality of the sides; or why its effect follows any given cause; or why the truth of the conclusion is evident from the truth of the premises. Every explanation which does not ultimately lead to a relation of which no "why" can further be demanded, stops at an accepted *qualitas occulta*; but this is the character of every original force of nature. Every explanation in natural science must ultimately end with such a *qualitas occulta*, and thus with complete obscurity. It must leave the inner nature of a stone just as much unexplained as that

[1] Cf. Ch. 7 of the Supplement.

of a human being; it can give as little account of the weight, the cohesion, the chemical qualities, &c., of the former, as of the knowing and acting of the latter. Thus, for example, weight is a *qualitas occulta,* for it can be thought away, and does not proceed as a necessity from the form of knowledge; which, on the contrary, is not the case with the law of inertia, for it follows from the law of causality, and is therefore sufficiently explained if it is referred to that law. There are two things which are altogether inexplicable,—that is to say, do not ultimately lead to the relation which the principle of sufficient reason expresses. These are, first, the principle of sufficient reason itself in all its four forms, because it is the principle of all explanation, which has meaning only in relation to it; secondly, that to which this principle does not extend, but which is the original source of all phenomena; the thing-in-itself, the knowledge of which is not subject to the principle of sufficient reason. We must be content for the present not to understand this thing-in-itself, for it can only be made intelligible by means of the following book, in which we shall resume this consideration of the possible achievements of the sciences. But at the point at which natural science, and indeed every science, leaves things, because not only its explanation of them, but even the principle of this explanation, the principle of sufficient reason, does not extend beyond this point; there philosophy takes them up and treats them after its own method, which is quite distinct from the method of science. In my essay on the principle of sufficient reason, § 51, I have shown how in the different sciences the chief guiding clue is one or other form of that principle; and, in fact, perhaps the most appropriate classification of the sciences might be based upon this circumstance. Every explanation arrived at by the help of this clue is, as we have said, merely relative; it explains things in relation to each other, but something which indeed is presupposed is always left unexplained. In mathematics, for example, this is space and time; in mechanics, physics, and chemistry it is matter, qualities, original forces and laws of nature; in botany and zoology it is the difference of species, and life itself; in history it is the human race with all its properties of thought and will: in all it is that form of the principle of sufficient reason which is respectively applicable. It is peculiar to *philosophy* that it presupposes nothing as known, but treats everything as equally external and a problem; not merely the relations of phenomena, but also the phenomena themselves, and even the principle of sufficient reason to which the other sciences are content to refer everything. In philosophy nothing would be gained by such a reference, as one member of the series is just as external to it as another; and, moreover, that kind of connection is just as much a problem for philosophy as what is joined together by it, and the latter again is just as much a problem after its combination has been explained as before it. For, as we have said, just what the sciences presuppose and lay down as the basis and the limits of their explanation, is precisely and peculiarly the problem of philosophy, which may therefore be said to begin where science ends. It cannot be founded upon demonstrations, for they lead from known principles to unknown, but everything is equally unknown and external to philosophy. There can be no principle in consequence of which the world with all its phenomena first came into existence, and therefore it is not possible to construct, as Spinoza wished, a philosophy which demonstrates *ex firmis principiis*. Philosophy is the most general rational knowledge, the first principles of which cannot therefore be derived from another principle still more general. The principle of contradiction establishes merely the agreement of concepts, but does not itself produce concepts. The principle of sufficient reason explains the connections of phenomena, but not the phenomena themselves;

therefore philosophy cannot proceed upon these principles to seek a *causa efficiens* or a *causa finalis* of the whole world. My philosophy, at least, does not by any means seek to know *whence* or *wherefore* the world exists, but merely *what* the world is. But the *why* is here subordinated to the *what*, for it already belongs to the world, as it arises and has meaning and validity only through the form of its phenomena, the principle of sufficient reason. We might indeed say that every one knows what the world is without help, for he is himself that subject of knowledge of which the world is the idea; and so far this would be true. But that knowledge is empirical, is in the concrete; the task of philosophy is to reproduce this in the abstract, to raise to permanent rational knowledge the successive changing perceptions, and in general, all that is contained under the wide concept of feeling and merely negatively defined as not abstract, distinct, rational knowledge. It must therefore consist of a statement in the abstract, of the nature of the whole world, of the whole, and of all the parts. In order then that it may not lose itself in the endless multitude of particular judgments, it must make use of abstraction and think everything individual in the universal, and its differences also in the universal. It must therefore partly separate and partly unite, in order to present to rational knowledge the whole manifold of the world generally, according to its nature, comprehended in a few abstract concepts. Through these concepts, in which it fixes the nature of the world, the whole individual must be known as well as the universal, the knowledge of both therefore must be bound together to the minutest point. Therefore the capacity for philosophy consists just in that in which Plato placed it, the knowledge of the one in the many, and the many in the one. Philosophy will therefore be a sum total of general judgments, whose ground of knowledge is immediately the world itself in its entirety, without ex-

:epting anything; thus all that is to be found in human consciousness; it will be *a complete recapitulation, as it were, a reflection, of the world in abstract concepts*, which is only possible by the union of the essentially identical in *one* concept and the relegation of the different to another.

The agreement which all the sides and parts of the world have with each other, just because they belong to a whole, must also be found in this abstract copy of it. Therefore the judgments in this sum-total could to a certain extent be deduced from each other, and indeed always reciprocally so deduced. Yet to make the first judgment possible, they must all be present, and thus implied as prior to it in the knowledge of the world in the concrete, especially as all direct proof is more certain than indirect proof; their harmony with each other by virtue of which they come together into the unity of *one* thought, and which arises from the harmony and unity of the world of perception itself, which is their common ground of knowledge, is not therefore to be made use of to establish them, as that which is prior to them, but is only added as a confirmation of their truth. This problem itself can only become quite clear in being solved.[1]

The many-sided view of life as a whole which man, as distinguished from the lower animals, possesses through reason, may be compared to a geometrical, colourless, abstract, reduced plan of his actual life. He, therefore, stands to the lower animals as the navigator who, by means of chart, compass, and quadrant, knows accurately his course and his position at any time upon the sea, stands to the uneducated sailors who see only the waves and the heavens. Thus it is worth noticing, and indeed wonderful, how, besides his life in the concrete, man always lives another life in the abstract. In the former he is given as a prey to all the storms of actual life, and to the influence of

[1] Cf. Ch. 7 of Supplement

the present; he must struggle, suffer, and die like the brute. But his life in the abstract, as it lies before his rational consciousness, is the still reflection of the former, and of the world in which he lives; it is just that reduced chart or plan to which we have referred. Here in the sphere of quiet deliberation, what completely possessed him and moved him intensely before, appears to him cold, colour-less, and for the moment external to him; he is merely the spectator, the observer. In respect of this withdrawal into reflection he may be compared to an actor who has played his part in one scene, and who takes his place among the audience till it is time for him to go upon the stage again, and quietly looks on at whatever may happen, even though it be the preparation for his own death (in the piece), but afterwards he again goes on the stage and acts and suffers as he must. From this double life proceeds that quietness peculiar to human beings, so very different from the thoughtlessness of the brutes, and with which, in accordance with previous reflection, or a formed determination, or a recognised necessity, a man suffers or accomplishes in cold blood, what is of the utmost and often terrible importance to him; suicide, execution, the duel, enterprises of every kind fraught with danger to life, and, in general, things against which his whole animal nature rebels. Under such circumstances we see to what an extent reason has mastered the animal nature, and we say to the strong: σιδηρειον νυ τοι ητορ! (*ferreum certe tibi cor*), Il. 24, 521.[1] Here we can say truly that reason manifests itself practically, and thus wherever action is guided by reason, where the motives are abstract concepts, wherever we are not determined by particular ideas of perception, nor by the impression of the moment which guides the brutes, there *practical reason* shows itself.

The ideal explained in the *Stoical philosophy* is the most

[1] Surely your heart is of iron.

complete development of *practical reason* in the true and
genuine sense of the word; it is the highest summit to which
man can attain by the mere use of his reason, and in it his
difference from the brutes shows itself most distinctly. For
the ethics of Stoicism are, originally and essentially, not a
doctrine of virtue, but merely a guide to a rational life,
the end and aim of which is happiness through peace of
mind. Virtuous conduct appears in it as it were merely by
accident, as the means, not as the end. Therefore the
ethical theory of Stoicism is in its whole nature and point
of view fundamentally different from the ethical systems
which lay stress directly upon virtue, such as the doctrines
of the Vedas, of Plato, of Christianity, and of Kant.
Yet the ethics of Stoicism teach that happiness can only be
attained with certainty through inward peace and quietness
of spirit (αταραζια), and that this again can only be reached
through virtue; this is the whole meaning of the saying that
virtue is the highest good. But if indeed by degrees the end
is lost sight of in the means, and virtue is inculcated in a
way which discloses an interest entirely different from that
of one's own happiness, for it contradicts this too distinctly;
this is just one of those inconsistencies by means of which,
in every system, the immediately known, or, as it is called,
felt truth, leads us back to the right way in defiance of
syllogistic reasoning; as, for example, we see clearly in
the ethical teaching of Spinoza, which deduces a pure
doctrine of virtue from the egoistical *suum utile quærere*
by means of palpable sophisms. According to this, as I conceive the spirit of the Stoical ethics, their source lies in the
question whether the great prerogative of man, reason,
which, by means of planned action and its results, relieves
life and its burdens so much, might not also be capable of
freeing him at once, directly, *i.e.*, through mere knowledge,
completely, or nearly so, of the sorrows and miseries of
every kind of which his life is full. They held that it was

not in keeping with the prerogative of reason that the nature given with it, which by means of it comprehends and contemplates an infinity of things and circumstances, should yet, through the present, and the accidents that can be contained in the few years of a life that is short, fleeting, and uncertain, be exposed to such intense pain, to such great anxiety and suffering, as arise from the tempestuous strain of the desires and the antipathies; and they believed that the due application of reason must raise men above them, and can make them invulnerable. Therefore Antisthenes says: Δει κτασθαι νουν, η βροχον (aut mentem parandam, aut laqueum,[1] i.e., life is so full of troubles and vexations, that one must either rise above it by means of corrected thoughts, or leave it. It was seen that want and suffering did not directly and of necessity spring from not having, but from desiring to have and not having; that therefore this desire to have is the necessary condition under which alone it becomes a privation not to have and begets pain. Men learned also from experience that it is only the hope of what is claimed that begets and nourishes the wish; therefore neither the many unavoidable evils which are common to all, nor unattainable blessings, disquiet or trouble us, but only the trifling more or less of those things which we can avoid or attain; indeed, not only what is absolutely unavoidable or unattainable, but also what is merely relatively so, leaves us quite undisturbed; therefore the ills that have once become joined to our individuality, or the good things that must of necessity always be denied us, are treated with indifference, in accordance with the peculiarity of human nature that every wish soon dies and can no more beget pain if it is not nourished by hope. It followed from all this that happiness always depends upon the proportion between our claims and what we receive. It is all one whether the quantities thus related be great or

[1] Either a prepared mind, or death.

small, and the proportion can be established just as well by diminishing the amount of the first as by increasing the amount of the second; and in the same way it also follows that all suffering proceeds from the want of proportion between what we demand and expect and what we get. Now this want of proportion obviously lies only in knowledge, and it could be entirely abolished through fuller insight.[1] Therefore Chrysippus says: one ought to live with a due knowledge of the transitory nature of the things of the world. For as often as a man loses self-command, or is struck down by a misfortune, or grows angry, or becomes faint-hearted, he shows that he finds things different from what he expected, consequently that he was caught in error, and did not know the world and life, did not know that the will of the individual is crossed at every step by the chance of inanimate nature and the antagonism of aims and the wickedness of other individuals: he has therefore either not made use of his reason in order to arrive at a general knowledge of this characteristic of life, or he lacks judgment, in that he does not recognise in the particular what he knows in general, and is therefore surprised by it and loses his self-command.[2] Thus also every keen pleasure is an error and an illusion, for no attained wish can give lasting satisfaction; and, moreover, every possession and every happiness is but lent by chance for an uncertain time, and may therefore be demanded back the next hour. All pain rests on the passing away of such an illusion; thus both arise from defective knowledge; the wise man there-

---

[1] Omnes perturbationes judicio censent fieri et opinione. Cic. Tusc., 4, 6. Ταρασσει τους ανθρωπους ου τα πραγματα, αλλα τα περι των πραγματων δογματα (Perturbant homines non res ipsæ, sed de rebus opiniones). Epictet., c. v.

[2] Τουτο γαρ εστι το αιτιρν τοις ανθρωποις παντων των κακων, το τας προληψεις τας κοινας μη δυνασθαι εφαρμοξειν ταις επι μερους (Hæc est causa mortalibus omnium malorum, non posse communes notiones aptare singularibus). Epict. dissert., ii., 26.

fore holds himself equally aloof from joy and sorrow, and no event disturbs his αταραξια.

The ethical system of Stoicism, regarded as a whole, is in fact a very valuable and estimable attempt to use the great prerogative of man, reason, for an important and salutary end; to raise him above the suffering and pain to which all life is exposed, by means of a maxim—

> "Qua ratione queas traducere leniter ævum:
> Ne te semper inops agitet vexetque cupido,
> Ne pavor et rerum mediocriter utilium spes," [1]

and thus to make him partake, in the highest degree, of the dignity which belongs to him as a rational being, as distinguished from the brutes; a dignity of which, in this sense at any rate, we can speak, though not in any other. It is a consequence of my view of the ethical system of Stoicism that it must be explained at the part of my work at which I consider what reason is and what it can do. But although it may to a certain extent be possible to attain that end through the application of reason, and through a purely rational system of ethics, and although experience shows that the happiest men are those purely rational characters commonly called practical philosophers,—and rightly so, because just as the true, that is, the theoretical philosopher carries life into the concept, they carry the concept into life,—yet it is far from the case that perfection can be attained in this way, and that the reason, rightly used, can really free us from the burden and sorrow of life, and lead us to happiness. Rather, there lies an absolute contradiction in wishing to live without suffering, and this contradiction is also implied in the commonly used expression, "blessed life." This will become perfectly clear to whoever compre-

---

[1] Would you learn how to pass your years tranquilly; do not let greedy desire always vex and agitate you, nor fear nor hope of mediocre wealth.

hends the whole of the following exposition. In this purely rational system of ethics the contradiction reveals itself thus, the Stoic is obliged in his doctrine of the way to the blessed life (for that is what his ethical system always remains) to insert a recommendation of suicide (as among the magnificent ornaments and apparel of Eastern despots there is always a costly vial of poison) for the case in which the sufferings of the body, which cannot be philosophised away by any principles or syllogistic reasonings, are paramount and incurable; thus its one aim, blessedness, is rendered vain, and nothing remains as a mode of escape from suffering except death; in such a case then death must be voluntarily accepted, just as we would take any other medicine. Here then a marked antagonism is brought out between the ethical system of Stoicism and all those systems referred to above which make virtue in itself directly, and accompanied by the most grievous sorrows, their aim, and will not allow a man to end his life in order to escape from suffering. Not one of them, however, was able to give the true reason for the rejection of suicide, but they laboriously collected illusory explanations from all sides: the true reason will appear in the Fourth Book in the course of the development of our system. But the antagonism referred to reveals and establishes the essential difference in fundamental principle between Stoicism, which is just a special form of endæmonism, and those doctrines we have mentioned, although both are often at one in their results, and are apparently related. And the inner contradiction referred to above, with which the ethical system of Stoicism is affected even in its fundamental thought, shows itself further in the circumstance that its ideal, the Stoic philosopher, as the system itself represents him, could never obtain life or inner poetic truth, but remains a wooden, stiff lay-figure of which nothing can be made. He cannot himself make use of his wisdom, and his perfect peace, contentment, and blessedness directly contradict the nature of man, and preclude us from forming any concrete idea of him. When compared with him, how entirely different appear the overcomers of the world, and voluntary hermits that Indian philosophy presents to us, and has actually produced; or indeed, the holy man of Christianity, that excellent form full of deep life, of the greatest poetic truth, and the highest significance, which stands before us in perfect virtue, holiness, and sublimity, yet in a state of supreme suffering.[1]

[1] Cf. Ch. 16 of Supplement.

Second Book

THE WORLD AS WILL

FIRST ASPECT

THE OBJECTIFICATION OF THE WILL

Nos habitat, non tartara, sed nec sidera coeli:
Spiritus, in nobis qui viget, illa facit.

II

§ 17. IN the first book we considered the idea merely as such, that is, only according to its general form. It is true that as far as the abstract idea, the concept, is concerned, we obtained a knowledge of it in respect of its content also, because it has content and meaning only in relation to the idea of perception, without which it would be worthless and empty. Accordingly, directing our attention exclusively to the idea of perception, we shall now endeavour to arrive at a knowledge of its content, its more exact definition, and the forms which it presents to us. And it will specially interest us to find an explanation of its peculiar significance, that significance which is otherwise merely felt, but on account of which it is that these pictures do not pass by us entirely strange and meaningless, as they must otherwise do, but speak to us directly, are understood, and obtain an interest which concerns our whole nature.

We direct our attention to mathematics, natural science, and philosophy, for each of these holds out the hope that it will afford us a part of the explanation we desire. Now, taking philosophy first, we find that it is like a monster with many heads, each of which speaks a different language. They are not, indeed, all at variance on the point we are here considering, the significance of the idea of perception. For, with the exception of the Sceptics and the Idealists, the others, for the most part, speak very much in the same way of an *object* which constitutes the *basis* of the idea, and which is indeed different in its whole being and nature from the idea, but yet is in all points as like it as one egg is to another. But this does not help us, for we are quite unable

to distinguish such an object from the idea; we find that
they are one and the same; for every object always and
for ever presupposes a subject, and therefore remains idea,
so that we recognised objectivity as belonging to the most
universal form of the idea, which is the division into subject
and object. Further, the principle of sufficient reason, which
is referred to in support of this doctrine, is for us merely
the form of the idea, the orderly combination of one idea
with another, but not the combination of the whole finite
or infinite series of ideas with something which is not idea
at all, and which cannot therefore be presented in perception. Of the Sceptics and Idealists we spoke above, in examining the controversy about the reality of the outer
world.

If we turn to mathematics to look for the fuller knowledge we desire of the idea of perception, which we have,
as yet, only understood generally, merely in its form, we
find that mathematics only treats of these ideas so far as
they fill time and space, that is, so far as they are quantities.
It will tell us with the greatest accuracy the how-many and
the how-much; but as this is always merely relative, that is
to say, merely a comparison of one idea with others, and a
comparison only in the one respect of quantity, this also
is not the information we are principally in search of.

Lastly, if we turn to the wide province of natural science,
which is divided into many fields, we may, in the first place,
make a general division of it into two parts. It is either
the description of forms, which I call *Morphology*, or the
explanation of changes, which I call *Etiology*. The first
treats of the permanent forms, the second of the changing
matter, according to the laws of its transition from one
form to another. The first is the whole extent of what is
generally called natural history. It teaches us, especially in
the sciences of botany and zoology, the various permanent,
organised, and therefore definitely determined forms in the

constant change of individuals; and these forms constitute
a great part of the content of the idea of perception. In
natural history they are classified, separated, united, arranged according to natural and artificial systems, and
brought under concepts which make a general view and
knowledge of the whole of them possible. Further, an infinitely fine analogy both in the whole and in the parts
of these forms, and running through them all (*unité de
plan*), is established, and thus they may be compared to
innumerable variations on a theme which is not given.
The passage of matter into these forms, that is to say, the
origin of individuals, is not a special part of natural science,
for every individual springs from its like by generation,
which is everywhere equally mysterious, and has as yet
evaded definite knowledge. The little that is known on
the subject finds its place in physiology, which belongs to
that part of natural science I have called etiology. Min-
eralogy also, especially where it becomes geology, inclines
towards etiology, though it principally belongs to morphology. Etiology proper comprehends all those branches
of natural science in which the chief concern is the knowledge of cause and effect. The sciences teach how, according
to an invariable rule, one condition of matter is necessarily
followed by a certain other condition; how one change
necessarily conditions and brings about a certain other
change; this sort of teaching is called *explanation*. The
principal sciences in this department are mechanics, physics,
chemistry, and physiology.

If, however, we surrender ourselves to its teaching, we
soon become convinced that etiology cannot afford us the
information we chiefly desire, any more than morphology.
The latter presents to us innumerable and infinitely varied
forms, which are yet related by an unmistakable family
likeness. These are for us ideas, and when only treated in
this way, they remain always strange to us, and stand before

us like hieroglyphics which we do not understand. Etiology, on the other hand, teaches us that, according to the law of cause and effect, this particular condition of matter brings about that other particular condition, and thus it has explained it and performed its part. However, it really does nothing more than indicate the orderly arrangement according to which the states of matter appear in space and time, and teach in all cases what phenomenon must necessarily appear at a particular time in a particular place. It thus determines the position of phenomena in time and space, according to a law whose special content is derived from experience, but whose universal form and necessity is yet known to us independently of experience. But it affords us absolutely no information about the inner nature of any one of these phenomena: this is called a *force of nature*, and it lies outside the province of causal explanation, which calls the constant uniformity with which manifestations of such a force appear whenever their known conditions are present, a *law of nature*. But this law of nature, these conditions, and this appearance in a particular place at a particular time, are all that it knows or ever can know. The force itself which manifests itself, the inner nature of the phenomena which appear in accordance with these laws, remains always a secret to it, something entirely strange and unknown in the case of the simplest as well as of the most complex phenomena. For although as yet etiology has most completely achieved its aim in mechanics, and least completely in physiology, still the force on account of which a stone falls to the ground or one body repels another is, in its inner nature, not less strange and mysterious than that which produces the movements and the growth of an animal. The science of mechanics presupposes matter, weight, impenetrability, the possibility of communicating motion by impact, inertia and so forth as ultimate facts, calls them forces of nature, and their necessary and orderly appearance under certain conditions a law of nature. Only after this does its explanation begin, and it consists in indicating truly and with mathematical exactness, how, where and when each force manifests itself, and in referring every phenomenon which presents itself to the operation of one of these forces. Physics, chemistry, and physiology proceed in the same way in their province, only they presuppose more and accomplish less. Consequently the most complete etiological explanation of the whole of nature can never be more than an enumeration of forces which cannot be explained, and a reliable statement of the rule according to which phenomena appear in time and space, succeed, and make way for each other. But the inner nature of the forces which thus appear remains unexplained by such an explanation, which must confine itself to phenomena and their arrangement, because the law which it follows does not extend further. In this respect it may be compared to a section of a piece of marble which shows many veins beside each other, but does not allow us to trace the course of the veins from the interior of the marble to its surface. Or, if I may use an absurd but more striking comparison, the philosophical investigator must always have the same feeling towards the complete etiology of the whole of nature as a man who, without knowing how, has been brought into a company quite unknown to him, each member of which in turn presents another to him as his friend and cousin, and therefore as quite well known, and yet the man himself, while at each introduction he expresses himself gratified, has always the question on his lips: "But how the deuce do I stand to the whole company?"

Thus we see that, with regard to those phenomena which we know only as our ideas, etiology can never give us the desired information that shall carry us beyond this point. For, after all its explanations, they still remain quite strange to us, as mere ideas whose significance we do not understand. The causal connection merely gives us the rule and the relative order of their appearance in space and time, but affords us no further knowledge of that which so appears. Moreover, the law of causality itself has only validity for ideas, for objects of a definite class, and it has meaning only in so far as it presupposes them. Thus, like these objects themselves, it always exists only in relation to a subject, that is, conditionally; and so it is known just as well if we start from the subject, *i.e., a priori,* as if we start from the object, *i.e., a posteriori.* Kant indeed has taught us this.

But what now impels us to inquiry is just that we are not satisfied with knowing that we have ideas, that they are such and such, and that they are connected according to certain laws, the general expression of which is the principle of sufficient reason. We wish to know the significance of these ideas; we ask whether this world is merely idea; in which case it would pass by us like an empty dream or a baseless vision, not worth our notice; or whether it is also something else, something more than idea, and if so, what. Thus much is certain, that this something we seek for must be completely and in its whole nature different from the idea; that the forms and laws of the idea must therefore be completely foreign to it; further, that we cannot arrive at it from the idea under the guidance of the laws which merely combine objects, ideas, among themselves, and which are the forms of the principle of sufficient reason.

Thus we see already that we can never arrive at the real nature of things from without. However much we investigate, we can never reach anything but images and names. We are like a man who goes round a castle seeking in vain for an entrance, and sometimes sketching the façades. And yet this is the method that has been followed by all philosophers before me.

§ 18. In fact, the meaning for which we seek of that
world which is present to us only as our idea, or the transition from the world as mere idea of the knowing subject
to whatever it may be besides this, would never be found
if the investigator himself were nothing more than the
pure knowing subject (a winged cherub without a body).
But he is himself rooted in that world; he finds himself in
it as an *individual*, that is to say, his knowledge, which is
the necessary supporter of the whole world as idea, is yet
always given through the medium of a body, whose affections are, as we have shown, the starting-point for the
understanding in the perception of that world. His body is,
for the pure knowing subject, an idea like every other idea,
an object among objects. Its movements and actions are so
far known to him in precisely the same way as the changes
of all other perceived objects, and would be just as strange
and incomprehensible to him if their meaning were not
explained for him in an entirely different way. Otherwise
he would see his actions follow upon given motives with
the constancy of a law of nature, just as the changes of
other objects follow upon causes, stimuli, or motives. But
he would not understand the influence of the motives any
more than the connection between every other effect which
he sees and its cause. He would then call the inner nature
of these manifestations and actions of his body which he
did not understand a force, a quality, or a character, as
he pleased, but he would have no further insight into it. But
all this is not the case; indeed the answer to the riddle is
given to the subject of knowledge who appears as an individual, and the answer is *will*. This and this alone gives him
the key to his own existence, reveals to him the significance,
shows him the inner mechanism of his being, of his action,
of his movements. The body is given in two entirely different ways to the subject of knowledge, who becomes an
individual only through his identity with it. It is given as

an idea in intelligent perception, as an object among objects and subject to the laws of objects. And it is also given in quite a different way as that which is immediately known to every one, and is signified by the word *will*. Every true act of his will is also at once and without exception a movement of his body. The act of will and the movement of the body are not two different things objectively known, which the bond of causality unites; they do not stand in the relation of cause and effect; they are one and the same, but they are given in entirely different ways,—immediately, and again in perception for the understanding. The action of the body is nothing but the act of the will objectified, *i.e.*, passed into perception. It will appear later that this is true of every movement of the body, not merely those which follow upon motives, but also involuntary movements which follow upon mere stimuli, and, indeed, that the whole body is nothing but objectified will, *i.e.*, will become idea. All this will be proved and made quite clear in the course of this work. In one respect, therefore, I shall call the body the *objectivity of will;* as in the previous book, and in the essay on the principle of sufficient reason, in accordance with the one-sided point of view intentionally adopted there (that of the idea), I called it *the immediate object*. Thus in a certain sense we may also say that will is the knowledge *a priori* of the body, and the body is the knowledge *a posteriori* of the will.

§ 19. In the first book we were reluctantly driven to explain the human body as merely idea of the subject which knows it, like all the other objects of this world of perception. But it has now become clear that what enables us consciously to distinguish our own body from all other objects which in other respects are precisely the same, is that our body appears in consciousness in quite another way *toto genere* different from idea, and this we denote by the word *will;* and that it is just this double knowledge which we have of our own body that affords us information about it, about its action and movement following on motives, and also about what it experiences by means of external impressions; in a word, about what it is, not as idea, but as more than idea; that is to say, what it is *in itself*. None of this information have we got directly with regard to the nature, action, and experience of other real objects.

It is just because of this special relation to one body that the knowing subject is an individual. For regarded apart from this relation, his body is for him only an idea like all other ideas. But the relation through which the knowing subject is an *individual*, is just on that account a relation which subsists only between him and one particular idea of all those which he has. Therefore he is conscious of this one idea, not merely as an idea, but in quite a different way as a will. If, however, he abstracts from that special relation, from that twofold and completely heterogeneous knowledge of what is one and the same, then that *one*, the body, is an idea like all other ideas. Therefore, in order to understand the matter, the individual who knows must either assume that what distinguishes that one idea from others is merely the fact that his knowledge stands in this double relation to it alone; that insight in two ways at the same time is open to him only in the case of this one object of perception, and that this is to be explained not by the difference of this object from all others, but only by the difference between the relation of his knowledge to this one object, and its relation to all other objects. Or else he must assume that this object is essentially different from all others; that it alone of all objects is at once both will and idea, while the rest are only ideas, *i.e.*, only phantoms. Thus he must assume that his body is the only real individual in the world, *i.e.*, the only phenomenon of will and the only immediate object of the subject. That other objects, considered merely as *ideas*, are like his body, that is, like it, fill space (which itself can only be present as idea), and also, like it, are causally active in space, is indeed demonstrably certain from the law of causality which is *a priori* valid for ideas, and which admits of no effect without a cause; but apart from the fact that we can only reason from an effect to a cause generally, and not to a similar cause, we are still in the sphere of mere ideas, in which alone the law of causality is valid, and beyond which it can never take us. But whether the objects known to the individual only as ideas are yet, like his own body, manifestations of a will, is, as was said in the First Book, the proper meaning of the question as to the reality of the external world. To deny this is *theoretical egoism*, which on that account regards all phenomena that are outside its own will as phantoms, just as in a practical reference exactly the same thing is done by practical egoism. For in it a man regards and treats himself alone as a person, and all other persons as mere phantoms. Theoretical egoism can never be demonstrably refuted, yet in philosophy it has never been used otherwise than as a sceptical sophism, *i.e.*, a pretence. As a serious conviction, on the other hand, it could only be found in a madhouse, and as such it stands in need of a cure rather than a refutation. We do not therefore combat it any further in this regard, but treat it as merely the last stronghold of scepticism, which is always polemical. Thus our knowledge, which is always bound to individuality and is limited by this circumstance, brings with it the necessity that each of us can only *be one*, while, on the other hand, each of us can *know all*; and it is this limitation that creates the need for philosophy. We therefore who, for this very reason, are striving to extend the limits of our knowledge through philosophy, will treat this sceptical argument of theoretical egoism which meets us, as an army would treat a small frontier fortress. The fortress cannot indeed be taken, but the garrison can never sally forth from it, and therefore we pass it by without danger, and are not afraid to have it in our rear.

The double knowledge which each of us has of the nature and activity of his own body, and which is given in two completely different ways, has now been clearly brought out. We shall accordingly make further use of it as a key to the nature of every phenomenon in nature, and shall judge of all objects which are not our own bodies, and are consequently not given to our consciousness in a double way but only as ideas, according to the analogy of our own bodies, and shall therefore assume that as in one aspect they are idea, just like our bodies, and in this respect are analogous to them, so in another aspect, what remains of objects when we set aside their existence as idea of the subject, must in its inner nature be the same as that in us which we call *will*. For what other kind of existence or reality should we attribute to the rest of the material world? Whence should we take the elements out of which we construct such a world? Besides will and idea nothing is known to us or thinkable. If we wish to attribute the greatest known reality to the material world which exists immediately only in our idea, we give it the reality which our own body has for each of us; for that is the most real thing for every one. But if we now analyse the reality of this body and its actions, beyond the fact that it is idea, we find nothing in it except the will; with this its reality is exhausted. Therefore we can nowhere find another kind of reality which we can attribute to the material world. Thus if we hold that the material world is something more than merely our idea, we must say that besides being idea, that is, in itself and according to its inmost nature, it is that which we find immediately in ourselves as *will*. I say according to its inmost nature; but we must first come to know more accurately this real nature of the will, in order that we may be able to distinguish from it what does not belong to itself, but to its manifestation, which has many grades. Such, for example, is the circumstance of its being accompanied by knowledge, and the determination by motives which is conditioned by this knowledge. As we shall see farther on, this does not belong to the real nature of will, but merely to its distinct manifestation as an animal or a human being. If, therefore, I say,—the force which attracts a stone to the earth is according to its nature, in itself, and apart from all idea, will, I shall not be supposed to express in this proposition the insane opinion that the stone moves itself in accordance with a known motive, merely because this is the way in which will appears in man. We shall now proceed more clearly and in detail to prove, establish, and develop to its full extent what as yet has only been provisionally and generally explained.

§ 20. As we have said, the will proclaims itself primarily in the voluntary movements of our own body, as the inmost nature of this body, as that which it is besides being object of perception, idea. For these voluntary movements are nothing else than the visible aspect of the individual acts of will, with which they are directly coincident and identical, and only distinguished through the form of knowledge into which they have passed, and in which alone they can be known, the form of idea.

But these acts of will have always a ground or reason outside themselves in motives. Yet these motives never determine more than what I will at *this* time, in *this* place, and under *these* circumstances, not *that* I will in general, or *what* I will in general, that is, the maxims which characterise my volition generally. Therefore the inner nature of my volition cannot be explained from these motives; but they merely determine its manifestation at a given point of time: they are merely the occasion of my will showing itself; but the will itself lies outside the province of the law of motivation, which determines nothing but its appearance at each point of time. It is only under the presupposition of my empirical character that the motive is a sufficient ground of explanation of my action. But if I abstract from my character, and then ask, why, in general, I will this and not that, no answer is possible, because it is only the manifestation of the will that is subject to the principle of sufficient reason, and not the will itself, which in this respect is to be called *groundless*.

If now every action of my body is the manifestation of an act of will in which my will itself in general, and as a whole, thus my character, expresses itself under given motives, manifestation of the will must be the inevitable condition and presupposition of every action. For the fact of its manifestation cannot depend upon something which does not exist directly and only through it, which consequently is for it merely accidental, and through which its manifestation itself would be merely accidental. Now that condition is just the whole body itself. Thus the body itself must be manifestation of the will, and it must be related to my will as a whole, that is, to my intelligible character, whose phenomenal appearance in time is my empirical character, as the particular action of the body is related to the particular act of the will. The whole body, then, must be simply my will become visible, must be my will itself, so far as this is object of perception, an idea of the first class. It has already been advanced in confirmation of this that every impression upon my body also affects my will at once and immediately, and in this respect is called pain or pleasure, or, in its lower degrees, agreeable or disagreeable sensation; and also, conversely, that every violent movement of the will, every emotion or passion, convulses the body and disturbs the course of its functions. Indeed we can also give an etiological account, though a very incomplete one, of the origin of my body, and a somewhat better account of its development and conservation, and this is the substance of physiology. But physiology merely explains its theme in precisely the same way as motives explain action. Thus the physiological explanation of the functions of the body detracts just as little from the philosophical truth that the whole existence of this body and the sum total of its functions are merely the objectification of that will which appears in its outward actions in accordance with a motive, as the establishment of the individual action through the motive and the necessary sequence of the action from the motive conflicts with the fact that action in general, and according to its nature, is only the manifestation of a will which itself has no ground. If, however, physiology tries to refer even these outward actions, the immediate voluntary movements, to causes in the organism,—for example, if it explains the movement of the muscles as resulting from the presence of fluids, even supposing it really could give a thorough explanation of this kind, yet this would never invalidate the immediately certain truth that every voluntary motion (*functiones animales*) is the manifestation of an act of will. Now, just as little can the physiological explanation of vegetative life (*functiones naturales vitales*), however far it may advance, ever invalidate the truth that the whole animal life which thus develops itself is the manifestation of will. In general, then, as we have shown above, no etiological explanation can ever give us more than the necessarily determined position in time and space of a particular manifestation, its necessary appearance there, according to a fixed law; but the inner nature of everything that appears in this way remains wholly inexplicable, and is presupposed by every etiological explanation, and merely indicated by the names, force, or law of nature, or, if we are speaking of action, character or will. Thus, although every particular action, under the presupposition of the definite character, necessarily follows from the given motive, and although growth, the process of nourishment, and all the changes of the animal body take place according to necessarily acting causes (stimuli), yet the whole series of actions, and consequently every individual act, and also its condition, the whole body itself which accomplishes it, and therefore also the process through which and in which it exists, are nothing but the manifestation of the will, the becoming visible, *the objectification of the will*. Upon this rests the perfect suitableness of the human and animal body to the human and animal will in general, resembling, though far surpassing, the correspondence between an instrument made for a purpose and the will of the maker, and on this account appearing as design, *i.e.*, the teleological explanation of the body. The parts of the body must, therefore, completely correspond to the principal desires through which the will manifests itself; they must be the visible expression of these desires. Teeth, throat, and bowels are objectified hunger; the organs of generation are objectified sexual desire; the grasping hand, the hurrying feet, correspond to the more indirect desires of the will which they express. As the human form generally corresponds to the human will generally, so the individual bodily structure corresponds to the individually modified will, the character of the individual, and therefore it is throughout and in all parts characteristic and full of expression.

§ 21. Whoever has now gained from all these expositions a knowledge *in abstracto*, and therefore clear and certain, of what every one knows directly *in concreto*, *i.e.*, as feeling, a knowledge that his will is the real inner nature of his phenomenal being, which manifests itself to him as idea, both in his actions and in their permanent substratum, his body, and that his will is that which is most immediate in his consciousness, though it has not as such completely passed into the form of idea in which object and subject stand over against each other, but makes itself known to

him in a direct manner, in which he does not quite clearly
distinguish subject and object, yet is not known as a whole
to the individual himself, but only in its particular acts,—
whoever, I say, has with me gained this conviction will
find that of itself it affords him the key to the knowledge
of the inmost being of the whole of nature; for he now
transfers it to all those phenomena which are not given to
him, like his own phenomenal existence, both in direct and
indirect knowledge, but only in the latter, thus merely one-
sidedly as *idea* alone. He will recognise this will of which
we are speaking not only in those phenomenal existences
which exactly resemble his own, in men and animals as
their inmost nature, but the course of reflection will lead
him to recognise the force which germinates and vegetates
in the plant, and indeed the force through which the crystal
is formed, that by which the magnet turns to the north
pole, the force whose shock he experiences from the contact
of two different kinds of metals, the force which appears
in the elective affinities of matter as repulsion and attraction,
decomposition and combination, and, lastly, even gravitation,
which acts so powerfully throughout matter, draws the
stone to the earth and the earth to the sun,—all these, I
say, he will recognise as different only in their phenomenal
existence, but in their inner nature as identical, as that
which is directly known to him so intimately and so much
better than anything else, and which in its most distinct
manifestation is called *will*. It is this application of reflection alone that prevents us from remaining any longer at the
phenomenon, and leads us to the *thing-in-itself*. Phenomenal
existence is idea and nothing more. All idea, of whatever
kind it may be, all *object*, is *phenomenal* existence, but the
will alone is a *thing-in-itself*. As such, it is throughout not
idea, but *toto genere* different from it; it is that of which
all idea, all object, is the phenomenal appearance, the
visibility, the objectification. It is the inmost nature, the

kernel, of every particular thing, and also of the whole. It appears in every blind force of nature and also in the preconsidered action of man; and the great difference between these two is merely in the degree of the manifestation, not in the nature of what manifests itself.

§ 22. Now, if we are to think as an object this thing-in-itself (we wish to retain the Kantian expression as a standing formula), which, as such, is never object, because all object is its mere manifestation, and therefore cannot be it itself, we must borrow for it the name and concept of an object, of something in some way objectively given, consequently of one of its own manifestations. But in order to serve as a clue for the understanding, this can be no other than the most complete of all its manifestations, *i.e.*, the most distinct, the most developed, and directly enlightened by knowledge. Now this is the human will. It is, however, well to observe that here, at any rate, we only make use of a *denominatio a potiori*, through which, therefore, the concept of will receives a greater extension than it has hitherto had. Knowledge of the identical in different phenomena, and of difference in similar phenomena, is, as Plato so often remarks, a *sine qua non* of philosophy. But hitherto it was not recognised that every kind of active and operating force in nature is essentially identical with will, and therefore the multifarious kinds of phenomena were not seen to be merely different species of the same genus, but were treated as heterogeneous. Consequently there could be no word to denote the concept of this genus. I therefore name the genus after its most important species, the direct knowledge of which lies nearer to us and guides us to the indirect knowledge of all other species. But whoever is incapable of carrying out the required extension of the concept will remain involved in a permanent misunderstanding. For by the word *will* he understands only that species of it which has hitherto been

exclusively denoted by it, the will which is guided by
knowledge, and whose manifestation follows only upon
motives, and indeed merely abstract motives, and thus takes
place under the guidance of the reason. This, we have said,
is only the most prominent example of the manifestation
of will. We must now distinctly separate in thought the
inmost essence of this manifestation which is known to
us directly, and then transfer it to all the weaker, less distinct manifestations of the same nature, and thus we shall
accomplish the desired extension of the concept of will.
From another point of view I should be equally misunder-
stood by any one who should think that it is all the same
in the end whether we denote this inner nature of all
phenomena by the word *will* or by any other. This would
be the case if the thing-in-itself were something whose
existence we merely *inferred*, and thus knew indirectly and
only in the abstract. Then, indeed, we might call it what
we pleased; the name would stand merely as the symbol
of an unknown quantity. But the word *will*, which, like
a magic spell, discloses to us the inmost being of everything
in nature, is by no means an unknown quantity, something
arrived at only by inference, but is fully and immediately
comprehended, and is so familiar to us that we know and
understand what will is far better than anything else whatever. The concept of will has hitherto commonly been
subordinated to that of force, but I reverse the matter
entirely, and desire that every force in nature should be
thought as will. It must not be supposed that this is mere
verbal quibbling or of no consequence; rather, it is of the
greatest significance and importance. For at the foundation of the concept of force, as of all other concepts, there
ultimately lies the knowledge in sense-perception of the
objective world, that is to say, the phenomenon, the idea;
and the concept is constructed out of this. It is an abstraction from the province in which cause and effect reign, *i.e.*,

from ideas of perception, and means just the causal nature of causes at the point at which this causal nature is no further etiologically explicable, but is the necessary presupposition of all etiological explanation. The concept will, on the other hand, is of all possible concepts the only one which has its source *not* in the phenomenal, *not* in the mere idea of perception, but comes from within, and proceeds from the most immediate consciousness of each of us, in which each of us knows his own individuality, according to its nature, immediately, apart from all form, even that of subject and object, and which at the same time is this individuality, for here the subject and the object of knowledge are one. If, therefore, we refer the concept of *force* to that of *will*, we have in fact referred the less known to what is infinitely better known; indeed, to the one thing that is really immediately and fully known to us, and have very greatly extended our knowledge. If, on the contrary, we subsume the concept of will under that of force, as has hitherto always been done, we renounce the only immediate knowledge which we have of the inner nature of the world, for we allow it to disappear in a concept which is abstracted from the phenomenal, and with which we can therefore never go beyond the phenomenal.

§ 23. The *will* as a thing-in-itself is quite different from its phenomenal appearance, and entirely free from all the forms of the phenomenal, into which it first passes when it manifests itself, and which therefore only concern its *objectivity*, and are foreign to the will itself. Even the most universal form of all idea, that of being object for a subject, does not concern it; still less the forms which are subordinate to this and which collectively have their common expression in the principle of sufficient reason, to which we know that time and space belong, and consequently multiplicity also, which exists and is possible only through these. In this last regard I shall call time and

space the *principium individuationis,* borrowing an expression from the old schoolmen, and I beg to draw
attention to this, once for all. For it is only through
the medium of time and space that what is one and the
same, both according to its nature and to its concept, yet
appears as different, as a multiplicity of co-existent and
successive phenomena. Thus time and space are the *principium individuationis,* the subject of so many subtleties and
disputes among the schoolmen. According to what has been
said, the will as a thing-in-itself lies outside the province
of the principle of sufficient reason in all its forms, and is
consequently completely groundless, although all its manifestations are entirely subordinated to the principle of sufficient reason. Further, it is free from all *multiplicity,*
although its manifestations in time and space are innumerable. It is itself one, though not in the sense in which
an object is one, for the unity of an object can only be
known in opposition to a possible multiplicity; nor yet in
the sense in which a concept is one, for the unity of a concept originates only in abstraction from a multiplicity; but
it is one as that which lies outside time and space, the
principium individuationis, i.e., the possibility of multiplicity.
Only when all this has become quite clear to us through
the subsequent examination of the phenomena and different manifestations of the will, shall we fully understand the meaning of the Kantian doctrine that time, space
and causality do not belong to the thing-in-itself, but are
only forms of knowing.

The uncaused nature of will has been actually recognised, where it manifests itself most distinctly, as the will
of man, and this has been called free, independent. But
on account of the uncaused nature of the will itself, the
necessity to which its manifestation is everywhere subjected has been overlooked, and actions are treated as free,
which they are not. For every individual action follows

with strict necessity from the effect of the motive upon the character. All necessity is, as we have already said, the relation of the consequent to the reason, and nothing more. The principle of sufficient reason is the universal form of all phenomena, and man in his action must be subordinated to it like every other phenomenon. But because in self-consciousness the will is known directly and in itself, in this consciousness lies also the consciousness of freedom. The fact is, however, overlooked that the individual, the person, is not will as a thing-in-itself, but is a *phenomenon* of will, is already determined as such, and has come under the form of the phenomenal, the principle of sufficient reason. Hence arises the strange fact that every one believes himself *a priori* to be perfectly free, even in his individual actions, and thinks that at every moment he can commence another manner of life, which just means that he can become another person. But *a posteriori*, through experience, he finds to his astonishment that he is not free, but subjected to necessity; that in spite of all his resolutions and reflections he does not change his conduct, and that from the beginning of his life to the end of it, he must carry out the very character which he himself condemns, and as it were play the part he has undertaken to the end. I cannot pursue this subject further at present, for it belongs, as ethical, to another part of this work. In the meantime, I only wish to point out here that the *phenomenon* of the will which in itself is uncaused, is yet as such subordinated to the law of necessity, that is, the principle of sufficient reason, so that in the necessity with which the phenomena of nature follow each other, we may find nothing to hinder us from recognising in them the manifestations of will.

Only those changes which have no other ground than a motive, *i.e.*, an idea, have hitherto been regarded as manifestations of will. Therefore in nature a will has only been attributed to man, or at the most to animals; for knowledge, the idea is, of course, as I have said elsewhere, the true and exclusive characteristic of animal life. But that the will is also active where no knowledge guides it, we see at once in the instinct and the mechanical skill of animals. That they have ideas and knowledge is here not to the point, for the end towards which they strive as definitely as if it were a known motive, is yet entirely unknown to them. Therefore in such cases their action takes place without motive, is not guided by the idea, and shows us first and most distinctly how the will may be active entirely without knowledge. The bird of a year old has no idea of the eggs for which it builds a nest; the young spider has no idea of the prey for which it spins a web; nor has the ant-lion any idea of the ants for which he digs a trench for the first time. The larva of the stag-beetle makes the hole in the wood, in which it is to await its metamorphosis, twice as big if it is going to be a male beetle as if it is going to be a female, so that if it is a male there may be room for the horns, of which, however, it has no idea. In such actions of these creatures the will is clearly operative as in their other actions, but it is in blind activity, which is indeed accompanied by knowledge but not guided by it. If now we have once gained insight into the fact, that idea as motive is not a necessary and essential condition of the activity of the will, we shall more easily recognise the activity of will where it is less apparent. For example, we shall see that the house of the snail is no more made by a will which is foreign to the snail itself, than the house which we build is produced through another will than our own; but we shall recognise in both houses the work of a will which objectifies itself in both the phenomena—a will which works in us according to motives, but in the snail still blindly as formative impulse directed outwards. In us also the same will is in many ways only blindly active: in all the functions of our body which are not guided by

THE WORLD AS WILL

knowledge, in all its vital and vegetative processes, digestion, circulation, secretion, growth, reproduction. Not only the actions of the body, but the whole body itself is, as we have shown above, phenomenon of the will, objectified will, concrete will. All that goes on in it must therefore proceed through will, although here this will is not guided by knowledge, but acts blindly according to causes, which in this case are called *stimuli*.

I call a *cause*, in the narrowest sense of the word, that state of matter, which, while it introduces another state with necessity, yet suffers just as great a change itself as that which it causes; which is expressed in the rule, "action and reaction are equal." Further, in the case of what is properly speaking a cause, the effect increases directly in proportion to the cause, and therefore also the reaction. So that, if once the mode of operation be known, the degree of the effect may be measured and calculated from the degree of the intensity of the cause; and conversely the degree of the intensity of the cause may be calculated from the degree of the effect. Such causes, properly so called, operate in all the phenomena of mechanics, chemistry, and so forth; in short, in all the changes of unorganised bodies. On the other hand, I call a *stimulus*, such a cause as sustains no reaction proportional to its effect, and the intensity of which does not vary directly in proportion to the intensity of its effect, so that the effect cannot be measured by it. On the contrary, a small increase of the stimulus may cause a very great increase of the effect, or conversely, it may eliminate the previous effect altogether, and so forth. All effects upon organised bodies as such are of this kind. All properly organic and vegetative changes of the animal body must therefore be referred to stimuli, not to mere causes. But the stimulus, like every cause and motive generally, never determines more than the point of time and space at which the manifestation of every force is to take place, and does not determine the inner nature of the force itself which is manifested. This inner nature we know, from our previous investigation, is will, to which therefore we ascribe both the unconscious and the conscious changes of the body. The stimulus holds the mean, forms the transition between the motive, which is causality accompanied throughout by knowledge, and the cause in the narrowest sense. In particular cases, it is sometimes nearer a motive, sometimes nearer a cause, but yet it can always be distinguished from both. Thus, for example, the rising of the sap in a plant follows upon stimuli, and cannot be explained from mere causes, according to the laws of hydraulics or capillary attraction; yet it is certainly assisted by these, and altogether approaches very near to a purely causal change. On the other hand, the movements of the *Hedysarum gyrans* and the *Mimosa pudica,* although still following upon mere stimuli, are yet very like movements which follow upon motives, and seem almost to wish to make the transition. The contraction of the pupils of the eyes as the light is increased is due to stimuli, but it passes into movement which is due to motive; for it takes place, because too strong lights would affect the retina painfully, and to avoid this we contract the pupils. The occasion of an erection is a motive, because it is an idea, yet it operates with the necessity of a stimulus, *i.e.,* it cannot be resisted, but we must put the idea away in order to make it cease to affect us. This is also the case with disgusting things, which excite the desire to vomit. Thus we have treated the instinct of animals as an actual link, of quite a distinct kind, between movement following upon stimuli and action following upon a known motive. Now we might be asked to regard breathing as another link of this kind. It has been disputed whether it belongs to the voluntary or the involuntary movements, that is to say, whether it follows upon motive or stimulus, and perhaps it may be explained as some-

THE WORLD AS WILL
Diseases of the Nervous System," § 293 sq.) explains it as
a mixed function, for it is partly under the influence of the
(non-voluntary) nerves. However, we are finally obliged
to number it with the expressions of will which result from
the will to check it or accelerate it, and, as is the case with
every other voluntary action, it seems to us that we could
in fact we could do so if any other motive influenced the
end to his life in this way. Certain negroes also are said to
have done this. If this be true, it affords us a good example
of the influence of abstract motives, *i.e.*, of the victory of
is shown by the fact that the primary cause of death from
prussic acid is that it paralyses the brain, and so, indirectly,
death will not ensue. We may also observe in passing that
that motives act with just as much necessity as stimuli, or as
causes in the narrowest sense of the word, and their opera-
breathing, the illusion that we can stop when we like is
very powerful, very near to us, and its satisfaction is very
nothing, as a rule, obstructs it, and the whole process is sup-

yet all motives act with the same necessity. The knowledge that necessity is common to movements following upon motives, and those following upon stimuli, makes it easier for us to understand that that also which takes place in our bodily organism in accordance with stimuli and in obedience to law, is yet, according to its inner nature—will, which in all its manifestations, though never in itself, is subordinated to the principle of sufficient reason, that is, to necessity.[1] Accordingly, we shall not rest contented with recognising that animals, both in their actions and also in their whole existence, bodily structure and organisation, are manifestations of will; but we shall extend to plants also this immediate knowledge of the essential nature of things which is given to us alone. Now all the movements of plants follow upon stimuli; for the absence of knowledge, and the movement following upon motives which is conditioned by knowledge, constitutes the only essential difference between animals and plants. Therefore, what appears for the idea as plant life, as mere vegetation, as blindly impelling force, we shall claim, according to its inner nature for will, and recognise it as just that which constitutes the basis of our own phenomenal being, as it expresses itself in our actions, and also in the whole existence of our body itself.

It only remains for us to take the final step, the extension of our way of looking at things to all those forces which act in nature in accordance with universal, unchangeable laws, in conformity with which the movements of all those bodies take place, which are wholly without organs, and have therefore no susceptibility for stimuli, and have no knowledge, which is the necessary condition of motives. Thus we must also apply the key to the understanding of the inner nature of things, which the immediate knowledge of our

[1] This subject is fully worked out in my prize essay on the freedom of the will, in which therefore (pp. 29-44 of the "Grundprobleme der Ethik") the relation of *cause, stimulus,* and *motive* has also been fully explained

own existence alone can give us, to those phenomena of the unorganised world which are most remote from us. And if we consider them attentively, if we observe the strong and unceasing impulse with which the waters hurry to the ocean, the persistency with which the magnet turns ever to the north pole, the readiness with which iron flies to the magnet, the eagerness with which the electric poles seek to be re-united, and which, just like human desire, is increased by obstacles; if we see the crystal quickly and suddenly take form with such wonderful regularity of construction, which is clearly only a perfectly definite and accurately determined impulse in different directions, seized and retained by crystallisation; if we observe the choice with which bodies repel and attract each other, combine and separate, when they are set free in a fluid state, and emancipated from the bonds of rigidness; lastly, if we feel directly how a burden which hampers our body by its gravitation towards the earth, unceasingly presses and strains upon it in pursuit of its one tendency; if we observe all this, I say, it will require no great effort of the imagination to recognise, even at so great a distance, our own nature. That which in us pursues its ends by the light of knowledge; but here, in the weakest of its manifestations, only strives blindly and dumbly in a one-sided and unchangeable manner, must yet in both cases come under the name of will, as it is everywhere one and the same —just as the first dim light of dawn must share the name of sunlight with the rays of the full mid-day. For the name *will* denotes that which is the inner nature of everything in the world, and the one kernel of every phenomenon.

Yet the remoteness, and indeed the appearance of abso-lute difference between the phenomena of unorganised na-ture and the will which we know as the inner reality of our own being arises chiefly from the contrast between the com-pletely determined conformity to law of the one species of phenomena, and the apparently unfettered freedom of the other. For in man, individuality makes itself powerfully felt. Every one has a character of his own; and therefore the same motive has not the same influence over all, and a thousand circumstances which exist in the wide sphere of the knowledge of the individual, but are unknown to others, modify its effect. Therefore action cannot be predetermined from the motive alone, for the other factor is wanting, the accurate acquaintance with the individual character, and with the knowledge which accompanies it. On the other hand, the phenomena of the forces of nature illustrate the opposite extreme. They act according to universal laws, without variation, without individuality in accordance with openly manifest circumstances, subject to the most exact predetermination; and the same force of nature appears in its million phenomena in precisely the same way. In order to explain this point and prove the identity of the *one* indivisible will in all its different phenomena, in the weakest as in the strongest, we must first of all consider the relation of the will as thing-in-itself to its phenomena, that is, the relation of the world as will to the world as idea; for this will open to us the best way to a more thorough investigation of the whole subject we are considering in this second book.

§ 24. We have learnt from the great Kant that time, space, and causality, with their entire constitution, and the possibility of all their forms, are present in our consciousness quite independently of the objects which appear in them, and which constitute their content; or, in other words, they can be arrived at just as well if we start from the subject as if we start from the object. Therefore, with equal accuracy, we may call them either forms of intuition or perception of the subject, or qualities of the object *as object* (with Kant, phenomena), *i.e.*, *idea*. We may also regard these forms as the irreducible boundary between object and subject. All objects must therefore exist in them, yet the subject, independently of the phenomenal object, possesses and surveys them completely. But if the objects appearing in these forms are not to be empty phantoms, but are to have a meaning, they must refer to something, must be the expression of something which is not, like themselves, object, idea, a merely relative existence for a subject, but which exists without such dependence upon something which stands over against it as a condition of its being, and independent of the forms of such a thing, *i.e., is not idea,* but a *thing-in-itself.* Consequently it may at least be asked: Are these ideas, these objects, something more than or apart from the fact that they are ideas, objects of the subject? And what would they be in this sense? What is that other side of them which is *toto genere* different from idea? What is the thing-in-itself? *The will,* we have answered, but for the present I set that answer aside.

Whatever the thing-in-itself may be, Kant is right in his conclusion that time, space, and causality (which we afterwards found to be forms of the principle of sufficient reason, the general expression of the forms of the phenomenon) are not its properties, but come to it only after, and so far as, it has become idea. That is, they belong only to its phenomenal existence, not to itself. For since the subject fully understands and constructs them out of itself, independently of all object, they must be dependent upon *existence as idea* as such, not upon that which becomes idea. They must be the form of the idea as such; but not qualities of that which has assumed this form. They must be already given with the mere antithesis of subject and object (not as concepts but as facts), and consequently they must be only the more exact determination of the form of knowledge in general, whose most universal determination is that antithesis itself. Now, that in the phenomenon, in the object, which is in its turn conditioned by time, space and causality, inasmuch as it can only become idea by means of them, namely *multiplicity,* through co-existence and succession, *change and permanence* through the law of causality, *matter* which can only become idea under the presupposition of causality, and lastly, all that becomes idea only by means of these,—all this, I say, as a whole, does not in reality belong to that which appears, to that which has passed into the form of idea, but belongs merely to this form itself. And conversely, that in the phenomenon which is not conditioned through time, space and causality, and which cannot be referred to them, nor explained in accordance with them, is precisely that in which the thing manifested, the thing-in-itself, directly reveals itself. It follows from this that the most complete capacity for being known, that is to say, the greatest clearness, distinctness, and susceptibility of exhaustive explanation, will necessarily belong to that which pertains to knowledge *as such,* and thus to the *form* of knowledge; but not to that which in itself is not idea, not object, but which has become knowledge only through entering these forms; in other words, has become idea, object. Thus only that which depends entirely upon being an object of knowledge, upon existing as idea in general and *as such* (not upon that which *becomes* known, and has only *become* idea), which therefore belongs without distinction to everything that is known, and which, on that account, is found just as well if we start from the subject as if we start from the object,—this alone can afford us without reserve a sufficient, exhaustive knowledge, a knowledge which is clear to the very foundation. But this consists of nothing but those forms of all phenomena of which we are conscious *a priori,* and which may be generally expressed as the principle of sufficient reason. Now, the forms of this principle which occur in knowledge of perception (with which alone we are here concerned) are time, space, and causality. The whole of pure mathematics and pure natural science *a priori* is based entirely upon these. Therefore it is only in these sciences that knowledge finds no obscurity, does not rest upon what is incomprehensible (groundless, *i.e.*, will), upon what cannot be further deduced. It is on this account that Kant wanted, as we have said, to apply the name science specially and even exclusively to these branches of knowledge together with logic. But, on the other hand, these branches of knowledge show us nothing more than mere connections, relations of one idea to another, form devoid of all content. All content which they receive, every phenomenon which fills these forms, contains something which is no longer completely knowable in its whole nature, something which can no longer be entirely explained through something else, something then which is groundless, through which consequently the knowledge loses its evidence and ceases to be completely lucid. This that withholds itself from investigation, however, is the thing-in-itself, is that which is essentially not idea, not object of knowledge, but has only become knowable by entering that form. The form is originally foreign to it, and the thing-in-itself can never become entirely one with it, can never be referred to mere form, and, since this form is the principle of sufficient reason, can never be completely explained. If therefore all mathematics affords us an exhaustive knowledge of that which in the phenomena is quantity, position, number, in a word, spatial and temporal relations; if all etiology gives us a complete account of the regular conditions under which phenomena, with all their determinations, appear in time and space, but, with it all, teaches us nothing more than why in each case this particular phenomena must appear just at this time here, and at this place now; it is clear that with their assistance we can never penetrate to the inner nature of things. There always remains something which no explanation can venture to attack, but which it always presupposes; the forces of nature, the definite mode of operation of things, the quality and character of every phenomenon, that which is without ground, that which does not depend upon the form of the phenomenal, the principle of sufficient reason, but is something to which this form in itself is foreign, something which has yet entered this form, and now appears according to its law, a law, however, which only determines the appearance, not that which appears, only the how, not the what, only the form, not the content. Mechanics, physics, and chemistry teach the rules and laws according to which the forces of impenetrability, gravitation, rigidity, fluidity, cohesion, elasticity, heat, light, affinity, magnetism, electricity, &c., operate; that is to say, the law, the rule which these forces observe whenever they enter time and space. But do what we will, the forces themselves remain *qualitates occultæ*. For it is just the thing-in-itself, which, because it is manifested, exhibits these phenomena, which are entirely different from itself. In its manifestation, indeed, it is completely subordinated to the principle of sufficient reason as the form of the idea, but it can never itself be referred to this form, and therefore cannot be fully explained etiologically, can never be completely fathomed. It is certainly perfectly comprehensible so far as it has assumed that form, that is, so far as it is phenomenon, but its inner nature is not in the least explained by the fact that it can thus be comprehended. Therefore the more necessity any knowledge carries with it, the more there is in it of that which cannot be otherwise thought or presented in perception—as, for example, space-relations—the clearer and more sufficing then it is, the less pure objective content it has, or the less reality, properly so called, is given in it. And conversely, the more there is in it which must be conceived as mere chance, and the more it impresses us as given merely empirically, the more proper objectivity and true reality is there in such knowledge, and at the same time, the more that is inexplicable, that is, that cannot be deduced from anything else.

It is true that at all times an etiology, unmindful of its real aim, has striven to reduce all organised life to chemism or electricity; all chemism, that is to say, quality, again to mechanism (action determined by the shape of the atom), this again sometimes to the object of phoronomy, *i.e.*, the combination of time and space, which makes motion possible, sometimes to the object of mere geometry, *i.e.*, position in space (much in the same way as we rightly deduce the diminution of an effect from the square of the distance, and the theory of the lever in a purely geometrical manner): geometry may finally be reduced to arithmetic, which, on account of its one dimension, is of all the forms of the principle of sufficient reason, the most intelligible, comprehensible, and completely susceptible of investigation. As instances of the method generally indicated here, we may refer to the atoms of Democritus, the vortex of Descartes, the mechanical physics of Lesage, which towards the end of last century tried to explain both chemical affinities and gravitation mechanically by impact and pressure, as may be seen in detail in *"Lucrèce Neutonien"*; Reil's form and combination as the cause of animal life, also tends in this direction. Finally, the crude materialism which even now in the middle of the nineteenth century has been served up again under the ignorant delusion that it is original, belongs distinctly to this class. It stupidly denies vital force, and first of all tries to explain the phenomena of life from physical and chemical forces, and those again from the mechanical effects of the matter, position, form, and motion of imagined atoms, and thus seeks to reduce all the forces of nature to action and reaction as its thing-in-itself. We shall soon have to speak again of this false reduction of the forces of nature to each other; so much for the present. Supposing this theory were possible, all would certainly be explained and established and finally reduced to an arithmetical problem, which would then be the holiest thing in the temple of wisdom, to which the principle of sufficient reason would at last have happily conducted us. But all content of the phenomenon would have disappeared, and the mere form would remain. The "what appears" would be referred to the "how it appears," and this "how" would be what is *a priori* knowable, therefore entirely dependent on the subject, therefore only for the subject, therefore, lastly, mere phantom, idea and form of idea, through and through: no thing-in-itself could be demanded. Supposing, then, that this were possible, the whole world would be derived from the subject, and, in fact, that would be accomplished which Fichte wanted to *seem* to accomplish by his empty bombast. But it is not possible: phantasies, sophisms, castles in the air, have been constructed in this way, but science never. The many and multifarious phenomena in nature have been successfully referred to particular original forces, and as often as this has been done, a real advance has been made. Several forces and qualities, which were at first regarded as different, have been derived from each other, and thus their number has been curtailed. (For example, magnetism from electricity.) Etiology will have reached its goal when it has recognised and exhibited as such all the original forces of nature, and established their mode of operation, *i.e.*, the law according to which, under the guidance of causality, their phenomena appear in time and space, and determine their position with regard to each other. But certain original forces will always remain over; there will always remain as an insoluble residuum a content of phenomena which cannot be referred to their form, and thus cannot be explained from something else in accordance with the principle of sufficient reason. For in everything in nature there is something of which no ground can ever be assigned, of which no explanation is possible, and no ulterior cause is to be sought. This is the specific nature of its action, *i.e.*, the nature of its existence, its being. Of each particular effect of the thing a cause may be certainly indicated, from which it follows that it must act just at this time and in this place;

but no cause can ever be found from which it follows that a thing acts in general, and precisely in the way it does. If it has no other qualities, if it is merely a mote in a sunbeam, it yet exhibits this unfathomable something, at least as weight and impenetrability. But this, I say, is to the mote what his will is to a man; and, like the human will, it is, according to its inner nature, not subject to explanation; nay, more—it is in itself identical with this will. It is true that a motive may be given for every manifestation of will, for every act of will at a particular time and in a particular place, upon which it must necessarily follow, under the presupposition of the character of the man. But no reason can ever be given that the man has this character; that he wills at all; that, of several motives, just this one and no other, or indeed that any motive at all, moves his will. That which in the case of man is the unfathomable character which is presupposed in every explanation of his actions from motives is, in the case of every unorganised body, its definitive quality—the mode of its action, the manifestations of which are occasioned by impressions from without, while it itself, on the contrary, is determined by nothing outside itself, and thus is also inexplicable. Its particular manifestations, through which alone it becomes visible, are subordinated to the principle of sufficient reason; it itself is groundless.

It is a greater and a commoner error that the phenomena which we best understand are those which are of most frequent occurrence, and which are most universal and simple; for, on the contrary, these are just the phenomena that we are most accustomed to see about us, and to be ignorant of. It is just as inexplicable to us that a stone should fall to the earth as that an animal should move itself. It has been supposed, as we have remarked above, that, starting from the most universal forces of nature (gravitation, cohesion, impenetrability), it was possible to explain from them the rarer forces, which only operate under a combination of circumstances (for example, chemical quality, electricity, magnetism), and, lastly, from these to understand the organism and the life of animals, and even the nature of human knowing and willing. Men resigned themselves without a word to starting from mere *qualitates occultæ*, the elucidation of which was entirely given up, for they intended to build upon them, not to investigate them. Such an intention cannot, as we have already said, be carried out. But apart from this, such structures would always stand in the air. What is the use of explanations which ultimately refer us to something which is quite as unknown as the problem with which we started? Do we in the end understand more of the inner nature of these universal natural forces than of the inner nature of an animal? Is not the one as much a sealed book to us as the other? Unfathomable because it is without ground, because it is the content, that which the phenomenon is, and which can never be referred to the form, to the how, to the principle of sufficient reason. But we, who have in view not etiology but philosophy, that is, not relative but unconditioned knowledge of the real nature of the world, take the opposite course, and start from that which is immediately and most completely known to us, and fully and entirely trusted by us—that which lies nearest to us, in order to understand that which is known to us only at a distance, one-sidedly and indirectly. From the most powerful, most significant, and most distinct phenomenon we seek to arrive at an understanding of those that are less complete and weaker. With the exception of my own body, all things are known to me only on *one* side, that of the idea. Their inner nature remains hidden from me and a profound secret, even if I know all the causes from which their changes follow. Only by comparison with that which goes on in me if my body performs an action when I am influenced by a motive—only by comparison, I say, with what is the inner nature of my own changes determined by external reasons, can I obtain insight into the way in which these lifeless bodies change under the influence of causes, and so understand what is their inner nature. For the knowledge of the causes of the manifestation of this inner nature affords me merely the rule of its appearance in time and space, and nothing more. I can make this comparison because my body is the only object of which I know not merely the *one* side, that of the idea, but also the other side which is called will. Thus, instead of believing that I would better understand my own organisation, and then my own knowing and willing, and my movements following upon motives, if I could only refer them to movements due to electrical, chemical, and mechanical causes, I must, seeing that I seek philosophy and not etiology, learn to understand from my own movements following upon motives the inner nature of the simplest and commonest movements of an unorganised body which I see following upon causes. I must recognise the inscrutable forces which manifest themselves in all natural bodies as identical in kind with that which in me is the will, and as differing from it only in degree. That is to say, the fourth class of ideas given in the Essay on the Principle of Sufficient Reason must be the key to the knowledge of the inner nature of the first class, and by means of the law of motivation I must come to understand the inner meaning of the law of causation.

Spinoza (Epist. 62) says that if a stone which has been projected through the air had consciousness, it would believe that it was moving of its own will. I add to this only that the stone would be right. The impulse given it is for the stone what the motive is for me, and what in the case of the stone appears as cohesion, gravitation, rigidity, is in its inner nature the same as that which I recognise in myself as will, and what the stone also, if knowledge were given to it, would recognise as will. In the passage referred to, Spinoza had in view the necessity with which the stone flies, and he rightly desires to transfer this necessity to that of the particular act of will of a person. I, on the other hand, consider the inner being, which alone imparts meaning and validity to all real necessity (*i.e.*, effect following upon a cause) as its presupposition. In the case of men this is called character; in the case of a stone it is called quality, but it is the same in both. When it is immediately known it is called will. In the stone it has the weakest, and in man the strongest degree of visibility, of objectivity.

§ 26. The lowest grades of the objectification of will are to be found in those most universal forces of nature which partly appear in all matter without exception, as gravity and impenetrability, and partly have shared the given matter among them, so that certain of them reign in one species of matter and others in another species, constituting its specific difference, as rigidity, fluidity, elasticity, electricity, magnetism, chemical properties and qualities of every kind. They are in themselves immediate manifestations of will, just as much as human action; and as such they are groundless, like human character. Only their particular manifestations are subordinated to the principle of sufficient reason, like the particular actions of men. They themselves, on the other hand, can never be called either effect or cause, but are the prior and presupposed conditions of all causes and effects through which their real nature unfolds and reveals itself. It is therefore senseless to demand a cause of gravity or electricity, for they are original forces. Their expressions, indeed, take place in accordance with the law of cause and effect, so that every one of their particular manifestations has a cause, which is itself again just a similar particular manifestation which determines that this force must express itself here, must appear in space and time; but the force itself is by no means the effect of a cause, nor the cause of an effect. It is therefore a mistake to say "gravity is the cause of a stone falling"; for the cause in this case is rather the nearness of the earth, because it attracts the stone. Take the earth away and the stone will not fall, although gravity remains. The force itself lies quite outside the chain of causes and effects, which presupposes time, because it only has meaning in relation to it; but the force lies outside time. The individual change always has for its cause another change just as individual as itself, and not the force of which it is the expression. For that which always gives its efficiency to a cause, however many times it may appear, is a force of nature. As such, it is groundless, *i.e.*, it lies outside the chain of causes and outside the province of the principle of sufficient reason in general, and is philosophically known as the immediate objectivity of will, which is the "in-itself" of the whole of nature; but in etiology, which in this reference is physics, it is set down as an original force, *i.e.*, a *qualitas occulta*.

In the higher grades of the objectivity of will we see individuality occupy a prominent position, especially in the case of man, where it appears as the great difference of individual characters, *i.e.*, as complete personality, outwardly expressed in strongly marked individual physiognomy, which influences the whole bodily form. None of the brutes have this individuality in anything like so high a degree, though the higher species of them have a trace of it; but the character of the species completely predominates over it, and therefore they have little individual physiognomy. The farther down we go, the more completely is every trace of the individual character lost in the common character of the species, and the physiognomy of the species alone remains. We know the physiological character of the species, and from that we know exactly what is to be expected from the individual; while, on the contrary, in the human species every individual has to be studied and fathomed for himself, which, if we wish to forecast his action with some degree of certainty, is, on account of the possibility of concealment

that first appears with reason, a matter of the greatest difficulty. It is probably connected with this difference of the
human species from all others, that the folds and convolu-
tions of the brain, which are entirely wanting in birds, and
very weakly marked in rodents, are even in the case of the
higher animals far more symmetrical on both sides, and
more constantly the same in each individual, than in the case
of human beings.[1] It is further to be regarded as a phenomenon of this peculiar individual character which distinguishes men from all the lower animals, that in the case
of the brutes the sexual instinct seeks its satisfaction without observable choice of objects, while in the case of man
this choice is, in a purely instinctive manner and independent of all reflection, carried so far that it rises into a powerful passion. While then every man is to be regarded as a
specially determined and characterised phenomenon of will,
and indeed to a certain extent as a special Idea, in the case
of the brutes this individual character as a whole is wanting,
because only the species has a special significance. And the
farther we go from man, the fainter becomes the trace of
this individual character, so that plants have no individual
qualities left, except such as may be fully explained from
the favourable or unfavourable external influences of soil,
climate, and other accidents. Finally, in the inorganic kingdom of nature all individuality disappears. The crystal alone
is to be regarded as to a certain extent individual. It is a unity
of the tendency in definite directions, fixed by crystallisation,
which makes the trace of this tendency permanent. It is at
the same time a cumulative repetition of its primitive form,
bound into unity by an idea, just as the tree is an aggregate
of the single germinating fibre which shows itself in every
rib of the leaves, in every leaf, in every branch; which

[1] Wenzel, De Structura Cerebri Hominis et Brutorum, 1812, ch.
ii.; Cuvier, Leçons d'Anat., comp. leçon 9, arts. 4 and 5; Vic.
d'Azyr, Hist. de l'Acad. de Sc. de Paris, 1783, pp. 470 and 483.

that must appear when invoked by it. On the other hand, if we have attained to the philosophical knowledge that a force of nature is a definite grade of the objectification of will, that is to say, a definite grade of that which we recognise as our own inmost nature, and that this will, in itself, and distinguished from its phenomena and their forms, lies outside time and space, and that, therefore, the multiplicity, which is conditioned by time and space, does not belong to it, nor directly to the grade of its objectification, *i.e.*, the Idea, but only to the phenomena of the Idea; and if we remember that the law of causality has significance only in relation to time and space, inasmuch as it determines the position of the multitude of phenomena of the different Ideas in which the will reveals itself, governing the order in which they must appear; if, I say, in this knowledge the inner meaning of the great doctrine of Kant has been fully grasped, the doctrine that time, space, and causality do not belong to the thing-in-itself, but merely to the phenomenon, that they are only the forms of our knowledge, not qualities of things in themselves; then we shall understand that this astonishment at the conformity to law and accurate opera- tion of a force of nature, this astonishment at the complete sameness of all its million phenomena and the infallibility of their occurrence, is really like that of a child or a savage who looks for the first time through a glass with many facets at a flower, and marvels at the complete similarity of the innumerable flowers which he sees, and counts the leaves of each of them separately.

Thus every universal, original force of nature is nothing but a low grade of the objectification of will, and we call every such grade an eternal *Idea* in Plato's sense. But a *law of nature* is the relation of the Idea to the form of its mani- festation. This form is time, space, and causality, which are necessarily and inseparably connected and related to each other. Through time and space the Idea multiplies itself in innumerable phenomena, but the order according to which it enters these forms of multiplicity is definitely determined by the law of causality; this law is as it were the norm of the limit of these phenomena of different Ideas, in accordance with which time, space, and matter are assigned to them. This norm is therefore necessarily related to the identity of the aggregate of existing matter, which is the common substratum of all those different phenomena. If all these were not directed to that common matter in the possession of which they must be divided, there would be no need for such a law to decide their claims. They might all at once and together fill a boundless space throughout an endless time. Therefore, because all these phenomena of the eternal Ideas are directed to one and the same matter, must there be a rule for their appearance and disappearance; for if there were not, they would not make way for each other. Thus the law of causality is essentially bound up with that of the permanence of substance; they reciprocally derive significance from each other. Time and space, again, are related to them in the same way. For time is merely the possibility of conflicting states of the same matter, and space is merely the possibility of the permanence of the same matter under all sorts of conflicting states. Accordingly, in the preceding book we explained matter as the union of space and time, and this union shows itself as change of the accidents in the permanence of the substance, of which causality or becoming is the universal possibility. And accordingly, we said that matter is through and through causality. We explained the understanding as the subjective correlative of causality, and said matter (and thus the whole world as idea) exists only for the understanding; the understanding is its condition, its supporter as its necessary correlative. I repeat all this in passing, merely to call to mind what was demonstrated in the First Book, for it is necessary for the complete understanding of these two books that their inner agreement should be observed, since what is inseparably united in the actual world as its two sides, will and idea, has, in order that we might understand each of them more clearly in isolation, been dissevered in these two books.

In any case Malebranche is right: every natural cause is only an occasional cause. It only gives opportunity or occasion for the manifestation of the one indivisible will which is the "in-itself" of all things, and whose graduated objectification is the whole visible world. Only the appearance, the becoming visible, in this place, at this time, is brought about by the cause and is so far dependent on it, but not the whole of the phenomenon, nor its inner nature. This is the will itself, to which the principle of sufficient reason has not application, and which is therefore groundless. Nothing in the world has a sufficient cause of its existence generally, but only a cause of existence just here and just now. That a stone exhibits now gravity, now rigidity, now electricity, now chemical qualities, depends upon causes, upon impressions upon it from without, and is to be explained from these. But these qualities themselves, and thus the whole inner nature of the stone which consists in them, and therefore manifests itself in all the ways referred to; thus, in general, that the stone is such as it is, that it exists generally —all this, I say, has no ground, but is the visible appearance of the groundless will. Every cause is thus an occasional cause. We have found it to be so in nature, which is without knowledge, and it is also precisely the same when motives and not causes or stimuli determine the point at which the phenomena are to appear, that is to say, in the actions of animals and human beings. For in both cases it is one and the same will which appears; very different in the grades of its manifestations, multiplied in the phenomena of these grades, and, in respect of these, subordinated to the principle of sufficient reason, but in itself free from all this. Motives do not determine the character of man, but only the phenomena of his character, that is, his actions; the outward fashion of his life, not its inner meaning and content. These proceed from the character which is the immediate manifestation of the will, and is therefore groundless. That one man is bad and another good, does not depend upon motives or outward influences, such as teaching and preaching, and is in this sense quite inexplicable. But whether a bad man shows his badness in petty acts of injustice, cowardly tricks, and low knavery which he practises in the narrow sphere of his circumstances, or whether as a conqueror he oppresses nations, throws a world into lamentation, and sheds the blood of millions; this is the outward form of his manifestation, that which is unessential to it, and depends upon the circumstances in which fate has placed him, upon his surroundings, upon external influences, upon motives; but his decision upon these motives can never be explained from them; it proceeds from the will, of which this man is a manifestation. Of this we shall speak in the Fourth Book. The manner in which the character discloses its qualities is quite analogous to the way in which those of every material body in unconscious nature are disclosed. Water remains water with its intrinsic qualities, whether as a still lake it reflects its banks, or leaps in foam from the cliffs, or, artificially confined, spouts in a long jet into the air. All that depends upon external causes; the one form is as natural to it as the other, but it will always show the same form in the same circumstances; it is equally ready for any, but in every case true to its character, and at all times revealing this alone. So will every human character under all circumstances reveal itself, but the phenomena which proceed from it will always be in accordance with the circumstances.

§ 27. If, from the foregoing consideration of the forces of nature and their phenomena, we have come to see clearly how far an explanation from causes can go, and where it must stop if it is not to degenerate into the vain attempt to reduce the content of all phenomena to their mere form, in which case there would ultimately remain nothing but form, we shall be able to settle in general terms what is to be demanded of etiology as a whole. It must seek out the causes of all phenomena in nature, *i.e.*, the circumstances under which they invariably appear. Then it must refer the multitude of phenomena which have various forms in various circumstances to what is active in every phenomenon, and is presupposed in the cause,—original forces of nature. It must correctly distinguish between a difference of the phenomenon which arises from a difference of the force, and one which results merely from a difference of the circumstances under which the force expresses itself; and with equal care it must guard against taking the expressions of one and the same force under different circumstances for the manifestations of different forces, and conversely against taking for manifestations of one and the same force what originally belongs to different forces. For physics demands causes, and the will is never a cause. Its whole relation to the phenomenon is not in accordance with the principle of sufficient reason. But that which in itself is the will exists in another aspect as idea; that is to say, is phenomenon. As such, it obeys the laws which constitute the form of the phenomenon. Every movement, for example, although it is always a manifestation of will, must yet have a cause from which it is to be explained in relation to a particular time and space; that is, not in general in its inner nature, but as a *particular* phenomenon. In the case of the stone, this is a mechanical cause; in that of the movement of a man, it is a motive; but in no case can it be wanting. On the other hand, the universal common nature of all phenomena of one particular kind, that which must be presupposed if the explanation from causes is to have any sense and meaning, is the general force of nature, which, in physics, must remain a *qualitas occulta*, because with it the etiological explanation ends and the metaphysical begins. But the chain of causes and effects is never broken by an original force to which it has been necessary to appeal. It does not run back to such a force as if it were its first link, but the nearest link, as well as the remotest, presupposes the original force, and could otherwise explain nothing. A series of causes and effects may be the manifestation of the most different kinds of forces, whose successive visible appearances are conducted through it. But the difference of these original forces, which cannot be referred to each other, by no means breaks the unity of that chain of causes, and the connection between all its links. The etiology and the philosophy of nature never do violence to each other, but go hand in hand, regarding the same object from different points of view. Etiology gives an account of the causes which necessarily produce the particular phenomenon to be explained. It exhibits, as the foundation of all its explanations, the universal forces which are active in all these causes and effects. It accurately defines, enumerates, and distinguishes these forces, and then indicates all the different effects in which each force appears, regulated by the difference of the circumstances, always in accordance with its own peculiar character, which it discloses in obedience to an invariable rule, called *a law of nature*. When all this has been thoroughly accomplished by physics in every particular, it will be complete, and its work will be done. There will then remain no unknown force in unorganised nature, nor any effect, which has not been proved to be the manifestation of one of these forces under definite circumstances, in accordance with a law of nature. Yet a law of nature remains merely the observed rule according to which nature invariably proceeds whenever certain definite circumstances occur. Therefore a law of nature may be defined as a fact expressed generally—*un fait généralisé*—and thus a complete enumeration of all the laws of nature would only be a complete register of facts. The consideration of nature as a whole is thus completed in *morphology*, which enumerates, compares, and arranges all the enduring forms of organised nature. Of the causes of the appearance of the individual creature it has little to say, for in all cases this is procreation (the theory of which is a separate matter), and in rare cases the *generatio æquivoca*. But to this last belongs, strictly speaking, the manner in which all the lower grades of the objectification of will, that is to say, physical and chemical phenomena, appear as individual, and it is precisely the task of etiology to point out the conditions of this appearance. Philosophy, on the other hand, concerns itself only with the universal, in nature as everywhere else. The original forces themselves are here its object, and it recognises in them the different grades of the objectivity of will, which is the inner nature, the "in-itself" of this world; and when it regards the world apart from will, it explains it as merely the idea of the subject. But if etiology, instead of preparing the way for philosophy, and supplying its doctrines with practical application by means of instances, supposes that its aim is rather to deny the existence of all original forces, except perhaps *one*, the most general, for example, impenetrability, which it imagines it thoroughly understands, and consequently seeks forcibly to refer all the others to it—it forsakes its own province and can only give us error instead of truth. The content of nature is supplanted by its form, everything is ascribed to the circumstances which work from without, and nothing to the inner nature of the thing. Now if it were possible to succeed by this method, a problem in arithmetic would ultimately, as we have already remarked, solve the riddle of the universe. But this is the method adopted by those, referred to above, who think that all physiological effects ought to be reduced to form and combination, this, perhaps, to electricity, and this again to chemism, and chemism to mechanism. The mistake of

Descartes, for example, and of all the Atomists, was of this last description. They referred the movements of the globe to the impact of a fluid, and the qualities of matter to the connection and form of the atoms, and hence they laboured to explain all the phenomena of nature as merely manifestations of impenetrability and cohesion. Although this has been given up, precisely the same error is committed in our own day by the electrical, chemical, and mechanical physiologists, who obstinately attempt to explain the whole of life and all the functions of the organism from "form and combination." In Meckel's "Archiv für Physiologie" (1820, vol. v, p. 185) we still find it stated that the aim of physiological explanation is the reduction of organic life to the universal forces with which physics deals. Lamarck also, in his *"Philosophie Zoologique,"* explains life as merely the effect of warmth and electricity: *le calorique et la matière électrique suffisent parfaitement pour composer ensemble cette cause essentielle de la vie* (p. 16). According to this, warmth and electricity would be the "thing-in-itself," and the world of animals and plants its phenomenal appearance. The absurdity of this opinion becomes glaringly apparent at the 306th and following pages of that work. It is well known that all these opinions, that have been so often refuted, have reappeared quite recently with renewed confidence. If we carefully examine the foundation of these views, we shall find that they ultimately involve the presupposition that the organism is merely an aggregate of phenomena of physical, chemical, and mechanical forces, which have come together here by chance, and produced the organism as a freak of nature without further significance. The organism of an animal or of a human being would therefore be, if considered philosophically, not the exhibition of a special Idea, that is, not itself immediate objectivity of the will at a definite higher grade, but in it would appear only those Ideas which objectify the will in electricity, in chemism, and in mechanism. Thus the organism would be as fortuitously constructed by the concurrence of these forces as the forms of men and beasts in clouds and stalactites, and would therefore in itself be no more interesting than they are. However, we shall see immediately how far the application of physical and chemical modes of explanation to the organism may yet, within certain limits, be allowable and useful; for I shall explain that the vital force certainly avails itself of and uses the forces of unorganised nature; yet these forces no more constitute the vital force than a hammer and anvil make a blacksmith. Therefore even the most simple example of plant life can never be explained from these forces by any theory of capillary attraction and endosmose, much less animal life. The following observations will prepare the way for this somewhat difficult discussion.

It follows from all that has been said that it is certainly an error on the part of natural science to seek to refer the higher grades of the objectification of will to the lower; for the failure to recognise, or the denial of, original and self-existing forces of nature is just as wrong as the ground-less assumption of special forces when what occurs is merely a peculiar kind of manifestation of what is already known. Thus Kant rightly says that it would be absurd to hope for a blade of grass from a Newton, that is, from one who reduced the blade of grass to the manifestations of physical and chemical forces, of which it was the chance product, and therefore a mere freak of nature, in which no special Idea appeared, *i.e.*, the will did not directly reveal itself in it in a higher and specific grade, but just as in the phenomena of unorganised nature and by chance in this form. The schoolmen, who certainly would not have allowed such a doctrine, would rightly have said that it was a complete denial of the *forma substantialis*, and a degradation of it to the *forma accidentalis*. For the *forma substantialis* of

Aristotle denotes exactly what I call the grade of the objectification of will in a thing. On the other hand, it is not to be overlooked that in all Ideas, that is, in all forces of unorganised, and all forms of organised nature, it is *one and the same* will that reveals itself, that is to say, which enters the form of the idea and passes into *objectivity*. Its unity must therefore be also recognisable through an inner relationship between all its phenomena. Now this reveals itself in the higher grades of the objectification of will, where the whole phenomenon is more distinct, thus in the vegetable and animal kingdoms, through the universally prevailing analogy of all forms, the fundamental type which recurs in all phenomena. This has, therefore, become the guiding principle of the admirable zoological system which was originated by the French in this century, and it is most completely established in comparative anatomy as *l'unité de plan, l'uniformité de l'élément anatomique*. To discover this fundamental type has been the chief concern, or at any rate the praiseworthy endeavour, of the natural philosophers of the school of Schelling, who have in this respect considerable merit, although in many cases their hunt after analogies in nature degenerated into mere conceits. They have, however, rightly shown that that general relationship and family likeness exists also in the ideas of unorganised nature; for example, between electricity and magnetism, the identity of which was afterwards established; between chemical attraction and gravitation, and so forth. They specially called attention to the fact that *polarity*, that is, the sundering of a force into two qualitatively different and opposed activities striving after reunion, which also shows itself for the most part in space as a dispersion in opposite directions, is a fundamental type of almost all the phenomena of nature, from the magnet and the crystal to man himself. Yet this knowledge has been current in China from the earliest times, in the doctrine of opposition of Yin and Yang. Indeed, since

all things in the world are the objectification of one and
the same will, and therefore in their inner nature identical,
it must not only be the case that there is that unmistakable
analogy between them, and that in every phenomenon the
trace, intimation, and plan of the higher phenomenon that
lies next to it in point of development shows itself, but also
because all these forms belong to the world as *idea*, it is
indeed conceivable that even in the most universal forms of
the idea, in that peculiar framework of the phenomenal
world, space and time, it may be possible to discern and
establish the fundamental type, intimation, and plan of what
fills the forms. It seems to have been a dim notion of this
that was the origin of the Cabala and all the mathematical
philosophy of the Pythagoreans, and also of the Chinese in
Y-King. In the school of Schelling also, to which we have
already referred, we find, among their efforts to bring to
light the similarity among the phenomena of nature, several
attempts (though rather unfortunate ones) to deduce laws
of nature from the laws of pure space and time. However,
one can never tell to what extent a man of genius will realise
both endeavours.

Now, although the difference between phenomenon and
thing-in-itself is never lost sight of, and therefore the
identity of the will which objectifies itself in all Ideas can
never (because it has different grades of its objectification)
be distorted to mean identity of the particular Ideas themselves in which it appears, so that, for example, chemical or
electrical attraction can never be reduced to the attraction
of gravitation, although this inner analogy is known, and
the former may be regarded as, so to speak, higher powers of
the latter, just as little does the similarity of the construction
of all animals warrant us in mixing and identifying the
species and explaining the more developed as mere variations
of the less developed; and although, finally, the physiological
functions are never to be reduced to chemical or physical

processes, yet, in justification of this procedure, within certain limits, we may accept the following observations as
highly probable.

If several of the phenomena of will in the lower grades
of its objectification—that is, in unorganised nature—come
into conflict because each of them, under the guidance of
causality, seeks to possess a given portion of matter, there
arises from the conflict the phenomenon of a higher Idea
which prevails over all the less developed phenomena previously there, yet in such a way that it allows the essence of
these to continue to exist in a subordinate manner, in that it
takes up into itself from them something which is analogous
to them. This process is only intelligible from the identity
of the will which manifests itself in all the Ideas, and which
is always striving after higher objectification. We thus see,
for example, in the hardening of the bones, an unmistakable
analogy to crystallisation, as the force which originally had
possession of the chalk, although ossification is never to be
reduced to crystallisation. The analogy shows itself in a
weaker degree in the flesh becoming firm. The combination
of humours in the animal body and secretion are also
analogous to chemical combination and separation. Indeed,
the laws of chemistry are still strongly operative in this
case, but subordinated, very much modified, and mastered by
a higher Idea; therefore mere chemical forces outside the
organism will never afford us such humours; but the more
developed Idea resulting from this victory over several lower
Ideas or objectifications of will, gains an entirely new character by taking up into itself from every Idea over which it
has prevailed a strengthened analogy. The will objectifies
itself in a new, more distinct way. It originally appears in
generatio æquivoca; afterwards in assimilation to the given
germ, organic moisture, plant, animal, man. Thus from the
strife of lower phenomena the higher arise, swallowing them
all up, but yet realising in the higher grade the tendency of

all the lower. Here, then, already the law applies—*Serpens nisi serpentem comederit non fit draco*.[1]

According to the view I have expressed, the traces of chemical and physical modes of operation will indeed be found in the organism, but it can never be explained from them; because it is by no means a phenomenon even accidentally brought about through the united actions of such forces, but a higher Idea which has overcome these lower Ideas by *subduing assimilation;* for the *one* will which objectifies itself in all Ideas always seeks the highest possible objectification, and has therefore in this case given up the lower grades of its manifestation after a conflict, in order to appear in a higher grade, and one so much the more powerful. No victory without conflict: since the higher Idea or objectification of will can only appear through the conquest of the lower, it endures the opposition of these lower Ideas, which, although brought into subjection, still constantly strive to obtain an independent and complete expression of their being. The magnet that has attracted a piece of iron carries on a perpetual conflict with gravitation, which, as the lower objectification of will, has a prior right to the matter of the iron; and in this constant battle the magnet indeed grows stronger, for the opposition excites it, as it were, to greater effort. In the same way every manifestation of the will, including that which expresses itself in the human organism, wages a constant war against the many physical and chemical forces which, as lower Ideas, have a prior right to that matter. Thus the arm falls which for a while, overcoming gravity, we have held stretched out; thus the pleasing sensation of health, which proclaims the victory of the Idea of the self-conscious organism over the physical and chemical laws, which originally governed the humours of the body, is so often interrupted, and is in-

---

[1] "Unless the serpent eats a serpent, he does not become a dragon."

deed always accompanied by greater or less discomfort, which arises from the resistance of these forces, and on account of which the vegetative part of our life is constantly attended by slight pain. Thus also digestion weakens all the animal functions, because it requires the whole vital force to overcome the chemical forces of nature by assimilation. Hence also in general the burden of physical life, the necessity of sleep, and, finally, of death; for at last these subdued forces of nature, assisted by circumstances, win back from the organism, wearied even by the constant victory, the matter it took from them, and attain to an unimpeded expression of their being. We may therefore say that every organism expresses the Idea of which it is the image, only after we have subtracted the part of its force which is expended in subduing the lower Ideas that strive with it for matter. This seems to have been running in the mind of Jacob Böhm when he says somewhere that all the bodies of men and animals, and even all plants, are really half dead. According as the subjection in the organism of these forces of nature, which express the lower grades of the objectification of will, is more or less successful, the more or the less completely does it attain to the expression of its Idea; that is to say, the nearer it is to the *ideal* or the further from it—the *ideal* of beauty in its species.

Thus everywhere in nature we see strife, conflict, and alternation of victory, and in it we shall come to recognise more distinctly that variance with itself which is essential to the will. Every grade of the objectification of will fights for the matter, the space, and the time of the others. The permanent matter must constantly change its form; for under the guidance of causality, mechanical, physical, chemical, and organic phenomena, eagerly striving to appear, wrest the matter from each other, for each desires to reveal its own Idea. This strife may be followed through the whole of nature; indeed nature exists only through it. Yet this

strife itself is only the revelation of that variance with itself
which is essential to the will. This universal conflict becomes
most distinctly visible in the animal kingdom. For animals
have the whole of the vegetable kingdom for their food,
and even within the animal kingdom every beast is the prey
and the food of another; that is, the matter in which its
Idea expresses itself must yield itself to the expression of
another Idea, for each animal can only maintain its existence by the constant destruction of some other. Thus the
will to live everywhere preys upon itself, and in different
forms is its own nourishment, till finally the human race,
because it subdues all the others, regards nature as a manufactory for its use. Yet even the human race, as we shall
see in the Fourth Book, reveals in itself with most terrible
distinctness this conflict, this variance with itself of the will,
and we find *homo homini lupus*. Meanwhile we can recognise this strife, this subjugation, just as well in the lower
grades of the objectification of will. Many insects (especially ichneumon-flies) lay their eggs on the skin, and even
in the body of the larvæ of other insects, whose slow destruction is the first work of the newly hatched brood. The
young hydra, which grows like a bud out of the old one,
and afterwards separates itself from it, fights while it is
still joined to the old one for the prey that offers itself, so
that the one snatches it out of the mouth of the other. But
the bulldog-ant of Australia affords us the most extraordinary example of this kind; for if it is cut in two, a battle
begins between the head and the tail. The head seizes the
tail with its teeth, and the tail defends itself bravely by
stinging the head: the battle may last for half an hour, until
they die or are dragged away by other ants. This contest
takes place every time the experiment is tried. On the banks
of the Missouri one sometimes sees a mighty oak the stem
and branches of which are so encircled, fettered, and inter-
laced by a gigantic wild vine, that it withers as if choked.

The same thing shows itself in the lowest grades; for ex·
ample, when water and carbon are changed into vegetable
sap, or vegetables or bread into blood by organic assimilation;
and so also in every case in which animal secretion takes
place, along with the restriction of chemical forces to a subordinate mode of activity. This also occurs in unorganised
nature, when, for example, crystals in process of formatior
meet, cross, and mutually disturb each other to such an extent
that they are unable to assume the pure crystalline form, so
that almost every cluster of crystals is an image of such a
conflict of will at this low grade of its objectification; or
again, when a magnet forces its magnetism upon iron, in
order to express its Idea in it; or when galvanism overcomes
chemical affinity, decomposes the closest combinations, and
so entirely suspends the laws of chemistry that the acid of a
decomposed salt at the negative pole must pass to the positive
pole without combining with the alkalies through which it
goes on its way, or turning red the litmus paper that touches
it. On a large scale it shows itself in the relation between
the central body and the planet, for although the planet is
in absolute dependence, yet it always resists, just like the
chemical forces in the organism; hence arises the constant
tension between centripetal and centrifugal force, which
keeps the globe in motion, and is itself an example of that
universal essential conflict of the manifestation of will
which we are considering. For as every body must be regarded as the manifestation of a will, and as will necessarily
expresses itself as a struggle, the original condition of every
world that is formed into a globe cannot be rest, but motion,
a striving forward in boundless space without rest and without end.

We should see the will express itself here in the lowest
grade as blind striving, an obscure, inarticulate impulse, far
from susceptible of being directly known. It is the simplest
and the weakest mode of its objectification. But it appears

as this blind and unconscious striving in the whole of un-organised nature, in all those original forces of which it is the work of physics and chemistry to discover and to study the laws, and each of which manifests itself to us in millions of phenomena which are exactly similar and regular, and show no trace of individual character, but are mere multi-plicity through space and time, *i.e.*, through the *principum individuationis*, as a picture is multiplied through the facets of a glass.

From grade to grade objectifying itself more distinctly, yet still completely without consciousness as an obscure striv-ing force, the will acts in the vegetable kingdom also, in which the bond of its phenomena consists no longer properly of causes, but of stimuli; and, finally, also in the vegetative part of the animal phenomenon, in the production and ma-turing of the animal and in sustaining its inner economy, in which the manifestation of will is still always necessarily determined by stimuli. The ever-ascending grades of the objectification of will bring us at last to the point at which the individual that expresses the Idea could no longer receive food for its assimilation through mere movement following upon stimuli. For such a stimulus must be waited for, but the food has now come to be of a more special and definite kind, and with the ever-increasing multiplicity of the indi-vidual phenomena, the crowd and confusion has become so great that they interfere with each other, and the chance of the individual that is moved merely by stimuli and must wait for its food would be too unfavourable. From the point, therefore, at which the animal has delivered itself from the egg or the womb in which it vegetated without consciousness, its food must be sought out and selected. For this purpose movement following upon motives, and there-fore consciousness, becomes necessary, and consequently it appears as an agent, μηχανη, called in at this stage of the objectification of will for the conservation of the individual and the propagation of the species. It appears represented by the brain or a large ganglion, just as every other effort or determination of the will which objectifies itself is represented by an organ, that is to say, manifests itself for the idea as an organ.[1] But with this means of assistance, this μηχανη, the *world as idea* comes into existence at a stroke, with all its forms, object and subject, time, space, multiplicity, and causality. The world now shows its second side. Till now *mere will*, it becomes also *idea*, object of the knowing subject. The will, which up to this point followed its tendency in the dark with unerring certainty, has at this grade kindled for itself a light as a means which became necessary for getting rid of the disadvantage which arose from the throng and the complicated nature of its manifestations, and which would have accrued precisely to the most perfect of them. The hitherto infallible certainty and regularity with which it worked in unorganised and merely vegetative nature, rested upon the fact that it alone was active in its original nature, as blind impulse, will, without assistance, and also without interruption, from a second and entirely different world, the world as idea, which is indeed only the image of its own inner being, but is yet of quite another nature, and now encroaches on the connected whole of its phenomena. Hence its infallible certainty comes to an end. Animals are already exposed to illusion, to deception. They have, however, merely ideas of perception, no conceptions, no reflections, and they are therefore bound to the present; they cannot have regard for the future. It seems as if this knowledge without reason was not in all cases sufficient for its end, and at times required, as it were, some assistance.

Finally, when the will has attained to the highest grade of its objectification, that knowledge of the understanding

[1] Cf chap xxii, of the Supplement, and also my work "Ueber den Willen in der Natur," p. 54 *et seq.*, and pp. 70-79 of the first edition, or p. 46 *et seq.*, and pp. 63-72 of the second, or p. 48 *et seq.*, and pp. 67-77 of the third edition.

given to brutes to which the senses supply the data, out of which there arises mere perception confined to what is immediately present, does not suffice. That complicated, many-sided, imaginative being, man, with his many needs, and exposed as he is to innumerable dangers, must, in order to exist, be lighted by a double knowledge; a higher power, as it were, of perceptive knowledge must be given him, and also reason, as the faculty of framing abstract conceptions. With this there has appeared reflection, surveying the future and the past, and, as a consequence, deliberation, care, the power of premeditated action independent of the present, and finally, the full and distinct consciousness of one's own deliberate volition as such. Now if with mere knowledge of perception there arose the possibility of illusion and deception, by which the previous infallibility of the blind striving of will was done away with, so that mechanical and other instincts, as expressions of unconscious will, had to lend their help in the midst of those that were conscious, with the entrance of reason that certainty and infallibility of the expressions of will (which at the other extreme in unorganised nature appeared as strict conformity to law) is almost entirely lost; instinct disappears altogether; deliberation, which is supposed to take the place of everything else, begets (as was shown in the First Book) irresolution and uncertainty; then error becomes possible, and in many cases obstructs the adequate objectification of the will in action. For although in the character the will has already taken its definite and unchangeable bent or direction, in accordance with which volition, when occasioned by the presence of a motive, invariably takes place, yet error can falsify its expressions, for it introduces illusive motives that take the place of the real ones which they resemble; [1] as, for example,

---

[1] The Scholastics therefore said very truly: *Causa finalis movet non secundum suum esse reale, sed secundum esse cognitum.* Cf. Suarez, Disp. Metaph., disp. xxiii, sec. 7 and 8.

when superstition forces on a man imaginary motives which impel him to a course of action directly opposed to the way in which the will would otherwise express itself in the given circumstances. Agamemnon slays his daughter; a miser dispenses alms, out of pure egotism, in the hope that he will some day receive an hundredfold; and so on.

Thus knowledge generally, rational as well as merely sensuous, proceeds originally from the will itself, belongs to the inner being of the higher grades of its objectification as a means of supporting the individual and the species, just like any organ of the body. Originally destined for the service of the will for the accomplishment of its aims, it remains almost throughout entirely subjected to its service: it is so in all brutes and in almost all men. Yet we shall see in the Third Book how in certain individual men knowledge can deliver itself from this bondage, throw off its yoke, and, free from all the aims of will, exist purely for itself, simply as a clear mirror of the world, which is the source of art. Finally, in the Fourth Book, we shall see how, if this kind of knowledge reacts on the will, it can bring about self-surrender, *i.e.*, resignation, which is the final goal, and indeed the inmost nature of all virtue and holiness, and is deliverance from the world.

§ 28. We have considered the great multiplicity and diversity of the phenomena in which the will objectifies itself, and we have seen their endless and implacable strife with each other. Yet, according to the whole discussion up to this point, the will itself, as thing-in-itself, is by no means included in that multiplicity and change. The diversity of the (Platonic) Ideas, *i.e.*, grades of objectification, the multitude of individuals in which each of these expresses itself, the struggle of forms for matter,—all this does not concern it, but is only the manner of its objectification, and only through this has an indirect relation to it, by virtue of which it belongs to the expression of the nature of will for the idea. As the magic-lantern shows many different pictures, which are all made visible by one and the same light, so in all the multifarious phenomena which fill the world together or throng after each other as events, only *one will* manifests itself, of which everything is the visibility, the objectivity, and which remains unmoved in the midst of this change; it alone is thing-in-itself; all objects are manifestations, or, to speak the language of Kant, phenomena. Although in man, as (Platonic) Idea, the will finds its clearest and fullest objectification, yet man alone could not express its being. In order to manifest the full significance of the will, the Idea of man would need to appear, not alone and sundered from everything else, but accompanied by the whole series of grades, down through all the forms of animals, through the vegetable kingdom to unorganised nature. All these supplement each other in the complete objectification of will; they are as much presupposed by the Idea of man as the blossoms of a tree presuppose leaves, branches, stem, and root; they form a pyramid, of which man is the apex. If fond of similes, one might also say that their manifestations accompany that of man as necessarily as the full daylight is accompanied by all the gradations of twilight, through which, little by little, it loses itself in darkness; or one might call them the echo of man, and say: Animal and plant are the descending fifth and third of man, the inorganic kingdom is the lower octave. The full truth of this last comparison will only become clear to us when, in the following book, we attempt to fathom the deep significance of music, and see how a connected, progressive melody, made up of high, quick notes, may be regarded as in some sense expressing the life and efforts of man connected by reflection, while the unconnected complemental notes and the slow bass, which make up the harmony necessary to perfect the music, represent the rest of the animal kingdom and the whole of nature that is without knowledge. But of this in its own place, where it will not sound so paradoxical. We find, however, that the *inner necessity* of the gradation of its manifestations, which is inseparable from the adequate objectification of the will, is expressed by an *outer necessity* in the whole of these manifestations themselves, by reason of which man has need of the beasts for his support, the beasts in their grades have need of each other as well as of plants, which in their turn require the ground, water, chemical elements and their combinations, the planet, the sun, rotation and motion round the sun, the curve of the ellipse, &c., &c. At bottom this results from the fact that the will must live on itself, for there exists nothing beside it, and it is a hungry will. Hence arise eager pursuit, anxiety, and suffering.

It is only the knowledge of the unity of will as thing-in-itself, in the endless diversity and multiplicity of the phenomena, that can afford us the true explanation of that wonderful, unmistakable analogy of all the productions of nature, that family likeness on account of which we may regard them as variations on the same ungiven theme. So in like measure, through the distinct and thoroughly comprehended knowledge of that harmony, that essential connection of all the parts of the world, that necessity of their gradation which we have just been considering, we shall obtain a true and sufficient insight into the inner nature and meaning of the undeniable *teleology* of all organised productions of nature, which, indeed, we presupposed *a priori*, when considering and investigating them.

This *teleology* is of a twofold description; sometimes an *inner teleology*, that is, an agreement of all the parts of a particular organism, so ordered that the sustenance of the individual and the species results from it, and therefore presents itself as the end of that disposition or arrangement. Sometimes, however, there is an *outward teleology*, a relation of unorganised to organised nature in general, or of particular parts of organised nature to each other, which makes the maintenance of the whole of organised nature, or of the particular animal species, possible, and therefore presents itself to our judgment as the means to this end.

Inner teleology is connected with the scheme of our work in the following way. If, in accordance with what has been said, all variations of form in nature, and all multiplicity of individuals, belong not to the will itself, but merely to its objectivity and the form of this objectivity, it necessarily follows that the will is indivisible and is present as a whole in every manifestation, although the grades of its objectification, the (Platonic) Ideas, are very different from each other. We may, for the sake of simplicity, regard these different Ideas as in themselves individual and simple acts of the will, in which it expresses its nature more or less. Individuals, however, are again manifestations of the Ideas, thus of these acts, in time, space, and multiplicity. Now, in the lowest grades of objectivity, such an act (or an Idea) retains its unity in the manifestation; while, in order to appear in higher grades, it requires a whole series of conditions and developments in time, which only collectively express its nature completely. Thus, for example, the Idea that reveals itself in any general force of nature has always one single expression, although it presents itself differently according to the external relations that are present: otherwise its identity could not be proved, for this is done by abstracting the diversity that arises merely from external relations. In the same way the crystal has only *one* manifestation of life, crystallisation, which afterwards has its fully adequate and exhaustive expression in the rigid form, the corpse of that momentary life. The plant, however, does not express the Idea, whose phenomenon it is, at once and through a single manifesta-

tion, but in a succession of developments of its organs in
time. The animal not only develops its organism in the
same manner, in a succession of forms which are often
very different (metamorphosis), but this form itself, although it is already objectivity of will at this grade, does
not attain to a full expression of its Idea. This expression
must be completed through the actions of the animal, in
which its empirical character, common to the whole species,
manifests itself, and only then does it become the full
revelation of the Idea, a revelation which presupposes
the particular organism as its first condition. In the case
of man, the empirical character is peculiar to every individual (indeed, as we shall see in the Fourth Book, even to
the extent of supplanting entirely the character of the
species, through the self-surrender of the whole will).
That which is known as the empirical character, through
the necessary development in time, and the division into
particular actions that is conditioned by it, is, when we
abstract from this temporal form of the manifestation the
intelligible character, according to the expression of Kant,
who shows his undying merit especially in establishing
this distinction and explaining the relation between freedom
and necessity, *i.e.*, between the will as thing-in-itself and
its manifestations in time.[1] Thus the intelligible character
coincides with the Idea, or, more accurately, with the
original act of will which reveals itself in it. So far then,
not only the empirical character of every man, but also
that of every species of animal and plant, and even of every
original force of unorganised nature, is to be regarded
as the manifestation of an intelligible character, that is, of

---

[1] Cf. "Critique of Pure Reason. Solution of the Cosmological Ideas
of the Totality of the Deduction of the Events in the Universe," pp.
560-586 of the fifth, and p. 532 and following of first edition; and
"Critique of Practical Reason," fourth edition, pp. 169-179; Rosen-
kranz' edition, p. 224 and following. Cf. my Essay on the Principle
of Sufficient Reason, § 43.

a timeless, indivisible act of will. I should like here to draw attention in passing to the naïveté with which every plant expresses and lays open its whole character in its mere form, reveals its whole being and will. This is why the physiognomy of plants is so interesting; while in order to know an animal in its Idea, it is necessary to observe the course of its action. As for man, he must be fully investigated and tested, for reason makes him capable of a high degree of dissimulation. The beast is as much more naïve than the man as the plant is more naïve than the beast. In the beast we see the will to live more naked, as it were, than in the man, in whom it is clothed with so much knowledge, and is, moreover, so veiled through the capacity for dissimulation, that it is almost only by chance, and here and there, that its true nature becomes apparent. In the plant it shows itself quite naked, but also much weaker, as mere blind striving for existence without end or aim. For the plant reveals its whole being at the first glance, and with complete innocence, which does not suffer from the fact that it carries its organs of generation exposed to view on its upper surface, though in all animals they have been assigned to the most hidden part. This innocence of the plant results from its complete want of knowledge. Guilt does not lie in willing, but in willing with knowledge. Every plant speaks to us first of all of its home, of the climate, and the nature of the ground in which it has grown. Therefore, even those who have had little practice easily tell whether an exotic plant belongs to the tropical or the temperate zone, and whether it grows in water, in marshes, on mountain, or on moor-land. Besides this, however, every plant expresses the special will of its species, and says something that cannot be uttered in any other tongue. But we must now apply what has been said to the teleological consideration of the organism, so far as it concerns its inner design. If in unorganised nature the Idea, which is everywhere to be regarded as a single act of will, reveals itself also in a single manifestation which is always the same, and thus one may say that here the empirical character directly partakes of the unity of the intelligible, coincides, as it were, with it, so that no inner design can show itself here; if, on the contrary, all organisms express their Ideas through a series of successive developments, conditioned by a multiplicity of co-existing parts, and thus only the sum of the manifestations of the empirical character collectively constitute the expression of the intelligible character; this necessary co-existence of the parts and succession of the stages of development does not destroy the unity of the appearing Idea, the act of will which expresses itself; nay, rather this unity finds its expression in the necessary relation and connection of the parts and stages of development with each other, in accordance with the law of causality. Since it is the will which is one, indivisible, and therefore entirely in harmony with itself, that reveals itself in the whole Idea as in act, its manifestation, although broken up into a number of different parts and conditions, must yet show this unity again in the thorough agreement of all of these. This is effected by a necessary relation and dependence of all the parts upon each other, by means of which the unity of the Idea is re-established in the manifestation. In accordance with this, we now recognise these different parts and functions of the organism as related to each other reciprocally as means and end, but the organism itself as the final end of all. Consequently, neither the breaking up of the Idea, which in itself is simple, into the multiplicity of the parts and conditions of the organism, on the one hand, nor, on the other hand, the re-establishment of its unity through the necessary connection of the parts and functions which arises from the fact that they are the cause and effect, the means and end, of each other, is peculiar and essential to the appearing will as such, to the thing-in-itself, but only to its manifestation in space, time, and causality (mere modes of the principle of sufficient reason, the form of the phenomenon). They belong to the world as idea, not to the world as will; they belong to the way in which the will becomes object, *i.e.*, idea at this grade of its objectivity. Every one who has grasped the meaning of this discussion— a discussion which is perhaps somewhat difficult—will now fully understand the doctrine of Kant, which follows from it, that both the design of organised and the conformity to law of unorganised nature are only introduced by our understanding, and therefore both belong only to the phenomenon, not to the thing-in-itself. The surprise, which was referred to above, at the infallible constancy of the conformity to law of unorganised nature, is essentially the same as the surprise that is excited by design in organised nature; for in both cases what we wonder at is only the sight of the original unity of the Idea, which, for the phenomenon, has assumed the form of multiplicity and diversity.[1]

As regards the second kind of teleology, according to the division made above, the *outer* design, which shows itself, not in the inner economy of the organisms, but in the support and assistance they receive from without, both from unorganised nature and from each other; its general explanation is to be found in the exposition we have just given. For the whole world, with all its phenomena, is the objectivity of the one indivisible will, the Idea, which is related to all other Ideas as harmony is related to the single voice. Therefore that unity of the will must show itself also in the agreement of all its manifestations. But we can very much increase the clearness of this insight if we go

[1] Cf. "Ueber den Willen in der Natur," at the end of the section on Comparative Anatomy.

somewhat more closely into the manifestations of that outer teleology and agreement of the different parts of nature with each other, an inquiry which will also throw some light on the foregoing exposition. We shall best attain this end by considering the following analogy.

The character of each individual man, so far as it is thoroughly individual, and not entirely included in that of the species, may be regarded as a special Idea, cor- responding to a special act of the objectification of will. This act itself would then be his intelligible character, and his empirical character would be the manifestation of it. The empirical character is entirely determined through the intelligible, which is without ground, *i.e.*, as thing-in- itself is not subordinated to the principle of sufficient reason (the form of the phenomenon). The empirical char- acter must in the course of life afford us the express image of the intelligible, and can only become what the nature of the latter demands. But this property extends only to the essential, not to the unessential in the course of life to which it applies. To this unessential belong the detailed events and actions which are the material in which the empirical character shows itself. These are determined by outward circumstances, which present the motives upon which the character reacts according to its nature; and as they may be very different, the outward form of the manifes- tation of the empirical character, that is, the definite actual or historical form of the course of life, will have to ac- commodate itself to their influence. Now this form may be very different, although what is essential to the manifesta- tion, its content, remains the same. Thus, for example, it is immaterial whether a man plays for nuts or for crowns; but whether a man cheats or plays fairly, that is the real matter; the latter is determined by the intelligible character, the former by outward circumstances. As the same theme may be expressed in a hundred different variations, so the same character may be expressed in a hundred very different lives. But various as the outward influence may be, the empirical character which expresses itself in the course of life must yet, whatever form it takes, accurately objectify the intelligible character, for the latter adapts its objectification to the given material of actual circumstances. We have now to assume something analogous to the influence of outward circumstances upon the life that is determined in essential matters by the character, if we desire to understand how the will, in the original act of its objectification, determines the various Ideas in which it objectifies itself, that is, the different forms of natural existence of every kind, among which it distributes its objectification, and which must therefore necessarily have a relation to each other in the manifestation. We must assume that between all these manifestations of the one will there existed a universal and reciprocal adaptation and accommodation of themselves to each other, by which, however, as we shall soon see more clearly, all time-determination is to be excluded, for the Idea lies outside time. In accordance with this, every manifestation must have adapted itself to the surroundings into which it entered, and these again must have adapted themselves to it, although it occupied a much later position in time; and we see this *consensus naturæ* everywhere. Every plant is therefore adapted to its soil and climate, every animal to its element and the prey that will be its food, and is also in some way protected, to a certain extent, against its natural enemy; the eye is adapted to the light and its refrangibility, the lungs and the blood to the air, the air-bladder of fish to water, the eye of the seal to the change of the medium in which it must see, the water-pouch in the stomach of the camel to the drought of the African deserts, the sail of the nautilus to the wind that is to drive its little bark, and so on down to the most special and astonishing outward adaptations.[1] We must abstract however here from all temporal relations, for these can only concern the manifestation of the Idea, not the Idea itself. Accordingly this kind of explanation must also be used retrospectively, and we must not merely admit that every species accommodated itself to the given environment, but also that this environment itself, which preceded it in time, had just as much regard for the being that would some time come into it. For it is one and the same will that objectifies itself in the whole world; it knows no time, for this form of the principle of sufficient reason does not belong to it, nor to its original objectivity, the Ideas, but only to the way in which these are known by the individuals who themselves are transitory, i.e., to the manifestation of the Ideas. Thus, time has no significance for our present examination of the manner in which the objectification of the will distributes itself among the Ideas, and the Ideas whose *manifestations* entered into the course of time earlier, according to the law of causality, to which as phenomena they are subject, have no advantage over those whose manifestation entered later; nay rather, these last are the completest objectifications of the will, to which the earlier manifestations must adapt themselves just as much as they must adapt themselves to the earlier. Thus the course of the planets, the tendency to the ellipse, the rotation of the earth, the division of land and sea, the atmosphere, light, warmth, and all such phenomena, which are in nature what bass is in harmony, adapted themselves in anticipation of the coming species of living creatures of which they were to become the supporter and sustainer. In the same way the ground adapted itself to the nutrition of plants, plants adapted themselves to the nutrition of animals, animals to that of other animals, and conversely they all adapted themselves to the

[1]Cf. "Ueber den Willen in der Natur," the section on Comparative Anatomy.

nutrition of the ground. All the parts of nature correspond to each other, for it is *one* will that appears in them all, but the course of time is quite foreign to its original and only *adequate objectification* (this expression will be explained in the following book), the Ideas. Even now, when the species have only to sustain themselves, no longer to come into existence, we see here and there some such forethought of nature extending to the future, and abstracting as it were from the process of time, a self-adaptation of what is to what is yet to come. The bird builds the nest for the young which it does not yet know; the beaver constructs a dam the object of which is unknown to it; ants, marmots, and bees lay in provision for the winter they have never experienced; the spider and the ant-lion make snares, as if with deliberate cunning, for future unknown prey; insects deposit their eggs where the coming brood finds future nourishment. In the springtime the female flower of the diœcian valisneria unwinds the spirals of its stalk, by which till now it was held at the bottom of the water, and thus rises to the surface. Just then the male flower, which grows on a short stalk from the bottom, breaks away, and so, at the sacrifice of its life, reaches the surface, where it swims about in search of the female. The latter is fructified, and then draws itself down again to the bottom by contracting its spirals, and there the fruit grows.[1] I must again refer here to the larva of the male stag-beetle, which makes the hole in the wood for its metamorphosis as big again as the female does, in order to have room for its future horns. The instinct of animals in general gives us the best illustration of what remains of teleology in nature. For as instinct is an action, like that which is guided by the conception of an end, and yet is entirely without this; so all construction of nature resembles that which is guided by the conception of an end, and yet is

[1] Chatin, Sur la Valisneria Spiralis, in the Comptes Rendus de l'Acad. de Sc., No. 13, 1855.

entirely without it. For in the outer as in the inner teleology of nature, what we are obliged to think as means and end is, in every case, *the manifestation of the unity of the one will so thoroughly agreeing with itself*, which has assumed multiplicity in space and time for our manner of knowing.

The reciprocal adaptation and self-accommodation of phenomena that springs from this unity cannot, however, annul the inner contradiction which appears in the universal conflict of nature described above, and which is essential to the will. That harmony goes only so far as to render possible the duration of the world and the different kinds of existences in it, which without it would long since have perished. Therefore it only extends to the continuance of the species, and the general conditions of life, but not to that of the individual. If, then, by reason of that harmony and accommodation, the *species* in organised nature and the *universal forces* in unorganised nature continue to exist beside each other, and indeed support each other reciprocally, on the other hand, the inner contradiction of the will which objectifies itself in all these ideas shows itself in the ceaseless internecine war of the *individuals* of these species, and in the constant struggle of the *manifestations* of these natural forces with each other, as we pointed out above. The scene and the object of this conflict is matter, which they try to wrest from each other, and also space and time, the combination of which through the form of causality is, in fact, matter, as was explained in the First Book.[1]

§ 29. I here conclude the second principal division of my exposition, in the hope that, so far as is possible in the case of an entirely new thought, which cannot be quite free from traces of the individuality in which it originated, I have succeeded in conveying to the reader the complete certainty that this world in which we live and have our being is in its whole nature through and through *will*, and at the same

[1] Cf. Chaps. xxvi. and xxvii. of the Supplement.

time through and through *idea:* that this idea, as such, already presupposes a form, object and subject, is therefore relative; and if we ask what remains if we take away this form, and all those forms which are subordinate to it, and which express the principle of sufficient reason, the answer must be that as something *toto genere* different from idea, this can be nothing but *will,* which is thus properly the *thing-in-itself.* Every one finds that he himself is this will, in which the real nature of the world consists, and he also finds that he is the knowing subject, whose idea the whole world is, the world which exists only in relation to his consciousness, as its necessary supporter. Every one is thus himself in a double aspect the whole world, the microcosm; finds both sides whole and complete in himself. And what he thus recognises as his own real being also exhausts the being of the whole world—the macrocosm; thus the world, like man, is through and through *will,* and through and through *idea,* and nothing more than this. So we see the philosophy of Thales, which concerned the macrocosm, unite at this point with that of Socrates, which dealt with the microcosm, for the object of both is found to be the same. But all the knowledge that has been communicated in the two first books will gain greater completeness, and consequently greater certainty from the two following books in which I hope that several questions that have more or less distinctly arisen in the course of our work will also be sufficiently answered.

In the meantime *one* such question may be more particularly considered, for it can only properly arise so long as one has not fully penetrated the meaning of the foregoing exposition, and may so far serve as an illustration of it. It is this: Every will is a will towards something, has an object, an end of its willing; what then is the final end, or towards what is that will striving that is exhibited to us as the thing-in-itself of the world? This question rests, like so many others, upon the confusion of the thing-in-itself with the manifestation. The principle of sufficient reason, of which the law of motivation is also a form, extends only to the latter, not to the former. It is only of phenomena, of individual things, that a ground can be given, never of the will itself, nor of the Idea in which it adequately objectifies itself. So then of every particular movement or change of any kind in nature, a cause is to be sought, that is, a condition that of necessity produced it, but never of the natural force itself which is revealed in this and innumerable similar phenomena; and it is therefore simple misunderstanding, arising from want of consideration, to ask for a cause of gravity, electricity, and so on. Only if one had somehow shown that gravity and electricity were not original special forces of nature, but only the manifestations of a more general force already known, would it be allowable to ask for the cause which made this force produce the phenomena of gravity or of electricity here. All this has been explained at length above. In the same way every particular act of will of a knowing individual (which is itself only a manifestation of will as the thing-in-itself) has necessarily a motive without which that act would never have occurred; but just as material causes contain merely the determination that at this time, in this place, and in this matter, a manifestation of this or that natural force must take place, so the motive determines only the act of will of a knowing being, at this time, in this place, and under these circumstances, as a particular act, but by no means determines that that being wills in general or wills in this manner; this is the expression of his intelligible character, which, as will itself, the thing-in-itself, is without ground, for it lies outside the province of the principle of sufficient reason. Therefore every man has permanent aims and motives by which he guides his conduct, and he can always give an account of his particular actions; but if he were asked why he wills at all, or why in general he wills to exist, he would have no answer, and the question would indeed seem to him meaningless; and this would be just the expression of his consciousness that he himself is nothing but will, whose willing stands by itself and requires more particular determination by motives only in its individual acts at each point of time.

In fact, freedom from all aim, from all limits, belongs to the nature of the will, which is an endless striving. This was already touched on above in the reference to centrifugal force. It also discloses itself in its simplest form in the lowest grade of the objectification of will, in gravitation, which we see constantly exerting itself, though a final goal is obviously impossible for it. For if, according to its will, all existing matter were collected in one mass, yet within this mass gravity, ever striving towards the centre, would still wage war with impenetrability as rigidity or elasticity. The tendency of matter can therefore only be confined, never completed or appeased. But this is precisely the case with all tendencies of all phenomena of will. Every attained end is also the beginning of a new course, and so on *ad infinitum.* The plant raises its manifestation from the seed through the stem and the leaf to the blossom and the fruit, which again is the beginning of a new seed, a new individual, that runs through the old course, and so on through endless time. Such also is the life of the animal; procreation is its highest point, and after attaining to it, the life of the first individual quickly or slowly sinks, while a new life ensures to nature the endurance of the species and repeats the same phenomena. Indeed, the constant renewal of the matter of every organism is also to be regarded as merely the manifestation of this continual pressure and change, and physiologists are now ceasing to hold that it is the necessary reparation of the matter wasted in motion, for the possible wearing out of the machine can by no means be equivalent to the support it is constantly receiving through nourishment. Eternal becoming. endless flux, characterises the revelation of the inner nature of will. Finally, the same thing shows itself in human endeavours and desires, which always delude us by presenting their satisfaction as the final end of will. As soon as we attain to them they no longer appear the same, and therefore they soon grow stale, are forgotten, and though not openly disowned, are yet always thrown aside as vanished illusions. We are fortunate enough if there still remains something to wish for and to strive after, that the game may be kept up of constant transition from desire to satisfaction, and from satisfaction to a new desire, the rapid course of which is called happiness, and the slow course sorrow, and does not sink into that stagnation that shows itself in fearful ennui that paralyses life, vain yearning without a definite object, deadening languor. According to all this, when the will is enlightened by knowledge, it always knows what it wills now and here, never what it wills in general; every particular act of will has its end, the whole will has none; just as every particular phenomenon of nature is determined by a sufficient cause so far as concerns its appearance in this place at this time, but the force which manifests itself in it has no general cause, for it belongs to the thing-in-itself, to the groundless will. The single example of self-knowledge of the will as a whole is the idea as a whole, the whole world of perception. It is the objectification, the revelation, the mirror of the will. What the will expresses in it will be the subject of our further consideration.

Third Book

THE WORLD AS IDEA

———

SECOND ASPECT

THE IDEA INDEPENDENT OF THE PRINCIPLE OF SUFFICIENT
REASON: THE PLATONIC IDEA: THE OBJECT OF ART

THE PHILOSOPHY OF SCHOPENHAUER

III

§ 30. In the First Book the world was explained as mere *idea*, object for a subject. In the Second Book we considered it from its other side, and found that in this aspect it is *will*, which proved to be simply that which this world is besides being idea. In accordance with this knowledge we called the world as idea, both as a whole and in its parts, the *objectification of will*, which therefore means the will become object, *i.e.*, idea. Further, we remember that this objectification of will was found to have many definite grades, in which, with gradually increasing distinctness and completeness, the nature of will appears in the idea, that is to say, presents itself as object. In these grades we already recognised the Platonic Ideas, for the grades are just the determined species, or the original unchanging forms and qualities of all natural bodies, both organised and unorganised, and also the general forces which reveal themselves according to natural laws. These Ideas, then, as a whole express themselves in innumerable individuals and particulars, and are related to these as archetypes to their copies. The multiplicity of such individuals is only conceivable through time and space, their appearing and passing away through causality, and in all these forms we recognise merely the different modes of the principle of sufficient reason, which is the ultimate principle of all that is finite, of all individual existence, and the universal form of the idea as it appears in the knowledge of the individual as such. The Platonic Idea, on the other hand, does not come under this principle, and has therefore neither multiplicity nor change. While the individuals in which it expresses itself are innumerable, and unceasingly come into being and pass away, it remains unchanged as one and the same, and the principle of sufficient reason has for it no meaning. As, however, this is the form under which all knowledge of the subject comes, so far as the subject knows as an *individual*, the Ideas lie quite outside the sphere of its knowledge. If, therefore, the Ideas are to become objects of knowledge, this can only happen by transcending the individuality of the knowing subject. The more exact and detailed explanation of this is what will now occupy our attention.

§ 31. First, however, the following very essential remark. I hope that in the preceding book I have succeeded in producing the conviction that what is called in the Kantian philosophy the *thing-in-itself*, and appears there as so significant, and yet so obscure and paradoxical a doctrine, and especially on account of the manner in which Kant introduced it as an inference from the caused to the cause, was considered a stumbling-stone, and, in fact, the weak side of his philosophy,—that this, I say, if it is reached by the entirely different way by which we have arrived at it, is nothing but the *will* when the sphere of that conception is extended and defined in the way I have shown. I hope, further, that after what has been said there will be no hesitation in recognising the definite grades of the objectification of the will, which is the inner reality of the world, to be what Plato called the eternal Ideas or unchangeable forms (ειδη); a doctrine which is regarded as the principal, but at the same time the most obscure and paradoxical dogma of his system, and has been the subject of reflection and controversy, of ridicule and of reverence, to so many and such differently endowed minds in the course of many centuries.

If now the will is for us the *thing-in-itself*, and the Idea is the immediate objectivity of that will at a definite grade, we find that Kant's thing-in-itself, and Plato's Idea, which to him is the only οντως ον, these two great obscure paradoxes of the two greatest philosophers of the West are not indeed identical, but yet very closely related, and only distinguished by a single circumstance. The purport of these two great paradoxes, with all inner harmony and relationship, is yet so very different on account of the remarkable diversity of the individuality of their authors, that they are the best commentary on each other, for they are like two entirely different roads that conduct us to the same goal. This is easily made clear. What Kant says is in substance this:—"Time, space, and causality are not determinations of the thing-in-itself, but belong only to its phenomenal existence, for they are nothing but the forms of our knowledge. Since, however, all multiplicity, and all coming into being and passing away, are only possible through time, space, and causality, it follows that they also belong only to the phenomenon, not to the thing-in-itself. But as our knowledge is conditioned by these forms, the whole of experience is only knowledge of the phenomenon, not of the thing-in-itself; therefore its laws cannot be made valid for the thing-in-itself. This extends even to our own *ego,* and we know it only as phenomenon, and not according to what it may be in itself." This is the meaning and content of the doctrine of Kant in the important respect we are considering. What Plato says is this:—"The things of this world which our senses perceive have no true being; *they always become, they never are:* they have only a relative being; they all exist merely in and through their relations to each other; their whole being may, therefore, quite as well be called a non-being. They are consequently not objects of a true knowledge (επιστημη), for such a knowledge can only be of what exists for itself, and always in the same way; they, on the contrary, are only the objects of an opinion based on sensation (δοξα μετ' αισθησεως αλογου). So long as we are confined to the perception of these, we are like men who sit in a dark cave, bound so fast that they cannot turn their heads, and who see nothing but the shadows of real things which pass between them and a fire burning behind them, the light of which casts the shadows on the wall opposite them; and even of themselves and of each other they see only the shadows on the wall. Their wisdom would thus consist in predicting the order of the shadows learned from experience. The real archetypes, on the other hand, to which these shadows correspond, the eternal Ideas, the original forms of all things, can alone be said to have true being (οντως ον), because they *always are, but never become nor pass away.* To them belongs *no multiplicity;* for each of them is according to its nature only one, for it is the archetype itself, of which all particular transitory things of the same kind which are named after it are copies or shadows. They have also *no coming into being nor passing away,* for they are truly being, never becoming nor vanishing, like their fleeting shadows. (It is necessarily presupposed, however, in these two negative definitions, that time, space, and causality have no significance or validity for these Ideas, and that they do not exist in them.) Of these only can there be true knowledge, for the object of such knowledge can only be that which always and in every respect (thus in-itself) is; not that which is and again is not, according as we look at it." This is Plato's doctrine. It is clear, and requires no further proof that the inner meaning of both doctrines is entirely the same; that both explain the visible world as a manifestation, which in itself is nothing, and which only has meaning and a borrowed reality through that which expresses itself in it (in the one case the thing-in-itself, in the other the Idea). To this last, which has true being, all the forms of that phenomenal existence, even the most universal and essential, are, according to both doctrines, entirely foreign. In order to disown these forms Kant has directly expressed them even in abstract terms, and distinctly refused time, space, and causality as mere forms of the phenomenon to the thing-in-itself. Plato, on the other hand, did not attain to the fullest expression, and has only distinctly refused these forms to his Ideas in that he denies of the Ideas what is only possible through these forms, multiplicity of similar things, coming into being and passing away. Though it is perhaps superfluous, I should like to illustrate this remarkable and important agreement by an example. There stands before us, let us suppose, an animal in the full activity of life. Plato would say, "This animal has no true existence, but merely an apparent existence, a constant becoming, a relative existence which may just as well be called non-being as being. Only the Idea which expresses itself in that animal is truly 'being,' or the animal in-itself (αυτο το θηριον), which is dependent upon nothing, but is in and for itself (καθ᾽ εαυτο εαι ὡς αυτως); it has not become, it will not end, but always is in the same way (αει ον, χαι μηδεποιε ουτε γίγνομενον ουτε απολλυμενον). If now we recognise its Idea in this animal, it is all one and of no importance whether we have this animal now before us or its progenitor of a thousand years ago, whether it is here or in a distant land, whether it presents itself in this or that manner, position, or action; whether, lastly, it is this or any other individual of the same species; all this is nothing, and only concerns the phenomenon; the Idea of the animal alone has true being, and is the object of real knowledge." So Plato; Kant would say something of this kind, "This animal is a phenomenon in time, space, and causality, which are collectively the conditions a priori of the possibility of experience, lying in our faculty of knowledge, not determinations of the thing-in-itself. Therefore this animal as we perceive it at this definite point of time, in this particular place, as an individual in the connection of experience (i.e., in the chain of causes and effects), which has come into being, and will just as necessarily pass away, is not a thing-in-itself, but a phenomenon which only exists in relation to our knowledge. To know it as what it may be in itself, that is to say, independent of all the determinations which lie in time, space, and causality, would demand another kind of knowledge than that which is possible for us through the senses and the understanding."

In order to bring Kant's mode of expression nearer the Platonic, we might say: Time, space, and causality are that arrangement of our intellect by virtue of which the *one* being of each kind which alone really is, manifests itself to us as a multiplicity of similar beings, constantly appearing and disappearing in endless succession. The apprehension of things by means of and in accordance with this arrangement is *immanent* knowledge; that, on the other hand, which is conscious of the true state of the case, is *transcendental* knowledge. The latter is obtained *in abstracto* through the criticism of pure reason, but in exceptional cases it may also appear intuitively. This last is an addition of my own, which I am endeavouring in this Third Book to explain.

§ 32. It follows from our consideration of the subject, that, for us, Idea and thing-in-itself are not entirely one and the same, in spite of the inner agreement between Kant and Plato, and the identity of the aim they had before them, or the conception of the world which roused them and led them to philosophise. The Idea is for us rather the direct, and therefore adequate, objectivity of the thing-in-itself, which is, however, itself the *will*—the will as not yet objectified, not yet become idea. For the thing-in-itself must, even according to Kant, be free from all the forms connected with knowing as such; and it is merely an error on his part (as is shown in the Appendix) that he did not count among these forms, before all others, that of being object for a subject, for it is the first and most universal form of all phenomena, *i.e.*, of all idea; he should therefore have distinctly denied objective existence to his thing-in-itself, which would have saved him from a great inconsistency that was soon discovered. The Platonic Idea, on the other hand, is necessarily object, something known, an idea, and in that respect is different from the thing-in-itself, but in that respect only. It has merely laid aside the subordinate forms of the phenomenon, all of which we include in the principle of sufficient reason, or rather it has not yet assumed them; but it has retained the first and most universal form, that of the idea in general, the form of being object for a subject. It is the forms which are subordinate to this (whose general expression is the principle of sufficient reason) that multiply the Idea in particular transitory individuals, whose number is a matter of complete indifference to the Idea. The principle of sufficient reason is thus again the form into which the Idea enters when it appears in the knowledge of the subject as individual. The particular thing that manifests itself in accordance with the principle of sufficient reason is thus only an indirect objectification of the thing-in-itself (which is the will), for between it and the thing-in-itself stands the Idea as the only direct objectivity of the will, because it has assumed none of the special forms of knowledge as such, except that of the idea in general, *i.e.*, the form of being object for a subject. Therefore it alone is the most *adequate objectivity* of the will or thing-in-itself which is possible; indeed it is the whole thing-in-itself, only under the form of the idea; and here lies the ground of the great agreement between Plato and Kant, although, in strict accuracy, that of which they speak is not the same. But the particular things are no really adequate objectivity of the will, for in them it is obscured by those forms whose general expression is the principle of sufficient reason, but which are conditions of the knowledge which belongs to the individual as such. If it is allowable to draw conclusions from an impossible presupposition, we would, in fact, no longer know particular things, nor events, nor change, nor multiplicity, but would comprehend only Ideas,—only the grades of the objectification of that one will, of the thing-in-itself, in pure

unclouded knowledge. Consequently our world would be a
nunc stans, if it were not that, as knowing subjects, we are
also individuals, *i.e.*, our perceptions come to us through the
medium of a body, from the affections of which they proceed, and which is itself only concrete willing, objectivity
of the will, and thus is an object among objects, and as such
comes into the knowing consciousness in the only way in
which an object can, through the forms of the principle
of sufficient reason, and consequently already presupposes,
and therefore brings in, time, and all other forms which
that principle expresses. Time is only the broken and piece-
meal view which the individual being has of the Ideas,
which are outside time, and consequently *eternal*. Therefore
Plato says time is the moving picture of eternity.

§ 33. Since now, as individuals, we have no other knowledge than that which is subject to the principle of sufficient
reason, and this form of knowledge excludes the Ideas, it
is certain that if it is possible for us to raise ourselves from
the knowledge of particular things to that of the Ideas, this
can only happen by an alteration taking place in the subject
which is analogous and corresponds to the great change of
the whole nature of the object, and by virtue of which the
subject, so far as it knows an Idea, is no more individual.

It will be remembered from the preceding book that
knowledge in general belongs to the objectification of will
at its higher grades, and sensibility, nerves, and brain, just
like the other parts of the organised being, are the expression of the will at this stage of its objectivity, and therefore
the idea which appears through them is also in the same
way bound to the service of will as a mean (μήχανη)
for the attainment of its now complicated (πολυτελεστερα)
aims for sustaining a being of manifold requirements. Thus
originally and according to its nature, knowledge is completely subject to the will, and, like the immediate object
which, by means of the application of the law of causality

is its starting-point, all knowledge which proceeds in accordance with the principle of sufficient reason remains in a
closer or more distant relation to the will. For the individual
finds his body as an object among objects, to all of which
it is related and connected according to the principle of
sufficient reason. Thus all investigations of these relations
and connections lead back to his body, and consequently to
his will. Since it is the principle of sufficient reason which
places the objects in this relation to the body, and, through
it, to the will, the one endeavour of the knowledge which
is subject to this principle will be to find out the relations in
which objects are placed to each other through this principle, and thus to trace their innumerable connections in
space, time, and causality. For only through these is the object *interesting* to the individual, *i.e.*, related to the will.
Therefore the knowledge which is subject to the will knows
nothing further of objects than their relations, knows the
objects only so far as they exist at this time, in this place,
under these circumstances, from these causes, and with these
effects—in a word, as particular things; and if all these
relations were to be taken away, the objects would also have
disappeared for it, because it knew nothing more about them.
We must not disguise the fact that what the sciences consider in things is also in reality nothing more than this; their
relations, the connections of time and space, the causes of
natural changes, the resemblance of forms, the motives of
actions,—thus merely relations. What distinguishes science
from ordinary knowledge is merely its systematic form, the
facilitating of knowledge by the comprehension of all particulars in the universal, by means of the subordination of
concepts, and the completeness of knowledge which is thereby
attained. All relation has itself only a relative existence; for
example, all being in time is also non-being; for time is only
that by means of which opposite determinations can belong
to the same thing; therefore every phenomenon which is in

time again is not, for what separates its beginning from its end is only time, which is essentially a fleeting, inconstant, and relative thing, here called duration. But time is the most universal form of all subjects of the knowledge which is subject to the will, and the prototype of its other forms.

Knowledge now, as a rule, remains always subordinate to the service of the will, as indeed it originated for this service, and grew, so to speak, to the will, as the head to the body. In the case of the brutes this subjection of knowledge to the will can never be abolished. In the case of men it can be abolished only in exceptional cases, which we shall presently consider more closely. This distinction between man and brute is outwardly expressed by the difference of the relation of the head to the body. In the case of the lower brutes both are deformed: in all brutes the head is directed towards the earth, where the objects of its will lie; even in the higher species the head and the body are still far more one than in the case of man, whose head seems freely set upon his body, as if only carried by and not serving it. This human excellence is exhibited in the highest degree by the Apollo of Belvedere; the head of the god of the Muses, with eyes fixed on the far distance, stands so freely on his shoulders that it seems wholly delivered from the body, and no more subject to its cares.

§ 34. The transition which we have referred to as possible, but yet to be regarded as only exceptional, from the common knowledge of particular things to the knowledge of the Idea, takes place suddenly; for knowledge breaks free from the service of the will, by the subject ceasing to be merely individual, and thus becoming the pure will-less subject of knowledge, which no longer traces relations in accordance with the principle of sufficient reason, but rests in fixed contemplation of the object presented to it, out of its connection with all others, and rises into it.

If, raised by the power of the mind, a man relinquishes

the common way of looking at things, gives up tracing, under the guidance of the forms of the principle of sufficient reason, their relations to each other, the final goal of which is always a relation to his own will; if he thus ceases to consider the where, the when, the why, and the whither of things, and looks simply and solely at the *what*; if, further, he does not allow abstract thought, the concepts of the reason, to take possession of his consciousness, but, instead of all this, gives the whole power of his mind to perception, sinks himself entirely in this. and lets his whole consciousness be filled with the quiet contemplation of the natural object actually present, whether a landscape, a tree, a mountain, a building, or whatever it may be; inasmuch as he *loses* himself in this object (to use a pregnant German idiom), *i.e.*, forgets even his individuality, his will, and only continues to exist as the pure subject, the clear mirror of the object, so that it is as if the object alone were there, without any one to perceive it, and he can no longer separate the perceiver from the perception, but both have become one, because the whole consciousness is filled and occupied with one single sensuous picture; if thus the object has to such an extent passed out of all relation to something outside it, and the subject out of all relation to the will, then that which is so known is no longer the particular thing as such; but it is the *Idea*, the eternal form, the immediate objectivity of the will at this grade; and, therefore, he who is sunk in this perception is no longer individual, for in such perception the individual has lost himself; but he is *pure*, will-less, painless, timeless *subject of knowledge*. This, which in itself is so remarkable (which I well know confirms the saying that originated with Thomas Paine, *Du sublime au ridicule il n'y a qu'un pas*), will by degrees become clearer and less surprising from what follows. It was this that was running in Spinoza's mind when he wrote: *Meus æterna est, quatenus*

res sub æternitatis specie concipit (Eth. V. pr. 31, Schol.) [1]
In such contemplation the particular thing becomes at once
the *Idea* of its species, and the perceiving individual becomes
pure subject of knowledge. The individual, as such, knows
only particular things; the pure subject of knowledge knows
only Ideas. For the individual is the subject of knowledge
in its relation to a definite particular manifestation of will,
and in subjection to this. This particular manifestation of
will is, as such, subordinated to the principle of sufficient
reason in all its forms; therefore, all knowledge which
relates itself to it also follows the principle of sufficient
reason, and no other kind of knowledge is fitted to be of
use to the will but this, which always consists merely of
relations to the object. The knowing individual as such, and
the particular things known by him, are always in some
place, at some time, and are links in the chain of causes and
effects. The pure subject of knowledge and his correlative,
the Idea, have passed out of all these forms of the principle
of sufficient reason: time, place, the individual that knows,
and the individual that is known, have for them no meaning.
When an individual knower has raised himself in the manner described to be pure subject of knowledge, and at the
same time has raised the observed object to the Platonic Idea,
the *world as idea* appears complete and pure, and the full
objectification of the will takes place, for the Platonic Idea
alone is its *adequate objectivity*. The Idea includes object
and subject in like manner in itself, for they are its one
form; but in it they are absolutely of equal importance; for
as the object is here, as elsewhere, simply the idea of the
subject, the subject, which passes entirely into the perceived
object has thus become this object itself, for the whole con-

[1] I also recommend the perusal of what Spinoza says in his Ethics
(Book II., Prop. 40, Schol. 2, and Book V., Props. 25-38), concerning the *cognitio tertii generis, sive intuitiva,* in illustration of the
kind of knowledge we are considering, and very specially Prop. 29,
Schol.; Prop. 36, Schol., and Prop. 38, Demonst. et Schol.

sciousness is nothing but its perfectly distinct picture. Now this consciousness constitutes the whole *world as idea*, for one imagines the whole of the Platonic Ideas, or grades of the objectivity of will, in their series passing through it. The particular things of all time and space are nothing but Ideas multiplied through the principle of sufficient reason (the form of the knowledge of the individual as such), and thus obscured as regards their pure objectivity. When the Platonic Idea appears, in it subject and object are no longer to be distinguished, for the Platonic Idea, the adequate objectivity of will, the true world as idea, arises only when the subject and object reciprocally fill and penetrate each other completely; and in the same way the knowing and the known individuals, as things in themselves, are not to be distinguished. For if we look entirely away from the true *world as idea*, there remains nothing but *the world as will*. The will is the "in-itself" of the Platonic Idea, which fully objectifies it; it is also the "in-itself" of the particular thing and of the individual that knows it, which objectify it incompletely. As will, outside the idea and all its forms, it is one and the same in the object contemplated and in the individual, who soars aloft in this contemplation, and becomes conscious of himself as pure subject. These two are, therefore, in themselves not different, for in themselves they are will, which here knows itself; and multiplicity and difference exist only as the way in which this knowledge comes to the will, *i.e.*, only in the phenomenon, on account of its form, the principle of sufficient reason.

Now the known thing, without me as the subject of knowledge, is just as little an object, and not mere will, blind effort, as without the object, without the idea. I am a knowing subject and not mere blind will. This will is in itself, *i.e.*, outside the idea, one and the same with mine: only in the world as idea, whose form is always at least that of subject and object, we are separated as the known and the knowing individual. As soon as knowledge, the world as idea, is abolished, there remains nothing but mere will, blind effort. That it should receive objectivity, become idea, supposes at once both subject and object; but that this should be pure, complete, and adequate objectivity of the will, supposes the object as Platonic Idea, free from the forms of the principle of sufficient reason, and the subject as the pure subject of knowledge, free from individuality and subjection to the will.

Whoever now, has, after the manner referred to, become so absorbed and lost in the perception of nature that he only continues to exist as the pure knowing subject, becomes in this way directly conscious that, as such, he is the condition, that is, the supporter, of the world and all objective existence; for this now shows itself as dependent upon his existence. Thus he draws nature into himself, so that he sees it to be merely an accident of his own being. In this sense Byron says—

> "Are not the mountains, waves, and skies, a part
> Of me and of my soul, as I of them?"

But how shall he who feels this, regard himself as absolutely transitory, in contrast to imperishable nature? Such a man will rather be filled with the consciousness, which the Upanishads of the Vedas express: *Hæ omnes creaturæ in totum ego sum, et præter me aliud ens non est.* (Oupnek'hat, i. 22).[1]

§ 35. In order to gain a deeper insight into the nature of the world, it is absolutely necessary that we should learn to distinguish the will as thing-in-itself from its adequate objectivity, and also the different grades in which this appears more and more distinctly and fully, *i.e.*, the Ideas themselves, from the merely phenomenal existence of these Ideas

---

[1] Cf. Chap. xxx. of the Supplement. "I am all these creatures in toto and beside me there is nothing."

in the forms of the principle of sufficient reason, the restricted method of knowledge of the individual. We shall
then agree with Plato when he attributes actual being only
to the Ideas, and allows only an illusive, dream-like existence
to things in space and time, the real world for the individual.
Then we shall understand how one and the same Idea reveals
itself in so many phenomena, and presents its nature only bit
by bit to the individual, one side after another. Then we
shall also distinguish the Idea itself from the way in which
its manifestation appears in the observation of the individual,
and recognise the former as essential and the latter as unessential. Let us consider this with the help of examples
taken from the most insignificant things, and also from the
greatest. When the clouds move, the figures which they form
are not essential, but indifferent to them; but that as elastic
vapour they are pressed together, drifted along, spread out,
or torn asunder by the force of the wind: this is their nature,
the essence of the forces which objectify themselves in them,
the Idea; their actual forms are only for the individual observer. To the brook that flows over stones, the eddies, the
waves, the foam-flakes which it forms are indifferent and
unessential; but that it follows the attraction of gravity,
and behaves as inelastic, perfectly mobile, formless, transparent fluid: this is its nature; this, *if known through perception*, is its Idea; these accidental forms are only for us so
long as we know as individuals. The ice on the window-pane
forms itself into crystals according to the laws of crystallisation, which reveal the essence of the force of nature that
appears here, exhibit the Idea; but the trees and flowers
which it traces on the pane are unessential, and are only there
for us. What appears in the clouds, the brook, and the crystal
is the weakest echo of that will which appears more fully in
the plant, more fully still in the beast, and most fully in
man. But only the essential in all these grades of its objectification constitutes the Idea; on the other hand, its unfolding

or development, because broken up in the forms of the principle of sufficient reason into a multiplicity of many-sided phenomena, is unessential to the Idea, lies merely in the kind of knowledge that belongs to the individual and has reality only for this. The same thing necessarily holds good of the unfolding of that Idea which is the completest objectivity of will. Therefore, the history of the human race, the throng of events, the change of times, the multifarious forms of human life in different lands and countries, all this is only the accidental form of the manifestation of the Idea, does not belong to the Idea itself, in which alone lies the adequate objectivity of the will, but only to the phenomenon which appears in the knowledge of the individual, and is just as foreign, unessential, and indifferent to the Idea itself as the figures which they assume are to the clouds, the form of its eddies and foam-flakes to the brook, or its trees and flowers to the ice.

To him who has thoroughly grasped this, and can distinguish between the will and the Idea, and between the Idea and its manifestation, the events of the world will have significance only so far as they are the letters out of which we may read the Idea of man, but not in and for themselves. He will not believe with the vulgar that time may produce something actually new and significant; that through it, or in it, something absolutely real may attain to existence, or indeed that it itself as a whole has beginnng and end, plan and development, and in some way has for its final aim the highest perfection (according to their conception) of the last generation of man, whose life is a brief thirty years. Therefore he will just as little, with Homer, people a whole Olympus with gods to guide the events of time, as, with Ossian, he will take the forms of the clouds for individual beings; for, as we have said, both have just as much meaning as regards the Idea which appears in them. In the manifold forms of human life and in the unceasing change of events, he will regard the Idea only as the abiding and essential, in which the will to live has its fullest objectivity, and which shows its different sides in the capacities, the passions, the errors and the excellences of the human race; in self-interest, hatred, love, fear, boldness, frivolity, stupidity, slyness, wit, genius, and so forth, all of which crowding together and combining in thousands of forms (individuals), continually create the history of the great and the little world, in which it is all the same whether they are set in motion by nuts or by crowns. Finally, he will find that in the world it is the same as in the dramas of Gozzi, in all of which the same persons appear, with like intention, and with a like fate; the motives and incidents are certainly different in each piece, but the spirit of the incidents is the same; the actors in one piece know nothing of the incidents of another, although they performed in it themselves; therefore, after all experience of former pieces, Pantaloon has become no more agile or generous, Tartaglia no more conscientious, Brighella no more courageous, and Columbine no more modest.

Suppose we were allowed for once a clearer glance into the kingdom of the possible, and over the whole chain of causes and effects; if the earth-spirit appeared and showed us in a picture all the greatest men, enlighteners of the world, and heroes, that chance destroyed before they were ripe for their work; then the great events that would have changed the history of the world and brought in periods of the highest culture and enlightenment, but which the blindest chance, the most insignificant accident, hindered at the outset; lastly, the splendid powers of great men, that would have enriched whole ages of the world, but which, either misled by error or passion, or compelled by necessity, they squandered uselessly on unworthy or unfruitful objects, or even wasted in play. If we saw all this, we would shudder and lament at the thought of the lost treasures of whole periods of the world. But the earth-spirit would smile and say, "The source from which the individuals and their powers proceed is inexhaustible and unending as time and space; for, like these forms of all phenomena, they also are only phenomena, visibility of the will. No finite measure can exhaust that infinite source; therefore an undiminished eternity is always open for the return of any event or work that was nipped in the bud. In this world of phenomena true loss is just as little possible as true gain. The will alone is; it is the thing-in-itself, and the source of all these phenomena. Its self-knowledge and its assertion or denial, which is then decided upon, is the only event-in-itself." [1]

§ 36. History follows the thread of events; it is pragmatic so far as it deduces them in accordance with the law of motivation, a law that determines the self-manifesting will wherever it is enlightened by knowledge. At the lowest grades of its objectivity, where it still acts without knowledge, natural science, in the form of etiology, treats of the laws of the changes of its phenomena, and, in the form of morphology, of what is permanent in them. This almost endless task is lightened by the aid of concepts, which comprehend what is general in order that we may deduce what is particular from it. Lastly, mathematics treats of the mere forms, time and space, in which the Ideas, broken up into multiplicity, appear for the knowledge of the subject as individual. All these, of which the common name is science, proceed according to the principle of sufficient reason in its different forms, and their theme is always the phenomenon, its laws, connections, and the relations which result from them. But what kind of knowledge is concerned with that which is outside and independent of all relations, that which alone is really essential to the world, the true content of its phenomena, that which is subject to no change, and there-

---

[1] This last sentence cannot be understood without some acquaintance with the next book.

unceasing desire for new things, and for the contemplation
of lofty things, and also that longing that is hardly ever
satisfied, for men of similar nature and of like stature, to
whom they might communicate themselves; whilst the common mortal, entirely filled and satisfied by the common
present, ends in it, and finding everywhere his like, en-
joys that peculiar satisfaction in daily life that is denied to
genius.

Imagination has rightly been recognised as an essential
element of genius; it has sometimes even been regarded as
identical with it; but this is a mistake. As the objects of
genius are the eternal Ideas, the permanent, essential forms
of the world and all its phenomena, and as the knowledge
of the Idea is necessarily knowledge through perception, is
not abstract, the knowledge of the genius would be limited
to the Ideas of the objects actually present to his person, and
dependent upon the chain of circumstances that brought these
objects to him, if his imagination did not extend his horizon
far beyond the limits of his actual personal existence, and
thus enable him to construct the whole out of the little that
comes into his own actual apperception, and so to let almost
all possible scenes of life pass before him in his own consciousness. Further, the actual objects are almost always very
imperfect copies of the Ideas expressed in them; therefore
the man of genius requires imagination in order to see in
things, not that which Nature has actually made, but that
which she endeavoured to make, yet could not because of
that conflict of her forms among themselves which we referred to in the last book. We shall return to this farther on
in treating of sculpture. The imagination then extends the
intellectual horizon of the man of genius beyond the objects
which actually present themselves to him, both as regards
quality and quantity. Therefore extraordinary strength of
imagination accompanies, and is indeed a necessary condition of genius. But the converse does not hold, for strength

of imagination does not indicate genius; on the contrary, men who have no touch of genius may have much imagination. For as it is possible to consider a real object in two opposite ways, purely objectively, the way of genius grasping its Idea, or in the common way, merely in the relations in which it stands to other objects and to one's own will, in accordance with the principle of sufficient reason, it is also possible to perceive an imaginary object in both of these ways. Regarded in the first way, it is a means to the knowledge of the Idea, the communication of which is the work of art; in the second case, the imaginary object is used to build castles in the air congenial to egotism and the individual humour, and which for the moment delude and gratify; thus only the relations of the phantasies so linked together are known. The man who indulges in such an amusement is a dreamer; he will easily mingle those fancies that delight his solitude with reality, and so unfit himself for real life: perhaps he will write them down, and then we shall have the ordinary novel of every description, which entertains those who are like him and the public at large, for the readers imagine themselves in the place of the hero, and then find the story very agreeable.

The common mortal, that manufacture of Nature which she produces by the thousand every day, is, as we have said, not capable, at least not continuously so, of observation that in every sense is wholly disinterested, as sensuous contemplation, strictly so called, is. He can turn his attention to things only so far as they have some relation to his will, however indirect it may be. Since in this respect, which never demands anything but the knowledge of relations, the abstract conception of the thing is sufficient, and for the most part even better adapted for use; the ordinary man does not linger long over the mere perception, does not fix his attention long on one object, but in all that is presented to him hastily seeks merely the concept under which it is to be brought, as the lazy man seeks a chair, and then it interests him no further. This is why he is so soon done with everything, with works of art, objects of natural beauty, and indeed everywhere with the truly significant contemplation of all the scenes of life. He does not linger; only seeks to know his own way in life, together with all that might at any time become his way. Thus he makes topographical notes in the widest sense; over the consideration of life itself as such he wastes no time. The man of genius, on the other hand, whose excessive power of knowledge frees it at times from the service of will, dwells on the consideration of life itself, strives to comprehend the Idea of each thing, not its relations to other things; and in doing this he often forgets to consider his own path in life, and therefore for the most part pursues it awkwardly enough. While to the ordinary man his faculty of knowledge is a lamp to lighten his path, to the man of genius it is the sun which reveals the world. This great diversity in their way of looking at life soon becomes visible in the outward appearance both of the man of genius and of the ordinary mortal. The man in whom genius lives and works is easily distinguished by his glance, which is both keen and steady, and bears the stamp of perception, of contemplation. This is easily seen from the likenesses of the few men of genius whom Nature has produced here and there among countless millions. On the other hand, in the case of an ordinary man, the true object of his contemplation, what he is prying into, can be easily seen from his glance, if indeed it is not quite stupid and vacant, as is generally the case. Therefore the expression of genius in a face consists in this, that in it a decided predominance of knowledge over will is visible, and consequently there also shows itself in it a knowledge that is entirely devoid of relation to will, *i.e., pure knowing.* On the contrary, in ordinary countenances there is a predominant expression of will; and we see that knowledge only comes into activity under the impulse of will, and thus is directed merely by motives.

§ 37. Genius, then, consists, according to our explanation, in the capacity for knowing, independently of the principle of sufficient reason, not individual things, which have their existence only in their relations, but the Ideas of such things, and of being oneself the correlative of the Idea, and thus no longer an individual, but the pure subject of knowledge. Yet this faculty must exist in all men in a smaller and different degree; for if not, they would be just as incapable of enjoying works of art as of producing them; they would have no susceptibility for the beautiful or the sublime; indeed, these words could have no meaning for them. We must therefore assume that there exists in all men this power of knowing the Ideas in things, and consequently of transcending their personality for the moment, unless indeed there are some men who are capable of no æsthetic pleasure at all. The man of genius excels ordinary men only by possessing this kind of knowledge in a far higher degree and more continuously. Thus, while under its influence he retains the presence of mind which is necessary to enable him to repeat in a voluntary and intentional work what he has learned in this manner; and this repetition is the work of art. Through this he communicates to others the Idea he has grasped. This Idea remains unchanged and the same, so that æsthetic pleasure is one and the same whether it is called forth by a work of art or directly by the contemplation of nature and life. The work of art is only a means of facilitating the knowledge in which this pleasure consists. That the Idea comes to us more easily from the work of art than directly from nature and the real world, arises from the fact that the artist, who knew only the Idea, no longer the actual, has reproduced in his work the pure Idea, has abstracted it from the actual, omitting all disturbing accidents. The artist lets us see the world through his eyes. That he has these eyes, that he knows the inner nature of things apart from all their relations, is the gift of genius, is inborn; but that he is able to lend us this gift, to let us see with his eyes, is acquired, and is the technical side of art. Therefore, after the account which I have given in the preceding pages of the inner nature of æsthetical knowledge in its most general outlines, the following more exact philosophical treatment of the beautiful and the sublime will explain them both, in nature and in art, without separating them further. First of all we shall consider what takes place in a man when he is affected by the beautiful and the sublime; whether he derives this emotion directly from nature, from life, or partakes of it only through the medium of art, does not make any essential, but merely an external, difference.

§ 38. In the æsthetical mode of contemplation we have found *two inseparable constituent parts*—the knowledge of the object, not as individual thing but as Platonic Idea, that is, as the enduring form of this whole species of things; and the self-consciousness of the knowing person, not as individual, but as *pure will-less subject of knowledge*. The condition under which both these constituent parts appear always united was found to be the abandonment of the method of knowing which is bound to the principle of sufficient reason, and which, on the other hand, is the only kind of knowledge that is of value for the service of the will and also for science. Moreover, we shall see that the pleasure which is produced by the contemplation of the beautiful arises from these two constituent parts, sometimes more from the one, sometimes more from the other, according to what the object of the æsthetical contemplation may be.

All *willing* arises from want, therefore from deficiency, and therefore from suffering. The satisfaction of a wish ends it; yet for one wish that is satisfied there remain at least ten which are denied. Further, the desire lasts long, the demands are infinite; the satisfaction is short and scantily measured out. But even the final satisfaction is itself only apparent; every satisfied wish at once makes room for a new one; both are illusions; the one is known to be so, the other not yet. No attained object of desire can give lasting satisfaction, but merely a fleeting gratification; it is like the alms thrown to the beggar, that keeps him alive to-day that his misery may be prolonged till the morrow. Therefore, so long as our consciousness is filled by our will, so long as we are given up to the throng of desires with their constant hopes and fears, so long as we are the subject of willing, we can never have lasting happiness nor peace. It is essentially all the same whether we pursue or flee, fear injury or seek enjoyment; the care for the constant demands of the will, in whatever form it may be, continually occupies and sways the consciousness; but without peace no true well-being is possible. The subject of willing is thus constantly stretched on the revolving wheel of Ixion, pours water into the sieve of the Danaids, is the ever-longing Tantalus.

But when some external cause or inward disposition lifts us suddenly out of the endless stream of willing, delivers knowledge from the slavery of the will, the attention is no longer directed to the motives of willing, but comprehends things free from their relation to the will, and thus observes them without personal interest, without subjectivity, purely objectively, gives itself entirely up to them so far as they are ideas, but not in so far as they are motives. Then all at once the peace which we were always seeking, but which always fled from us on the former path of the desires, comes to us of its own accord, and it is well with us. It is the painless state which Epicurus prized as the highest good and as the state of the gods; for we are for the moment set free from the miserable striving of the will; we keep the Sabbath of the penal servitude of willing; the wheel of Ixion stands still.

But this is just the state which I described above as necessary for the knowledge of the Idea, as pure contemplation, as sinking oneself in perception, losing oneself in the object, forgetting all individuality, surrendering that kind of knowledge which follows the principle of sufficient reason, and comprehends only relations; the state by means of which at once and inseparably the perceived particular thing is raised to the Idea of its whole species, and the knowing individual to the pure subject of will-less knowledge, and as such they are both taken out of the stream of time and all other relations. It is then all one whether we see the sun set from the prison or from the palace.

Inward disposition, the predominance of knowing over willing, can produce this state under any circumstances. This is shown by those admirable Dutch artists who directed this purely objective perception to the most insignificant objects, and established a lasting monument of their objectivity and spiritual peace in their pictures of *still life*, which the æsthetic beholder does not look on without emotion; for they present to him the peaceful, still, frame of mind of the artist, free from will, which was needed to contemplate such insignificant things so objectively, to observe them so attentively, and to repeat this perception so intelligently; and as the picture enables the onlooker to participate in this state, his emotion is often increased by the contrast between it and the unquiet frame of mind, disturbed by vehement willing, in which he finds himself. In the same spirit, landscape-painters, and particularly Ruisdael, have often painted very insignificant country scenes, which produce the same effect even more agreeably.

All this is accomplished by the inner power of an artistic nature alone; but that purely objective disposition is facilitated and assisted from without by suitable objects, by the abundance of natural beauty which invites contemplation, and even presses itself upon us. Whenever it discloses itself suddenly to our view, it almost always succeeds in delivering us, though it may be only for a moment, from subjectivity, from the slavery of the will, and in raising us to the state of pure knowing. This is why the man who is tormented by passion, or want, or care, is so suddenly revived, cheered, and restored by a single free glance into nature: the storm of passion, the pressure of desire and fear, and all the miseries of willing are then at once, and in a marvellous manner, calmed and appeased. For at the moment at which, freed from the will, we give ourselves up to pure will-less knowing, we pass into a world from which everything is absent that influenced our will and moved us so violently through it. This freeing of knowledge lifts us as wholly and entirely away from all that, as do sleep and dreams; happiness and unhappiness have disappeared; we are no longer individual; the individual is forgotten; we are only pure subject of knowledge; we are only that *one* eye of the world which looks out from all knowing creatures, but which can become perfectly free from the service of will in man alone. Thus all difference of individuality so entirely disappears, that it is all the same whether the perceiving eye belongs to a mighty king or to a wretched beggar; for neither joy nor complaining can pass that boundary with us. So near us always lies a sphere in which we escape from all our misery; but who has the strength to continue long in it? As soon as any single relation to our will, to our person, even of these objects of our pure contemplation, comes again into consciousness, the magic is at an end; we fall back into the knowledge which is governed by the principle of sufficient reason; we know no longer the Idea, but the particular thing, the link of a chain to which we also belong, and we are again abandoned to all our woe. Most men remain almost always at this standpoint because they entirely lack objectivity, *i.e.*, genius. Therefore they have no pleasure in being alone with nature; they need company, or at least a book. For their knowledge remains subject to their will;

they seek, therefore, in objects, only some relation to their will, and whenever they see anything that has no such relation, there sounds within them, like a ground bass in music, the constant inconsolable cry, "It is of no use to me"; thus in solitude the most beautiful surroundings have for them a desolate, dark, strange, and hostile appearance.

Lastly, it is this blessedness of will-less perception which casts an enchanting glamour over the past and distant, and presents them to us in so fair a light by means of self-deception. For as we think of days long gone by, days in which we lived in a distant place, it is only the objects which our fancy recalls, not the subject of will, which bore about with it then its incurable sorrows just as it bears them now; but they are forgotten, because since then they have often given place to others. Now, objective perception acts with regard to what is remembered just as it would in what is present, if we let it have influence over us, if we surrendered ourselves to it free from will. Hence it arises that, especially when we are more than ordinarily disturbed by some want, the remembrance of past and distant scenes suddenly flits across our minds like a lost paradise. The fancy recalls only what was objective, not what was individually subjective, and we imagine that that objective stood before us then just as pure and undisturbed by any relation to the will as its image stands in our fancy now; while in reality the relation of the objects to our will gave us pain then just as it does now. We can deliver ourselves from all suffering just as well through present objects as through distant ones whenever we raise ourselves to a purely objective contemplation of them, and so are able to bring about the illusion that only the objects are present and not we ourselves. Then, as the pure subject of knowledge, freed from the miserable self, we become entirely one with these objects, and, for the moment. our wants are as foreign to us as they are to them

The world as idea alone remains, and the world as will has disappeared.

§ 39. All these reflections are intended to bring out the subjective part of æsthetic pleasure; that is to say, that pleasure so far as it consists simply of delight in perceptive knowledge as such, in opposition to will. And as directly connected with this, there naturally follows the explanation of that disposition or frame of mind which has been called the sense of the *sublime*.

We have already remarked above that the transition to the state of pure perception takes place most easily when the objects bend themselves to it, that is, when by their manifold and yet definite and distinct form they easily become representatives of their Ideas, in which beauty, in the objective sense, consists. This quality belongs pre-eminently to natural beauty, which thus affords even to the most insensible at least a fleeting æsthetic satisfaction: indeed it is so remarkable how especially the vegetable world invites æsthetic observation, and, as it were, presses itself upon it, that one might say, that these advances are connected with the fact that these organisms, unlike the bodies of animals, are not themselves immediate objects of knowledge, and therefore require the assistance of a foreign intelligent individual in order to rise out of the world of blind will and enter the world of idea, and that thus they long, as it were, for this entrance, that they may attain at least indirectly what is denied them directly. But I leave this suggestion which I have hazarded, and which borders perhaps upon extravagance, entirely undecided, for only a very intimate and devoted consideration of nature can raise or justify it.[1] As long as that

---

[1] I am all the more delighted and astonished, forty years after I so timidly and hesitatingly advanced this thought, to discover that it has already been expressed by St. Augustine: *Arbusta formas suas varias, quibus mundi hujus visibilis structura formosa est, sentiendas sensibus præbent; ut, pro eo quod* NOSSE *non possunt, quasi* INNOTESCERE *velle videantur.—De civ. Dei, xi,* 27.

which raises us from the knowledge of mere relations subject to the will, to æsthetic contemplation, and thereby exalts
us to the position of the subject of knowledge free from
will, is this fittingness of nature, this significance and distinctness of its forms, on account of which the Ideas indi-
vidualised in them readily present themselves to us; so long
is it merely *beauty* that affects us and the sense of the *beautiful* that is excited. But if these very objects whose significant
forms invite us to pure contemplation, have a hostile relation
to the human will in general, as it exhibits itself in its
objectivity, the human body, if they are opposed to it, so
that it is menaced by the irresistible predominance of their
power, or sinks into insignificance before their immeasurable greatness; if, nevertheless, the beholder does not direct
his attention to this eminently hostile relation to his will,
but, although perceiving and recognising it, turns consciously
away from it, forcibly detaches himself from his will and
its relations, and, giving himself up entirely to knowledge,
quietly contemplates those very objects that are so terrible
to the will, comprehends only their Idea, which is foreign
to all relation, so that he lingers gladly over its contemplation, and is thereby raised above himself, his person, his will,
and all will:—in that case he is filled with the sense of the
sublime, he is in the state of spiritual exaltation, and therefore the object producing such a state is called *sublime.* Thus
what distinguishes the sense of the sublime from that of the
beautiful is this: in the case of the beautiful, pure knowledge has gained the upper hand without a struggle, for the
beauty of the object, *i.e.,* that property which facilitates
the knowledge of its Idea, has removed from consciousness
without resistance, and therefore imperceptibly, the will and
the knowledge of relations which is subject to it, so that
what is left is the pure subject of knowledge without even a
remembrance of will. On the other hand, in the case of the
sublime that state of pure knowledge is only attained by a

conscious and forcible breaking away from the relations of
the same object to the will, which are recognised as unfavourable, by a free and conscious transcending of the will
and the knowledge related to it.

This exaltation must not only be consciously won, but
also consciously retained, and it is therefore accompanied by
a constant remembrance of will; yet not of a single particular volition, such as fear or desire, but of human volition
in general, so far as it is universally expressed in its objectivity the human body. If a single real act of will were to
come into consciousness, through actual personal pressure
and danger from the object, then the individual will thus
actually influenced would at once gain the upper hand, the
peace of contemplation would become impossible, the impression of the sublime would be lost, because it yields to the
anxiety, in which the effort of the individual to right itself
has sunk every other thought. A few examples will help
very much to elucidate this theory to the æsthetic sublime
and remove all doubt with regard to it; at the same time
they will bring out the different degrees of this sense of the
sublime. It is in the main identical with that of the beautiful,
with pure will-less knowing, and the knowledge, that necessarily accompanies it of Ideas out of all relation determined
by the principle of sufficient reason, and it is distinguished
from the sense of the beautiful only by the additional quality
that it rises above the known hostile relation of the object
contemplated to the will in general. Thus there come to be
various degrees of the sublime, and transitions from the
beautiful to the sublime, according as this additional quality
is strong, bold, urgent, near, or weak, distant, and merely
indicated. I think it is more in keeping with the plan of my
treatise, first to give examples of these transitions, and of
the weaker degrees of the impression of the sublime, although persons whose æsthetical susceptibility in general is
not very great, and whose imagination is not very lively, will

only understand the examples given later of the higher and more distinct grades of that impression; and they should therefore confine themselves to these, and pass over the examples of the very weak degrees of the sublime that are to be given first.

As man is at once impetuous and blind striving of will (whose pole or focus lies in the genital organs), and eternal, free, serene subject of pure knowing (whose pole is the brain); so, corresponding to this antithesis, the sun is both the source of *light*, the condition of the most perfect kind of knowledge, and therefore of the most delightful of things—and the source of *warmth*, the first condition of life, *i.e.*, of all phenomena of will in its higher grades Therefore, what warmth is for the will, light is for knowl-edge. Light is the largest gem in the crown of beauty, and has the most marked influence on the knowledge of every beautiful object. Its presence is an indispensable condition of beauty; its favourable disposition increases the beauty of the most beautiful. Architectural beauty more than any other object is enhanced by favourable light, though even the most insignificant things become through its influence most beautiful. If, in the dead of winter, when all nature is frozen and stiff, we see the rays of the setting sun re-flected by masses of stone, illuminating without warming, and thus favourable only to the purest kind of knowledge, not to the will; the contemplation of the beautiful effect of the light upon these masses lifts us, as does all beauty, into a state of pure knowing. But, in this case, a certain transcending of the interests of the will is needed to enable us to rise into the state of pure knowing, because there is a faint recollection of the lack of warmth from these rays, that is, an absence of the principle of life; there is a slight challenge to persist in pure knowing, and to refrain from all willing, and therefore it is an example of a transition from the sense of the beautiful to that of the sublime. It is the faintest trace of the sublime in the beautiful; and beauty itself is indeed present only in a slight degree. The following is almost as weak an example.

Let us imagine ourselves transported to a very lonely place, with unbroken horizon, under a cloudless sky, trees and plants in the perfectly motionless air, no animals, no men, no running water, the deepest silence. Such surroundings are, as it were, a call to seriousness and contemplation, apart from all will and its cravings; but this is just what imparts to such a scene of desolate stillness a touch of the sublime. For, because it affords no object, either favourable or unfavourable, for the will which is constantly in need of striving and attaining, there only remains the state of pure contemplation, and whoever is incapable of this, is ignominiously abandoned to the vacancy of unoccupied will, and the misery of ennui. So far it is a test of our intellectual worth, of which, generally speaking, the degree of our power of enduring solitude, or our love of it, is a good criterion. The scene we have sketched affords us, then, an example of the sublime in a low degree, for in it, with the state of pure knowing in its peace and all-sufficiency, there is mingled, by way of contrast, the recollection of the dependence and poverty of the will which stands in need of constant action. This is the species of the sublime for which the sight of the boundless prairies of the interior of North America is celebrated.

But let us suppose such a scene, stripped also of vegetation, and showing only naked rocks; then from the entire absence of that organic life which is necessary for existence, the will at once becomes uneasy, the desert assumes a terrible aspect, our mood becomes more tragic; the elevation to the sphere of pure knowing takes place with a more decided tearing of ourselves away from the interests of the will; and because we persist in continuing in the state of pure knowing, the sense of the sublime distinctly appears.

The following situation may occasion this feeling in a still higher degree: Nature convulsed by a storm; the sky darkened by black threatening thunder-clouds; stupendous, naked, overhanging cliffs, completely shutting out the view; rushing, foaming torrents; absolute desert; the wail of the wind sweeping through the clefts of the rocks. Our dependence, our strife with hostile nature, our will broken in the conflict, now appears visibly before our eyes. Yet, so long as the personal pressure does not gain the upper hand, but we continue in æsthetic contemplation, the pure subject of knowing gazes unshaken and unconcerned through that strife of nature, through that picture of the broken will, and quietly comprehends the Ideas even of those objects which are threatening and terrible to the will. In this contrast lies the sense of the sublime.

But the impression becomes still stronger, if, when we have before our eyes, on a large scale, the battle of the raging elements, in such a scene we are prevented from hearing the sound of our own voice by the noise of a falling stream; or, if we are abroad in the storm of tempestuous seas, where the mountainous waves rise and fall, dash themselves furiously against steep cliffs, and toss their spray high into the air; the storm howls, the sea boils, the lightning flashes from black clouds, and the peals of thunder drown the voice of storm and sea. Then, in the undismayed beholder, the two-fold nature of his consciousness reaches the highest degree of distinctness. He perceives himself, on the one hand, as an individual, as the frail phenomenon of will, which the slightest touch of these forces can utterly destroy, helpless against powerful nature, dependent, the victim of chance, a vanishing nothing in the presence of stupendous might; and, on the other hand, as the eternal, peaceful, knowing subject, the condition of the object, and, therefore, the supporter of this whole world; the terrific strife of nature only his idea; the subject itself free and apart from all desire and necessities, in the quiet comprehension of the Ideas. This is the complete impression of the sublime. Here he obtains a glimpse of a power beyond all comparison superior to the individual, threatening it with annihilation.

The impression of the sublime may be produced in quite another way, by presenting a mere immensity in space and time; its immeasurable greatness dwindles the individual to nothing. Adhering to Kant's nomenclature and his accurate division, we may call the first kind the dynamical, and the second the mathematical sublime, although we entirely dissent from his explanation of the inner nature of the impression, and can allow no share in it either to moral reflections, or to hypostases from scholastic philosophy.

If we lose ourselves in the contemplation of the infinite greatness of the universe in space and time, meditate on the thousands of years that are past or to come, or if the heavens at night actually bring before our eyes innumerable worlds and so force upon our consciousness the immensity of the universe, we feel ourselves dwindle to nothing; as individuals, as living bodies, as transient phenomena of will, we feel ourselves pass away and vanish into nothing like drops in the ocean. But at once there rises against this ghost of our own nothingness, against such lying impossibility, the immediate consciousness that all these worlds exist only as our idea, only as modifications of the eternal subject of pure knowing, which we find ourselves to be as soon as we forget our individuality, and which is the necessary supporter of all worlds and all times the condition of their possibility. The vastness of the world which disquieted us before, rests now in us; our dependence upon it is annulled by its dependence upon us. All this, however, does not come at once into reflection, but shows itself merely as the felt consciousness that in some sense or other (which philosophy alone can explain) we are one with the world, and therefore not oppressed, but exalted by its immensity. It is the felt consciousness of this that the Upanishads of the Vedas repeatedly express in such a multitude of different ways; very admirably in the saying already quoted: *Hæ omnes creaturæ in totum ego sum, et præter me aliud ens non est* (Oupnek'hat, vol. i. p. 122.) It is the transcending of our own individuality, the sense of the sublime.

We receive this impression of the mathematical-sublime, quite directly, by means of a space which is small indeed as compared with the world, but which has become directly perceptible to us, and affects us with its whole extent in all its three dimensions, so as to make our own body seem almost infinitely small. An empty space can never be thus perceived, and therefore never an open space, but only space that is directly perceptible in all its dimensions by means of the limits which enclose it; thus for example a very high, vast dome, like that of St. Peter's at Rome, or St. Paul's in London. The sense of the sublime here arises through the consciousness of the vanishing nothingness of our own body in the presence of a vastness which, from another point of view, itself exists only in our idea, and of which we are, as knowing subject, the supporter. Thus here as everywhere it arises from the contrast between the insignificance and dependence of ourselves as individuals, as phenomena of will, and the consciousness of ourselves as pure subject of knowing. Even the vault of the starry heaven produces this if it is contemplated without reflection; but just in the same way as the vault of stone, and only by its apparent, not its real extent. Some objects of our perception excite in us the feeling of the sublime because, not only on account of their spatial vastness, but also of their great age, that is, their temporal duration, we feel ourselves dwarfed to insignificance in their presence, and yet revel in the pleasure of contemplating them: of this kind are very high mountains, the Egyptian pyramids, and colossal ruins of great antiquity.

§ 41. The course of the discussion has made it necessary

to insert at this point the treatment of the sublime, though we have only half done with the beautiful, as we have considered its subjective side only. For it was merely a special modification of this subjective side that distinguished the beautiful from the sublime. This difference was found to depend upon whether the state of pure will-less knowing, which is presupposed and demanded by all æsthetic contemplation, was reached without opposition, by the mere disappearance of the will from consciousness, because the object invited and drew us towards it; or whether it was only attained through the free, conscious transcending of the will, to which the object contemplated had an unfavourable and even hostile relation, which would destroy contemplation altogether, if we were to give ourselves up to it. This is the distinction between the beautiful and the sublime. In the object they are not essentially different, for in every case the object of æsthetical contemplation is not the individual thing, but the Idea in it which is striving to reveal itself; that is to say, adequate objectivity of will at a particular grade. Its necessary correlative, independent, like itself, of the principle of sufficient reason, is the pure subject of knowing; just as the correlative of the particular thing is the knowing individual, both of which lie within the province of the principle of sufficient reason.

When we say that a thing is *beautiful*, we thereby assert that it is an object of our æsthetic contemplation, and this has a double meaning; on the one hand, it means that the sight of the thing makes us *objective*, that is to say, that in contemplating it we are no longer conscious of ourselves as individuals, but as pure will-less subjects of knowledge; and, on the other hand, it means that we recognise in the object, not the particular thing, but an Idea; and this can only happen, so far as our contemplation of it is not subordinated to the principle of sufficient reason, does not follow the relation of the object to anything outside it (which is always ultimately connected with relations to our own will), but rests in the object itself. For the Idea and the pure subject of knowledge always appear at once in consciousness as necessary correlatives, and on their appearance all distinction of time vanishes, for they are both entirely foreign to the principle of sufficient reason in all its forms, and lie outside the relations which are imposed by it; they may be compared to the rainbow and the sun, which have no part in the constant movement and succession of the falling drops. Therefore, if, for example, I contemplate a tree æsthetically, *i.e.*, with artistic eyes, and thus recognise, not it, but its Idea, it becomes at once of no consequence whether it is this tree or its predecessor which flourished a thousand years ago, and whether the observer is this individual or any other that lived anywhere and at any time; the particular thing and the knowing individual are abolished with the principle of sufficient reason, and there remains nothing but the Idea and the pure subject of knowing, which together constitute the adequate objectivity of will at this grade. And the Idea dispenses not only with time, but also with space, for the Idea proper is not this special form which appears before me but its expression, its pure significance, its inner being, which discloses itself to me and appeals to me, and which may be quite the same though the spatial relations of its form be very different.

Since, on the one hand, every given thing may be observed in a purely objective manner and apart from all relations; and since, on the other hand, the will manifests itself in everything at some grade of its objectivity, so that everything is the expression of an Idea; it follows that everything is also *beautiful*. That even the most insignificant things admit of pure objective and will-less contemplation, and thus prove that they are beautiful, is shown by what was said above in this reference about the Dutch pictures of still life (§ 38). But one thing is more beautiful than another, because it makes this pure objective contemplation easier, it lends itself to it, and, so to speak, even compels it, and then we call it very beautiful. This is the case sometimes because, as an individual thing, it expresses in its purity the Idea of its species by the very distinct, clearly defined, and significant relation of its parts, and also fully reveals that Idea through the completeness of all the possible expressions of its species united in it, so that it makes the transition from the individual thing to the Idea, and therefore also the condition of pure contemplation, very easy for the beholder. Sometimes this possession of special beauty in an object lies in the fact that the Idea itself which appeals to us in it is a high grade of the objectivity of will, and therefore very significant and expressive. Therefore it is that man is more beautiful than all other objects, and the revelation of his nature is the highest aim of art. Human form and expression are the most important objects of plastic art, and human action the most important object of poetry. Yet each thing has its own peculiar beauty, not only every organism which expresses itself in the unity of an individual being, but also everything unorganised and formless, and even every manufactured article. For all these reveal the Ideas through which the will objectifies itself at its lowest grades; they give, as it were, the deepest resounding bass notes of nature. Gravity, rigidity, fluidity, light, and so forth, are the Ideas which express themselves in rocks, in buildings, in waters. Landscape gardening or architecture can do no more than assist them to unfold their qualities distinctly, fully, and variously; they can only give them the opportunity of expressing themselves purely, so that they lend themselves to æsthetic contemplation and make it easier. Inferior buildings or ill-favoured localities, on the contrary, which nature has neglected or art has spoiled, perform this task in a very slight degree or not at all; yet even from them these universal, fundamental Ideas of nature cannot altogether disappear. To the careful ob-

server they present themselves here also, and even bad buildings and the like are capable of being æsthetically considered;
the Ideas of the most universal properties of their materials
are still recognisable in them, only the artificial form which
has been given them does not assist but hinders æsthetic contemplation. Manufactured articles also serve to express Ideas,
only it is not the Idea of the manufactured article which
speaks in them, but the Idea of the material to which this
artificial form has been given. This may be very conveniently
expressed in two words, in the language of the schoolmen,
thus,—the manufactured article expresses the Idea of its
forma substantialis, but not that of its *forma accidentalis;*
the latter leads to no Idea, but only to a human conception
of which it is the result. It is needless to say that by manufactured article no work of plastic art is meant. The schoolmen understand, in fact, by *forma substantialis* that which
I call the grade of the objectification of will in a thing. We
shall return immediately, when we treat of architecture, to
the Idea of the material.

§42. I return to the exposition of the æsthetic impression.
The knowledge of the beautiful always supposes at once and
inseparably the pure knowing subject and the known Idea as
object. Yet the source of æsthetic satisfaction will sometimes
lie more in the comprehension of the known idea, sometimes
more in the blessedness and spiritual peace of the pure knowing subject freed from all willing, and therefore from all
individuality, and the pain that proceeds from it. And, indeed, this predominance of one or the other constituent part
of æsthetic feeling will depend upon whether the intuitively
grasped Idea is a higher or a lower grade of the objectivity
of will. Thus in æsthetic contemplation (in the real, or
through the medium of art) of the beauty of nature in the
inorganic and vegetable worlds, or in works of architecture,
the pleasure of pure will-less knowing will predominate,
because the Ideas which are here apprehended are only low

grades of the objectivity of will, and are therefore not manifestations of deep significance and rich content. On the other hand, if animals and man are the objects of æsthetic contemplation or representation, the pleasure will consist rather in the comprehension of these Ideas, which are the most distinct revelation of will; for they exhibit the greatest multiplicity of forms, the greatest richness and deep significance of phenomena, and reveal to us most completely the nature of will, whether in its violence, its terribleness, its satisfaction or its aberration (the latter in tragic situations), or finally in its change and self-surrender, which is the peculiar theme of Christian painting; as the Idea of the will enlightened by full knowledge is the object of historical painting in general, and of the drama. We shall now go through the fine arts one by one, and this will give completeness and distinctness to the theory of the beautiful which we have advanced.

If now we consider *architecture* simply as a fine art and apart from its application to useful ends, in which it serves the will and not pure knowledge, and therefore ceases to be art in our sense; we can assign to it no other aim than that of bringing to greater distinctness some of those ideas which are the lowest grades of the objectivity of will; such as gravity, cohesion, rigidity, hardness, those universal qualities of stone, those first, simplest, most inarticulate manifestations of will; the bass notes of nature; and after these light, which in many respects is their opposite. Even at these low grades of the objectivity of will we see its nature revealing itself in discord; for properly speaking the conflict between gravity and rigidity is the sole æsthetic material of architecture; its problem is to make this conflict appear with perfect distinctness in a multitude of different ways. It solves it by depriving these indestructible forces of the shortest way to their satisfaction, and conducting them to it by a circuitous route, so that the conflict is lengthened and the inex-

haustible efforts of both forces become visible in many
different ways. The whole mass of the building, if left to its
original tendency, would exhibit a mere heap or clump,
bound as closely as possible to the earth, to which gravity,
the form in which the will appears here, continually presses,
while rigidity, also objectivity of will, resists. But this very
tendency, this effort, is hindered by architecture from obtaining direct satisfaction, and only allowed to reach it indirectly and by roundabout ways. The roof, for example,
can only press the earth through columns, the arch must support itself, and can only satisfy its tendency towards the
earth through the medium of the pillars, and so forth. But
just by these enforced digressions, just by these restrictions,
the forces which reside in the crude mass of stone unfold
themselves in the most distinct and multifarious ways; and
the purely æsthetic aim of architecture can go no further
than this. Therefore the beauty, at any rate, of a building
lies in the obvious adaptation of every part, not to the outward arbitrary end of man (so far the work belongs to
practical architecture), but directly to the stability of the
whole, to which the position, dimensions, and form of every
part must have so necessary a relation that, where it is possible, if any one part were taken away, the whole would
fall to pieces. For just because each part bears just as much
as it conveniently can, and each is supported just where it
requires to be and just to the necessary extent, this opposition
unfolds itself, this conflict between rigidity and gravity,
which constitutes the life, the manifestation of will, in the
stone, becomes completely visible, and these lowest grades of
the objectivity of will reveal themselves distinctly. In the
same way the form of each part must not be determined arbitrarily, but by its end, and its relation to the whole.

Now, because the Ideas which architecture brings to clear
perception, are the lowest grades of the objectivity of will,
and consequently their objective significance, which archi-

tecture reveals to us, is comparatively small; the æsthetic pleasure of looking at a beautiful building in a good light will lie, not so much in the comprehension of the Idea, as in the subjective correlative which accompanies this comprehension; it will consist pre-eminently in the fact that the beholder, set free from the kind of knowledge that belongs to the individual, and which serves the will and follows the principle of sufficient reason, is raised to that of the pure subject of knowing free from will. It will consist then principally in pure contemplation itself, free from all the suffering of will and of individuality. In this respect the opposite of architecture, and the other extreme of the series of the fine arts, is the drama, which brings to knowledge the most significant Ideas. Therefore in the æsthetic pleasure afforded by the drama the objective side is throughout predominant.

Architecture has this distinction from plastic art and poetry: it does not give us a copy but the thing itself. It does not repeat, as they do, the known Idea, so that the artist lends his eyes to the beholder, but in it the artist merely presents the object to the beholder, and facilitates for him the comprehension of the Idea by bringing the actual, individual object to a distinct and complete expression of its nature.

Unlike the works of the other arts, those of architecture are very seldom executed for purely æsthetic ends. These are generally subordinated to other useful ends which are foreign to art itself. Thus the great merit of the architect consists in achieving and attaining the pure æsthetic ends, in spite of their subordination to other ends which are foreign to them. This he does by cleverly adapting them in a variety of ways to the arbitrary ends in view, and by rightly judging which form of æsthetical architectonic beauty is compatible and may be associated with a temple, which with a palace, which with a prison, and so forth. The more a harsh climate increases these demands of necessity and utility, determines them definitely, and prescribes them more inevitably, the less free play has beauty in architecture. In the mild climate of India, Egypt, Greece, and Rome, where the demands of necessity were fewer and less definite, architecture could follow its æsthetic ends with the greatest freedom. But under a northern sky this was sorely hindered. Here, wher. caissons, pointed roofs and towers were what was demanded, architecture could only unfold its own beauty within very narrow limits, and therefore it was obliged to make amends by resorting all the more to the borrowed ornaments of sculpture, as is seen in Gothic architecture.

§ 45. The great problem of historical painting and sculpture is to express directly and for perception the Idea in which the will reaches the highest grade of its objectification. The objective side of the pleasure afforded by the beautiful is here always predominant, and the subjective side has retired into the background. It is further to be observed that at the next grade below this, animal painting, the characteristic is entirely one with the beautiful; the most characteristic lion, wolf, horse, sheep, or ox, was always the most beautiful also. The reason of this is that animals have only the character of their species, no individual character. In the representation of men the character of the species is separated from that of the individual; the former is now called beauty (entirely in the objective sense), but the latter retains the name, character, or expression, and the new difficulty arises of representing both, at once and completely, in the same individual.

Human beauty is an objective expression, which means the fullest objectification of will at the highest grade at which it is knowable, the Idea of man in general, completely expressed in the sensible form. But however much the objective side of the beautiful appears here, the subjective side still always accompanies it. And just because no object transports us so quickly into pure æsthetic contemplation, as the most beautiful human countenance and form, at the sight of which we are instantly filled with unspeakable satis- faction, and raised above ourselves and all that troubles us; this is only possible because this most distinct and purest knowledge of will raises us most easily and quickly to the state of pure knowing, in which our personality, our will with its constant pain, disappears, so long as the pure æsthetic pleasure lasts. Therefore it is that Goethe says: "No evil can touch him who looks on human beauty; he feels himself at one with himself and with the world." That a beautiful human form is produced by nature must be explained in this way. At this its highest grade the will objectifies itself in an individual; and therefore through circumstances and its own power it completely overcomes all the hindrances and oppo- sition which the phenomena of the lower grades present to it. Such are the forces of nature, from which the will must always first extort and win back the matter that belongs to all its manifestations. Further, the phenomenon of will at its higher grades always has multiplicity in its form. Even the tree is only a systematic aggregate of innumerably re- peated sprouting fibres. This combination assumes greater complexity in higher forms and the human body is an ex- ceedingly complex system of different parts, each of which has a peculiar life of its own, *vita propria*, subordinate to the whole. Now that all these parts are in the proper fashion subordinate to the whole, and co-ordinate to each other, that they all work together harmoniously for the expression of the whole, nothing superfluous, nothing restricted; all these are the rare conditions, whose result is beauty, the completely expressed character of the species. So is it in nature. But how in art? One would suppose that art achieved the beautiful by imitating nature. But how is the artist to recognise the perfect work which is to be imitated, and distinguish it from the failures, if he does not anticipate the beautiful *before experience?* And besides this, has nature ever produced a human being perfectly beautiful in all his parts? It has accordingly been thought that the artist must seek out the beautiful parts, distributed among a number of different human beings, and out of them construct a beautiful whole; a perverse and foolish opinion. For it will be asked, how is he to know that just these forms and not others are beautiful? We also see what kind of success attended the efforts of the old German painters to achieve the beautiful by imitating nature. Observe their naked figures. No knowledge of the beautiful is possible purely *a posteriori*, and from mere experience; it is always, at least in part, *a priori*, although quite different in kind, from the forms of the principle of sufficient reason, of which we are conscious *a priori*. These concern the universal form of phenomena as such, as it constitutes the possibility of knowledge in general, the universal *how* of all phenomena, and from this knowledge proceed mathematics and pure natural science. But this other kind of knowledge *a priori*, which makes it possible to express the beautiful, concerns, not the form but the content of phenomena, not the *how* but the *what* of the phenomenon. That we all recognise human beauty when we see it, but that in the true artist this takes place with such clearness that he shows it as he has never seen it, and surpasses nature in his representation; this is only possible because *we ourselves are* the will whose adequate objectification at its highest grade is here to be judged and discovered. Thus alone have we in fact an anticipation of that which nature (which is just the will that constitutes our own being) strives to express. And in the true genius this anticipation is accompanied by so great a degree of intelligence that he recognises the Idea in the particular thing, and thus, as it were, *understands the half-uttered speech of nature*, and articulates clearly what she only stammered forth. He expresses in the hard marble that beauty of form which in a thousand attempts she failed to produce, he presents it to Nature, saying, as it were, to her, "That is what you wanted to say!" And whoever is able to judge replies, "Yes, that is it." Only in this way was it possible for the genius of the Greeks to find the type of human beauty and establish it as a canon for the school of sculpture; and only by virtue of such an anticipation is it possible for all of us to recognise beauty, when it has actually been achieved by nature in the particular case. This anticipation is the *Ideal*. It is the *Idea* so far as it is known *a priori*, at least half, and it becomes practical for art, because it corresponds to and completes what is given *a posteriori* through nature. The possibility of such an anticipation of the beautiful *a priori* in the artist, and of its recognition *a posteriori* by the critic, lies in the fact that the artist and the critic are themselves the "in-itself" of nature, the will which objectifies itself. For, as Empedocles said, like can only be known by like: only nature can understand itself: only nature can fathom itself: but only spirit also can understand spirit.[1]

Human beauty was explained above as the fullest objectification of will at the highest grade at which it is knowable. It expresses itself through the form; and this lies in space alone, and has no necessary connection with time, as, for example, motion has. Thus far then we may say: the adequate objectification of will through a merely spatial phenomenon is beauty, in the objective sense. A plant is nothing but such a merely spatial phenomenon of will; for no motion, and consequently no relation to time (regarded apart from its development), belongs to the expression of its nature; its mere form expresses its whole being and displays it

[1] The last sentence is the German of the *il n'y a que l'esprit qui sente l'esprit*, of Helvetius. In the first edition there was no occasion to point this out, but since then the age has become so degraded and ignorant through the stupefying influence of the Hegelian sophistry, that some might quite likely say that an antithesis was intended here between "spirit and nature." I am therefore obliged to guard myself in express terms against the suspicion of such vulgar sophisms.

openly. But brutes and men require, further, for the full revelation of the will which is manifested in them, a series of actions, and thus the manifestation in them takes on a direct relation to time. All this has already been explained in the preceding book; it is related to what we are consider-ing at present in the following way. As the merely spatial manifestation of will can objectify it fully or defectively at each definite grade,——and it is this which constitutes beauty or ugliness,——so the temporal objectification of will, *i.e.*, the action, and indeed the direct action, the movement, may correspond to the will, which objectifies itself in it, purely and fully without foreign admixture, without superfluity, without defect, only expressing exactly the act of will de-termined in each case;——or the converse of all this may oc-cur. In the first case the movement is made with *grace*, in the second case without it. Thus as beauty is the adequate representation of will generally, through its merely spatial manifestation; *grace* is the adequate representation of will through its temporal manifestation, that is to say, the per-fectly accurate and fitting expression of each act of will, through the movement and position which objectify it. Since movement and position presuppose the body, Winckel-mann's expression is very true and suitable, when he says, "Grace is the proper relation of the acting person to the ac-tion" (Works, vol. i. p. 258). It is thus evident that beauty may be attributed to a plant, but no grace, unless in a figura-tive sense; but to brutes and men, both beauty and grace. Grace consists, according to what has been said, in every movement being performed, and every position assumed, in the easiest, most appropriate and convenient way, and there-fore being the pure, adequate expression of its intention, or of the act of will, without any superfluity, which exhibits itself as aimless, meaningless bustle, or as wooden stiffness. Grace presupposes as its condition a true proportion of all the limbs, and a symmetrical, harmonious figure; for complete ease and evident appropriateness of all positions and movements are only possible by means of these. Grace is therefore never without a certain degree of beauty of person. The two, complete and united, are the most distinct manifestation of will at the highest grade of its objectification.

§ 51. If now, with the exposition which has been given of art in general, we turn from plastic and pictorial art to poetry, we shall have no doubt that its aim also is the revelation of the Ideas, the grades of the objectification of will, and the communication of them to the hearer with the distinctness and vividness with which the poetical sense comprehends them. Ideas are essentially perceptible; if, therefore, in poetry only abstract conceptions are directly communicated through words, it is yet clearly the intention to make the hearer perceive the Ideas of life in the representatives of these conceptions, and this can only take place through the assistance of his own imagination. But in order to set the imagination to work for the accomplishment of this end, the abstract conceptions, which are the immediate material of poetry as of dry prose, must be so arranged that their spheres intersect each other in such a way that none of them can remain in its abstract universality; but, instead of it, a perceptible representative appears to the imagination; and this is always further modified by the words of the poet according to what his intention may be. As the chemist obtains solid precipitates by combining perfectly clear and transparent fluids; the poet understands how to precipitate, as it were, the concrete, the individual, the perceptible idea, out of the abstract and transparent universality of the concepts by the manner in which he combines them. For the Idea can only be known by perception; and knowledge of the Idea is the end of art. The skill of a master, in poetry as in chemistry, enables us always to obtain the precise precipitate we intended. This end is assisted by the numerous epithets in poetry, by means of which the universality of every concept is narrowed more and more till we reach the per‑ceptible. Homer attaches to almost every substantive an ad‑jective, whose concept intersects and considerably diminishes the sphere of the concept of the substantive, which is thus brought so much the nearer to perception: for example—

> "Where gentle winds from the blue heavens sigh,
> There stand the myrtles still, the laurel high,"—

calls up before the imagination by means of a few concepts the whole delight of a southern clime.

Rhythm and rhyme are quite peculiar aids to poetry. I can give no other explanation of their incredibly powerful effect than that our faculties of perception have received from time, to which they are essentially bound, some quality on account of which we inwardly follow, and, as it were, consent to each regularly recurring sound. In this way rhythm and rhyme are partly a means of holding our atten‑tion, because we willingly follow the poem read, and partly they produce in us a blind consent to what is read prior to any judgment, and this gives the poem a certain emphatic power of convincing independent of all reasons.

From the general nature of the material, that is, the con‑cepts, which poetry uses to communicate the Ideas, the ex‑tent of its province is very great. The whole of nature, the Ideas of all grades, can be represented by means of it, for it proceeds according to the Idea it has to impart, so that its representations are sometimes descriptive, sometimes nar‑rative, and sometimes directly dramatic. If, in the represen‑tation of the lower grades of the objectivity of will, plastic and pictorial art generally surpass it, because lifeless nature, and even brute nature, reveals almost its whole being in a single well-chosen moment; man, on the contrary, so far as he does not express himself by the mere form and expression of his person, but through a series of actions and the accom‑

panying thoughts and emotions, is the principal object of poetry, in which no other art can compete with it, for here the progress or movement which cannot be represented in plastic or pictorial art just suits its purpose.

The revelation of the Idea, which is the highest grade of the objectivity of will, the representation of man in the connected series of his efforts and actions, is thus the great problem of poetry. It is true that both experience and history teach us to know man; yet oftener men than man, *i.e.*, they give us empirical notes of the behaviour of men to each other, from which we may frame rules for our own conduct, oftener than they afford us deep glimpses of the inner nature of man. The latter function, however, is by no means entirely denied them; but as often as it is the nature of mankind itself that discloses itself to us in history or in our own experience, we have comprehended our experience, and the historian has comprehended history, with artistic eyes, poetically, *i.e.*, according to the Idea, not the phenomenon, in its inner nature, not in its relations. Our own experience is the indispensable condition of understanding poetry as of understanding history; for it is, so to speak, the dictionary of the language that both speak. But history is related to poetry as portrait-painting is related to historical painting; the one gives us the true in the individual, the other the true in the universal; the one has the truth of the phenomenon, and can therefore verify it from the phenomenal, the other has the truth of the Idea, which can be found in no particular phenomenon, but yet speaks to us from them all. The poet from deliberate choice represents significant characters in significant situations; the historian takes both as they come. Indeed, he must regard and select the circumstances and the persons, not with reference to their inward and true significance, which expresses the Idea, but according to the outward, apparent, and relatively important significance with regard to the connection and the consequences. He must consider nothing in and for itself in its essential character and expression, but must look at everything in its relations, in its connection, in its influence upon what follows, and especially upon its own age. Therefore he will not overlook an action of a king, though of little significance, and in itself quite common, because it has results and influence. And, on the other hand, actions of the highest significance of particular and very eminent individuals are not to be recorded by him if they have no consequences. For his treatment follows the principle of sufficient reason, and apprehends the phenomenon, of which this principle is the form. But the poet comprehends the Idea, the inner nature of man apart from all relations, outside all time, the adequate objectivity of the thing-in-itself, at its highest grade. Even in that method of treatment which is necessary for the historian, the inner nature and significance of the phenomena, the kernel of all these shells, can never be entirely lost. He who seeks for it, at any rate, may find it and recognise it. Yet that which is significant in itself, not in its relations, the real unfolding of the Idea, will be found far more accurately and distinctly in poetry than in history, and, therefore, however paradoxical it may sound, far more really genuine inner truth is to be attributed to poetry than to history. For the historian must accurately follow the particular event according to life, as it develops itself in time in the manifold tangled chains of causes and effects. It is, however, impossible that he can have all the data for this; he cannot have seen all and discovered all. He is forsaken at every moment by the original of his picture, or a false one substitutes itself for it, and this so constantly that I think I may assume that in all history the false outweighs the true. The poet, on the contrary, has comprehended the Idea of man from some definite side which is to be represented; thus it is the nature of his own self that objectifies itself in it for him. His knowledge, as

we explained above when speaking of sculpture, is half
a priori; his ideal stands before his mind firm, distinct,
brightly illuminated, and cannot forsake him; therefore he
shows us, in the mirror of his mind, the Idea pure and distinct, and his delineation of it down to the minutest particular is true as life itself. The great ancient historians are,
therefore, in those particulars in which their data fail them,
for example, in the speeches of their heroes—poets; indeed
their whole manner of handling their material approaches
to the epic. But this gives their representations unity, and
enables them to retain inner truth, even when outward
truth was not accessible, or indeed was falsified. And as we
compared history to portrait-painting, in contradistinction to
poetry, which corresponds to historical painting, we find
that Winckelmann's maxim, that the portrait ought to be
the ideal of the individual, was followed by the ancient
historians, for they represent the individual in such a way
as to bring out that side of the Idea of man which is expressed in it. Modern historians, on the contrary, with few
exceptions, give us in general only "a dust-bin and a lumber-
room, and at the most a chronicle of the principal political
events." Therefore, whoever desires to know man in his
inner nature, identical in all its phenomena and developments, to know him according to the Idea, will find that the
works of the great, immortal poet present a far truer, more
distinct picture, than the historians can ever give. For even
the best of the historians are, as poets, far from the first;
and moreover their hands are tied. In this aspect the relation
between the historian and the poet may be illustrated by
the following comparison. The mere, pure historian, who
works only according to data, is like a man, who without
any knowledge of mathematics, has investigated the relations of certain figures, which he has accidentally found, by
measuring them; and the problem thus empirically solved
is affected of course by all the errors of the drawn figure.

The poet, on the other hand, is like the mathematician, who constructs these relations *a priori* in pure perception, and expresses them not as they actually are in the drawn figure, but as they are in the Idea, which the drawing is intended to render for the senses. Therefore Schiller says:—

> "What has never anywhere come to pass,
> That alone never grows old."

Indeed I must attribute greater value to biographies, and especially to autobiographies, in relation to the knowledge of the nature of man, than to history proper, at least as it is commonly handled. Partly because in the former the data can be collected more accurately and completely than in the latter; partly, because in history proper, it is not so much men as nations and heroes that act, and the individuals who do appear, seem so far off, surrounded with such pomp and circumstance, clothed in the stiff robes of state, or heavy, inflexible armour, that it is really hard through all this to recognise the human movements. On the other hand, the life of the individual when described with truth, in a narrow sphere, shows the conduct of men in all its forms and subtleties, the excellence, the virtue, and even holiness of a few, the perversity, meanness, and knavery of most, the dissolute profligacy of some. Besides, in the only aspect we are considering here, that of the inner significance of the phenomenal, it is quite the same whether the objects with which the action is concerned, are, relatively considered, trifling or important, farm-houses or kingdoms: for all these things in themselves are without significance, and obtain it only in so far as the will is moved by them. The motive has significance only through its relation to the will, while the relation which it has as a thing to other things like itself, does not concern us here. As a circle of one inch in diameter, and a circle of forty million miles in diameter, have precisely the same geometrical properties, so are the events and the history of a village and a kingdom essentially the same; and we may study and learn to know mankind as well in the one as in the other. It is also a mistake to suppose that autobiographies are full of deceit and dissimulation. On the contrary, lying (though always possible) is perhaps more difficult there than elsewhere. Dissimulation is easiest in mere conversation; indeed, though it may sound paradoxical, it is really more difficult even in a letter. For in the case of a letter the writer is alone, and looks into himself, and not out on the world, so that what is strange and distant does not easily approach him; and he has not the test of the impression made upon another before his eyes. But the receiver of the letter peruses it quietly in a mood unknown to the writer, reads it repeatedly and at different times, and thus easily finds out the concealed intention. We also get to know an author as a man most easily from his books, because all these circumstances act here still more strongly and permanently. And in an autobiography it is so difficult to dissimulate, that perhaps there does not exist a single one that is not, as a whole, more true than any history that ever was written. The man who writes his own life surveys it as a whole, the particular becomes small, the near becomes distant, the distant becomes near again, the motives that influenced him shrink; he seats himself at the confessional, and has done so of his own free will; the spirit of lying does not so easily take hold of him here, for there is also in every man an inclination to truth which has first to be overcome whenever he lies, and which here has taken up a specially strong position. The relation between biography and the history of nations may be made clear for perception by means of the following comparison: History shows us mankind as a view from a high mountain shows us nature; we see much at a time, wide stretches, great masses, but nothing is distinct nor recognisable in all the details of its own peculiar nature. On the other hand, the representation of the life of the individual shows us the man, as we see nature if we go about among her trees, plants, rocks, and waters. But in landscape-painting, in which the artist lets us look at nature with his eyes, the knowledge of the Ideas, and the condition of pure will-less knowing, which is demanded by these, is made much easier for us; and, in the same way, poetry is far superior both to history and biography, in the representation of the Ideas which may be looked for in all three. For here also genius holds up to us the magic glass, in which all that is essential and significant appears before us collected and placed in the clearest light, and what is accidental and foreign is left out.[1]

The representation of the Idea of man, which is the work of the poet, may be performed, so that what is represented is also the representer. This is the case in lyrical poetry, in songs, properly so called, in which the poet only perceives vividly his own state and describes it. Thus a certain subjectivity is essential to this kind of poetry from the nature of its object. Again, what is to be represented may be entirely different from him who represents it, as is the case in all other kinds of poetry, in which the poet more or less conceals himself behind his representation, and at last disappears altogether. In the ballad the poet still expresses to some extent his own state through the tone and proportion of the whole; therefore, though much more objective than the lyric, it has yet something subjective. This becomes less in the idyll, still less in the romantic poem, almost entirely disappears in the true epic, and even to the last vestige in the drama, which is the most objective and, in more than one respect, the completest and most difficult form of poetry. The lyrical form of poetry is consequently the easiest, and although art, as a whole, belongs only to the true man of genius, who so rarely appears, even a man who is not in general very remarkable may produce a beautiful song if,

[1] Cf. Ch. xxxviii. of Supplement.

by actual strong excitement from without, some inspiration raises his mental powers; for all that is required for this is a lively perception of his own state at a moment of emotional excitement. This is proved by the existence of many single songs by individuals who have otherwise remained unknown; especially the German national songs, of which we have an exquisite collection in the "Wunderhorn"; and also by innumerable lovesongs and other songs of the people in all languages;— for to seize the mood of a moment and embody it in a song is the whole achievement of this kind of poetry. Yet in the lyrics of true poets the inner nature of all mankind is reflected, and all that millions of past, present, and future men have found, or will find, in the same situations, which are constantly recurring, finds its exact expression in them. And because these situations, by constant recurrence, are permanent as man himself and always call up the same sensations, the lyrical productions of genuine poets remain through thousands of years true, powerful, and fresh. But if the poet is always the universal man, then all that has ever moved a human heart, all that human nature in any situation has ever produced from itself, all that dwells and broods in any human breast—is his theme and his material, and also all the rest of nature. Therefore the poet may just as well sing of voluptuousness as of mysticism, be Anacreon or Angelus Silesius, write tragedies or comedies, represent the sublime or the common mind—according to humour or vocation. And no one has the right to prescribe to the poet what he ought to be—noble and sublime, moral, pious, Christian, one thing or another, still less to reproach him because he is one thing and not another. He is the mirror of mankind, and brings to its consciousness what it feels and does.

In the more objective kinds of poetry, especially in the romance, the epic, and the drama, the end, the revelation of the Idea of man, is principally attained by two means, by true and profound representation of significant characters, and by the invention of pregnant situations in which they disclose themselves. For as it is incumbent upon the chemist not only to exhibit the simple elements, pure and genuine, and their principal compounds, but also to expose them to the influence of such reagents as will clearly and strikingly bring out their peculiar qualities, so is it incumbent on the poet not only to present to us significant characters truly and faithfully as nature itself; but, in order that we may get to know them, he must place them in those situations in which their peculiar qualities will fully unfold themselves, and appear distinctly in sharp outline; situations which are therefore called significant. In real life, and in history, situations of this kind are rarely brought about by chance, and they stand alone, lost and concealed in the multitude of those which are insignificant. The complete significance of the situations ought to distinguish the romance, the epic, and the drama from real life as completely as the arrangement and selection of significant characters. In both, however, absolute truth is a necessary condition of their effect, and want of unity in the characters, contradiction either of themselves or of the nature of humanity in general, as well as impossibility, or very great improbability in the events, even in mere accessories, offend just as much in poetry as badly drawn figures, false perspective, or wrong lighting in painting. For both in poetry and painting we demand the faithful mirror of life, of man, of the world, only made more clear by the representation, and more significant by the arrangement. For there is only one end of all the arts, the representation of the Ideas; and their essential difference lies simply in the different grades of the objectification of will to which the Ideas that are to be represented belong. This also determines the material of the representation. Thus the arts which are most widely separated may yet throw light on each other. For example, in order to comprehend fully the Ideas of water it is not sufficient to see it in the quiet pond or in the evenly-flowing stream; but these Ideas disclose themselves fully only when the water appears under all circumstances and exposed to all kinds of obstacles. The effects of the varied circumstances and obstacles give it the opportunity of fully exhibiting all its qualities. This is why we find it beautiful when it tumbles, rushes, and foams, or leaps into the air, or falls in a cataract or spray; or, lastly, if artificially confined it springs up in a fountain. Thus showing itself different under different circumstances, it yet always faithfully asserts its character; it is just as natural to it to spout up as to lie in glassy stillness; it is as ready for the one as for the other as soon as the circumstances appear. Now, what the engineer achieves with the fluid matter of water, the architect achieves with the rigid matter of stone, and just this the epic or dramatic poet achieves with the Idea of man. Unfolding and rendering distinct the Idea expressing itself in the object of every art, the Idea of the will which objectifies itself at each grade, is the common end of all the arts. The life of man, as it shows itself for the most part in the real world, is like the water, as it is generally seen in the pond and the river; but in the epic, the romance, the tragedy, selected characters are placed in those circumstances in which all their special qualities unfold themselves, the depths of the human heart are revealed, and become visible in extraordinary and very significant actions. Thus poetry objectifies the Idea of man, an Idea which has the peculiarity of expressing itself in highly individual characters.

Tragedy is to be regarded, and is recognised as the summit of poetical art, both on account of the greatness of its effect and the difficulty of its achievement. It is very significant for our whole system, and well worthy of observation, that the end of this highest poetical achievement is the representation of the terrible side of life. The unspeakable pain, the wail of humanity, the triumph of evil, the scornful mastery of chance, and the irretrievable fall of the just and innocent, is here presented to us; and in this lies a significant hint of the nature of the world and of existence. It is the strife of will with itself, which here, completely unfolded at the highest grade of its objectivity, comes into fearful prominence. It becomes visible in the suffering of men, which is now introduced, partly through chance and error, which appear as the rulers of the world, personified as fate, on account of their insidiousness, which even reaches the appearance of design; partly it proceeds from man himself, through the self-mortifying efforts of a few, through the wickedness and perversity of most. It is one and the same will that lives and appears in them all, but whose phenomena fight against each other and destroy each other. In one individual it appears powerfully, in another more weakly; in one more subject to reason, and softened by the light of knowledge, in another less so, till at last, in some single case, this knowledge, purified and heightened by suffering itself, reaches the point at which the phenomenon, the veil of Mâyâ, no longer deceives it. It sees through the form of the phenomenon, the *principium individuationis*. The egoism which rests on this perishes with it, so that now the *motives* that were so powerful before have lost their might, and instead of them the complete knowledge of the nature of the world, which has a *quieting* effect on the will, produces resignation, the surrender not merely of life, but of the very will to live. Thus we see in tragedies the noblest men, after long conflict and suffering, at last renounce the ends they have so keenly followed, and all the pleasures of life for ever, or else freely and joyfully surrender life itself. So is it with the steadfast prince of Calderon; with Gretchen in "Faust"; with Hamlet, whom his friend Horatio would willingly follow, but is bade remain a while, and in this harsh world draw his breath in pain, to tell the story of Hamlet, and clear his memory; so also is it with the Maid of Orleans, the Bride of Messina; they all die purified by suffering, *i.e.*, after the will to live which was formerly in them is dead. In the "Mohammed" of Voltaire this is actually expressed in the concluding words which the dying Palmira addresses to Mohammed: "The world is for tyrants: live!" On the other hand, the demand for so-called poetical justice rests on entire misconception of the nature of tragedy, and, indeed, of the nature of the world itself. It boldly appears in all its dulness in the criticisms which Dr. Samuel Johnson made on particular plays of Shakespeare, for he very naïvely laments its entire absence. And its absence is certainly obvious, for in what has Ophelia, Desdemona, or Cordelia offended? But only the dull, optimistic, Protestant-rationalistic, or peculiarly Jewish view of life will make the demand for poetical justice, and find satisfaction in it. The true sense of tragedy is the deeper insight, that it is not his own individual sins that the hero atones for, but original sin, *i.e.*, the crime of existence itself:

> "Pues el delito mayor
> Del hombre es haber nacido";
>
> ("For the greatest crime of man
> Is that he was born";)

as Calderon exactly expresses it.

§ 52. Now that we have considered all the fine arts in the general way that is suitable to our point of view, beginning with architecture, the peculiar end of which is to elucidate the objectification of will at the lowest grades of its visibility, in which it shows itself as the dumb unconscious tendency of the mass in accordance with laws, and yet already reveals a breach of the unity of will with itself in a conflict between gravity and rigidity—and ending with the consideration of tragedy, which presents to us at the highest grades of the objectification of will this very conflict with itself in terrible magnitude and distinctness; we find that there is still another fine art which has been excluded from our consideration, and had to be excluded, for in the systematic connection of our exposition there was no fitting place for it—I mean *music*. It stands alone, quite cut off from all the other arts. In it we do not recognise the copy or repetition of any Idea of existence in the world. Yet it is such a great and exceedingly noble art, its effect on the inmost nature of man is so powerful, and it is so entirely and deeply understood by him in his inmost consciousness as a perfectly universal language, the distinctness of which surpasses even that of the perceptible world itself, that we certainly have more to look for in it than an *exercitium arithmeticæ occultum nescientis se numerare animi*,[1] which Leibnitz called it. Yet he was perfectly right, as he considered only its immediate external significance, its form. But if it were nothing more, the satisfaction which it affords would be like that which we feel when a sum in arithmetic comes out right, and could not be that intense pleasure with which we see the deepest recesses of our nature find utterance. From our standpoint, therefore, at which the æsthetic effect is the criterion, we must attribute to music a far more serious and deep significance, connected with the inmost nature of the world and our own self, and in reference to which the arithmetical proportions, to which it may be reduced, are related, not as the thing signified, but merely as the sign. That in some sense music must be related to the world as the representation to the thing represented, as the copy to the original, we may conclude from the analogy of the other arts, all of which possess this character, and affect us on the whole in the same way as it does, only that the effect of music is stronger, quicker, more necessary and infallible. Further, its representative relation to the world must be very deep, absolutely true, and strikingly

[1] Leibnitii epistolæ, collectio Kortholti, ep. 154.

accurate, because it is instantly understood by every one, and has the appearance of a certain infallibility, because its form may be reduced to perfectly definite rules expressed in numbers, from which it cannot free itself without entirely ceasing to be music. Yet the point of comparison between music and the world, the respect in which it stands to the world in the relation of a copy or repetition, is very obscure. Men have practised music in all ages without being able to account for this; content to understand it directly, they renounce all claim to an abstract conception of this direct understanding itself.

I gave my mind entirely up to the impression of music in all its forms, and then returned to reflection and the system of thought expressed in the present work, and thus I arrived at an explanation of the inner nature of music and of the nature of its imitative relation to the world—which from analogy had necessarily to be presupposed—an explanation which is quite sufficient for myself, and satisfactory to my investigation, and which will doubtless be equally evident to any one who has followed me thus far and has agreed with my view of the world. Yet I recognise the fact that it is essentially impossible to prove this explanation, for it assumes and establishes a relation of music, as idea, to that which from its nature can never be idea, and music will have to be regarded as the copy of an original which can never itself be directly presented as idea. I can therefore do no more than state here, at the conclusion of this third book, which has been principally devoted to the consideration of the arts, the explanation of the marvellous art of music which satisfies myself, and I must leave the acceptance or denial of my view to the effect produced upon each of my readers both by music itself and by the whole system of thought communicated in this work. Moreover, I regard it as necessary, in order to be able to assent with full conviction to the exposition of the significance of music I am about to give, that one should often listen to music with constant reflection upon my theory concerning it, and for this again it is necessary to be very familiar with the whole of my system of thought.

The (Platonic) Ideas are the adequate objectification of will. To excite or suggest the knowledge of these by means of the representation of particular things (for works of art themselves are always representations of particular things) is the end of all the other arts, which can only be attained by a corresponding change in the knowing subject. Thus all these arts objectify the will indirectly only by means of the Ideas; and since our world is nothing but the manifestation of the Ideas in multiplicity, though their entrance into the *principium individuationis* (the form of the knowledge possible for the individual as such), music also, since it passes over the Ideas, is entirely independent of the phenomenal world, ignores it altogether, could to a certain extent exist if there was no world at all, which cannot be said of the other arts. Music is as *direct* an objectification and copy of the whole *will* as the world itself, nay, even as the Ideas, whose multiplied manifestation constitutes the world of individual things. Music is thus by no means like the other arts, the copy of the Ideas, but the *copy of the will itself,* whose objectivity the Ideas are. This is why the effect of music is so much more powerful and penetrating than that of the other arts, for they speak only of shadows, but it speaks of the thing itself. Since, however, it is the same will which objectifies itself both in the Ideas and in music, though in quite different ways, there must be, not indeed a direct likeness, but yet a parallel, an analogy, between music and the Ideas whose manifestation in multiplicity and incompleteness is the visible world. The establishing of this analogy will facilitate, as an illustration, the understanding of this exposition, which is so difficult on account of the obscurity of the subject.

I recognise in the deepest tones of harmony, in the bass, the lowest grades of the objectification of will, unorganised nature, the mass of the planet. It is well known that all the high notes which are easily sounded, and die away more quickly, are produced by the vibration in their vicinity of the deep bass note. When, also, the low notes sound, the high notes always sound faintly, and it is a law of harmony that only those high notes may accompany a bass note which actually already sound along with it of themselves (its *sons harmoniques*) on account of its vibration. This is analogous to the fact that the whole of the bodies and organisations of nature must be regarded as having come into existence through gradual development out of the mass of the planet; this is both their supporter and their source, and the same relation subsists between the high notes and the bass. There is a limit of depth, below which no sound is audible. This corresponds to the fact that no matter can be perceived without form and quality, *i.e.*, without the manifestation of a force which cannot be further explained, in which an Idea expresses itself, and, more generally, that no matter can be entirely without will. Thus, as a certain pitch is inseparable from the note as such, so a certain grade of the manifestation of will is inseparable from matter. Bass is thus, for us, in harmony what unorganised nature, the crudest mass, upon which all rests, and from which everything originates and develops, is in the world. Now, further, in the whole of the complemented parts which make up the harmony between the bass and the leading voice singing the melody, I recognise the whole gradation of the Ideas in which the will objectifies itself. Those nearer to the bass are the lower of these grades, the still unorganised, but yet manifold phenomenal things; the higher represent to me the world of plants and beasts. The definite intervals of the scale are parallel to the definite grades of the objectification of will, the definite species in nature. The departure from the arith-

metical correctness of the intervals, through some temperament, or produced by the key selected, is analogous to the
departure of the individual from the type of the species.
Indeed, even the impure discords, which give no definite interval, may be compared to the monstrous abortions produced by beasts of two species, or by man and beast. But to
all these bass and complemental parts which make up the
harmony there is wanting that connected progress which
belongs only to the high voice singing the melody, and it
alone moves quickly and lightly in modulations and runs,
while all these others have only a slower movement without
a connection in each part for itself. The deep bass moves
most slowly, the representative of the crudest mass. Its rising and falling occurs only by large intervals, in thirds,
fourths, fifths, never by *one* tone, unless it is a bass inverted
by double counterpoint. This slow movement is also physically essential to it; a quick run or shake in the low notes
cannot even be imagined. The higher complemental parts,
which are parallel to animal life, move more quickly, but
yet without melodious connection and significant progress.
The disconnected course of all the complemental parts, and
their regulation by definite laws, is analogous to the fact
that in the whole irrational world, from the crystal to the
most perfect animal, no being has a connected consciousness
of its own which would make its life into a significant
whole, and none experiences a succession of mental developments, none perfects itself by culture, but everything exists
always in the same way according to its kind, determined by
fixed law. Lastly, in the *melody*, in the high, singing, principal voice leading the whole and progressing with unre-
strained freedom, in the unbroken significant connection of
one thought from beginning to end representing a whole, I
recognise the highest grade of the objectification of will,
the intellectual life and effort of man. As he alone, because
endowed with reason, constantly looks before and after on

the path of his actual life and its innumerable possibilities, and so achieves a course of life which is intellectual, and therefore connected as a whole; corresponding to this, I say, the *melody* has significant intentional connection from beginning to end. It records, therefore, the history of the intellectually-enlightened will. This will expresses itself in the actual world as the series of its deeds; but melody says more, it records the most secret history of this intellectually-enlightened will, pictures every excitement, every effort, every movement of it, all that which the reason collects under the wide and negative concept of feeling, and which it cannot apprehend further through its abstract concepts. Therefore it has always been said that music is the language of feeling and of passion, as words are the language of reason. Plato explains it as ἡ τῶν μελῶν κίνησις μεμιμημένη, εν τοις παθημασιν ὁταν ψυχη γινηται (*melodiarum motus, animi affectus imitans*), De Leg. vii.; and also Aristotle says: δια τι οἱ ρυθμοι και τα μελη, φωνη ονσα, ηθεσιν εοικε (*cur numeri musici et modi, qui voces sunt, moribus similes sese exhibent?*), Probl. c. 19.

Now the nature of man consists in this, that his will strives, is satisfied and strives anew, and so on for ever. Indeed, his happiness and well-being consist simply in the quick transition from wish to satisfaction, and from satisfaction to a new wish. For the absence of satisfaction is suffering, the empty longing for a new wish, languor, *ennui*. And corresponding to this the nature of melody is a constant digression and deviation from the keynote in a thousand ways, not only to the harmonious intervals to the third and dominant, but to every tone, to the dissonant sevenths and to the superfluous degrees; yet there always follows a constant return to the keynote. In all these deviations melody expresses the multifarious efforts of will, but always its satisfaction also by the final return to an harmonious interval, and still more, to the keynote. The composition of melody,

the disclosure in it of all the deepest secrets of human willing and feeling, is the work of genius, whose action, which
is more apparent here than anywhere else, lies far from all
reflection and conscious intention, and may be called an
inspiration. The conception is here, as everywhere in art,
unfruitful. The composer reveals the inner nature of the
world, and expresses the deepest wisdom in a language which
his reason does not understand; as a person under the influence of mesmerism tells things of which he has no conception
when he awakes. Therefore in the composer, more than in
any other artist, the man is entirely separated and distinct
from the artist. Even in the explanation of this wonderful
art, the concept shows its poverty and limitation. I shall try,
however, to complete our analogy. As quick transition from
wish to satisfaction, and from satisfaction to a new wish, is
happiness and well-being, so quick melodies without great
deviations are cheerful; slow melodies, striking painful discords, and only winding back through many bars to the keynote are, as analogous to the delayed and hardly won satisfaction, sad. The delay of the new excitement of will, languor, could have no other expression than the sustained keynote, the effect of which would soon be unbearable; very
monotonous and unmeaning melodies approach this effect.
The short intelligible subjects of quick dance-music seem to
speak only of easily attained common pleasure. On the other
hand, the *Allegro maestoso*, in elaborate movements, long
passages, and wide deviations, signifies a greater, nobler effort towards a more distant end, and its final attainment.
The *Adagio* speaks of the pain of a great and noble effort
which despises all trifling happiness. But how wonderful is
the effect of the *minor* and *major*! How astounding that the
change of half a tone, the entrance of a minor third instead
of a major, at once and inevitably forces upon us an anxious
painful feeling, from which again we are just as instan-
taneously delivered by the major. The *Adagio* lengthens in

the minor the expression of the keenest pain, and becomes even a convulsive wail. Dance-music in the minor seems to indicate the failure of that trifling happiness which we ought rather to despise, seems to speak of the attainment of a lower end with toil and trouble. The inexhaustibleness of possible melodies corresponds to the inexhaustibleness of Nature in difference of individuals, physiognomies, and courses of life. The transition from one key to an entirely different one, since it altogether breaks the connection with what went before, is like death, for the individual ends in it; but the will which appeared in this individual lives after him as before him, appearing in other individuals, whose consciousness, however, has no connection with his.

But it must never be forgotten, in the investigation of all these analogies I have pointed out, that music has no direct, but merely an indirect relation to them, for it never expresses the phenomenon, but only the inner nature, the in-itself of all phenomena, the will itself. It does not therefore express this or that particular and definite joy, this or that sorrow, or pain, or horror, or delight, or merriment, or peace of mind; but joy, sorrow, pain, horror, delight, merriment, peace of mind *themselves*, to a certain extent in the abstract, their essential nature, without accessories, and therefore without their motives. Yet we completely understand them in this extracted quintessence. Hence it arises that our imagination is so easily excited by music, and now seeks to give form to that invisible yet actively moved spirit-world which speaks to us directly, and clothe it with flesh and blood, *i.e.*, to embody it in an analogous example. This is the origin of the song with words, and finally of the opera, the text of which should therefore never forsake that subordinate position in order to make itself the chief thing and the music a mere means of expressing it, which is a great misconception and a piece of utter perversity; for music always expresses only the quintessence of life and its events, never these

themselves, and therefore their differencs do not always affect it. It is precisely this universality, which belongs exclusively to it, together with the greatest determinateness, that
gives music the high worth which it has as the panacea for all
our woes. Thus, if music is too closely united to the words,
and tries to form itself according to the events, it is striving
to speak a language which is not its own. No one has kept so
free from this mistake as Rossini; therefore his music speaks
its own language so distinctly and purely that it requires no
words, and produces its full effect when rendered by instru-
ments alone.

According to all this, we may regard the phenomenal
world, or nature, and music as two different expressions of
the same thing, which is therefore itself the only medium of
their analogy, so that a knowledge of it is demanded in order
to understand that analogy. Music, therefore, if regarded as
an expression of the world, is in the highest degree a universal language, which is related indeed to the universality of
concepts, much as they are related to the particular things.
Its universality, however, is by no means that empty universality of abstraction, but quite of a different kind, and is
united with thorough and distinct definiteness. In this respect
it resembles geometrical figures and numbers, which are the
universal forms of all possible objects of experience and applicable to them all *a priori*, and yet are not abstract but perceptible and thoroughly determined. All possible efforts,
excitements, and manifestations of will, all that goes on in
the heart of man and that reason includes in the wide, negative concept of feeling, may be expressed by the infinite number of possible melodies, but always in the universal, in the
mere form, without the material, always according to the
thing-in-itself, not the phenomenon, the inmost soul, as it
were, of the phenomenon, without the body. This deep relation which music has to the true nature of all things also explains the fact that suitable music played to any scene, action,

event, or surrounding seems to disclose to us its most secret meaning, and appears as the most accurate and distinct commentary upon it. This is so truly the case, that whoever gives himself up entirely to the impression of a symphony, seems to see all the possible events of life and the world take place in himself, yet if he reflects, he can find no likeness between the music and the things that passed before his mind. For, as we have said, music is distinguished from all the other arts by the fact that it is not a copy of the phenomenon, or, more accurately, the adequate objectivity of will, but is the direct copy of the will itself, and therefore exhibits itself as the metaphysical to everything physical in the world, and as the thing-in-itself to every phenomenon. We might, therefore, just as well call the world embodied music as embodied will; and this is the reason why music makes every picture, and indeed every scene of real life and of the world, at once appear with higher significance, certainly all the more in proportion as its melody is analogous to the inner spirit of the given phenomenon. It rests upon this that we are able to set a poem to music as a song, or a perceptible representation as a pantomime, or both as an opera. Such particular pictures of human life, set to the universal language of music, are never bound to it or correspond to it with stringent necessity; but they stand to it only in the relation of an example chosen at will to a general concept. In the determinateness of the real, they represent that which music expresses in the universality of mere form. For melodies are to a certain extent, like general concepts, an abstraction from the actual. This actual world, then, the world of particular things, affords the object of perception, the special and individual, the particular case, both to the universality of the concepts and to the universality of the melodies. But these two universalities are in a certain respect opposed to each other; for the concepts contain particulars only as the first forms abstracted from perception, as it were, the separated shell of things; thus they are, strictly speaking, *ab-*

tracta; music, on the other hand, gives the inmost kernel which precedes all forms, or the heart of things. This relation may be very well expressed in the language of the schoolmen by saying the concepts are the *universalia post rem,* but music gives the *universalia ante rem,* and the real world the *universalia in re.* To the universal significance of a melody to which a poem has been set, it is quite possible to set other equally arbitrarily selected examples of the universal expressed in this poem corresponding to the significance of the melody in the same degree. This is why the same composition is suitable to many verses; and this is also what makes the *vaudeville* possible. But that in general a relation is possible between a composition and a perceptible representation rests, as we have said, upon the fact that both are simply different expressions of the same inner being of the world. When now, in the particular case, such a relation is actually given, that is to say, when the composer has been able to express in the universal language of music the emotions of will which constitute the heart of an event, then the melody of the song, the music of the opera, is expressive. But the analogy discovered by the composer between the two must have proceeded from the direct knowledge of the nature of the world unknown to his reason, and must not be an imitation produced with conscious intention by means of conceptions, otherwise the music does not express the inner nature of the will itself, but merely gives an inadequate imitation of its phenomenon. All specially imitative music does this; for example, "The Seasons," by Haydn; also many passages of his "Creation," in which phenomena of the external world are directly imitated; also all battle-pieces. Such music is entirely to be rejected.

The unutterable depth of all music by virtue of which it floats through our consciousness as the vision of a paradise firmly believed in yet ever distant from us, and by which also it is so fully understood and yet so inexplicable, rests on the fact that it restores to us all the emotions of our inmost nature, but entirely without reality and far removed from their pain. So also the seriousness which is essential to it, which excludes the absurd from its direct and peculiar province, is to be explained by the fact that its object is not the idea, with reference to which alone deception and absurdity are possible; but its object is directly the will, and this is essentially the most serious of all things, for it is that on which all depends. How rich in content and full of significance the language of music is, we see from the repetitions, as well as the *Da capo*, the like of which would be unbearable in works composed in a language of words, but in music are very appropriate and beneficial, for, in order to comprehend it fully, we must hear it twice.

In the whole of this exposition of music I have been trying to bring out clearly that it expresses in a perfectly universal language, in a homogeneous material, mere tones, and with the greatest determinateness and truth, the inner nature, the in-itself of the world, which we think under the concept of will, because will is its most distinct manifestation. Further, according to my view and contention, philosophy is nothing but a complete and accurate repetition or expression of the nature of the world in very general concepts, for only in such is it possible to get a view of that whole nature which will everywhere be adequate and applicable. Thus, whoever has followed me and entered into my mode of thought, will not think it so very paradoxical if I say, that supposing it were possible to give a perfectly accurate, complete explanation of music, extending even to particulars, that is to say, a detailed repetition in concepts of what it expresses, this would also be a sufficient repetition and explanation of the world in concepts, or at least entirely parallel to such an explanation, and thus it would be the true philosophy. Consequently the saying of Leibnitz quoted above, which is quite accurate from a lower standpoint, may be parodied in the following way to suit our higher view of music: *Musica est exercitium metaphysices occultum nescientis se philosophari animi;* for *scire,* to know, always means to have fixed in abstract concepts. But further, on account of the truth of the saying of Leibnitz, which is confirmed in various ways, music, regarded apart from its æsthetic or inner significance, and looked at merely externally and purely empirically, is simply the means of comprehending directly and in the concrete large numbers and complex relations of numbers, which otherwise we could only know indirectly by fixing them in concepts. Therefore by the union of these two very different but correct views of music we may arrive at a conception of the possibility of a philosophy of number, such as that of Pythagoras and of the Chinese in Y-King, and then interpret in this sense the saying of the Pythagoreans which Sextus Empiricus quotes (adv. Math., L. vii.): τῳ αριθμῳ δε τα παντ᾽ επεοικεν (*numero cuncta assimilantur*). And if, finally, we apply this view to the interpretation of harmony and melody given above, we shall find that a mere moral philosophy without an explanation of Nature, such as Socrates wanted to introduce, is precisely analogous to a mere melody without harmony, which Rousseau exclusively desired; and, in opposition to this mere physics and metaphysics without ethics, will correspond to mere harmony without melody. Allow me to add to these cursory observations a few more remarks concerning the analogy of music with the phenomenal world. We found in the second book that the highest grade of the objectification of will, man, could not appear alone and isolated, but presupposed the grades below him, as these again presupposed the grades lower still. In the same way music, which directly objectifies the will, just as the world does, is complete only in full harmony. In order to achieve its full effect, the high leading voice of the melody requires the accompaniment of all the other voices, even to the lowest bass, which is to be regarded as the origin of all. The melody itself enters as an integral part into the harmony, as the harmony enters into it, and only thus, in the full harmonious whole, music expresses what it aims at expressing. Thus also the one will outside of time finds its full objectification only in the complete union of all the steps which reveal its nature in the innumerable ascending grades of distinctness. The following analogy is also very remarkable. We have seen in the preceding book that notwithstanding the self-adaptation of all the phenomena of will to each other as regards their species, which constitutes their teleological aspect, there yet remains an unceasing conflict between those phenomena as individuals, which is visible at every grade, and makes the world a constant battle-field of all those manifestations of one and the same will, whose inner contradiction with itself becomes visible through it. In music also there is something corresponding to this. A complete, pure, harmonious system of tones is not only physically but arithmetically impossible. The numbers themselves by which the tones are expressed have inextricable irrationality. There is no scale in which, when it is counted, every fifth will be related to the keynote as 2 to 3, every major third as 4 to 5, every minor third as 5 to 6, and so on. For if they are correctly related to the keynote, they can no longer be so to each other; because, for example, the fifth must be the minor third to the third, &c. For the notes of the scale may be compared to actors who must play now one part, now another. Therefore a perfectly accurate system of music cannot even be thought, far less worked out; and on this account all possible music deviates from perfect purity; it can only conceal the discords essential to it by dividing them among all the notes, *i.e.*, by temperament. On this see Chladni's "Akustik," § 30, and his "Kurze Uebersicht der Schall- und Klanglehre." [1]

[1] Cf. Ch. xxxix. of Supplement.

I might still have something to say about the way in which music is perceived, namely, in and through time alone, with absolute exclusion of space, and also apart from the influence of the knowledge of causality, thus without understanding; for the tones make the æsthetic impression as effect, and without obliging us to go back to their causes, as in the case of perception. I do not wish, however, to lengthen this discussion, as I have perhaps already gone too much into detail with regard to some things in this Third Book, or have dwelt too much on particulars. But my aim made it necessary, and it will be the less disapproved if the importance and high worth of art, which is seldom sufficiently recognised, be kept in mind. For if, according to our view, the whole visible world is just the objectification, the mirror, of the will, conducting it to knowledge of itself, and, indeed, as we shall soon see, to the possibility of its deliverance; and if, at the same time, the world as idea, if we regard it in isolation, and, freeing ourselves from all volition, allow it alone to take possession of our consciousness, is the most joy-giving and the only innocent side of life; we must regard art as the higher ascent, the more complete development of all this, for it achieves essentially just what is achieved by the visible world itself, only with greater concentration, more perfectly, with intention and intelligence, and therefore may be called, in the full significance of the word, the flower of life. If the whole world as idea is only the visibility of will, the work of art is to render this visibility more distinct. It is the *camera obscura* which shows the objects more purely, and enables us to survey them and comprehend them better. It is the play within the play, the stage upon the stage in "Hamlet."

The pleasure we receive from all beauty, the consolation which art affords, the enthusiasm of the artist, which enables him to forget the cares of life,—the latter an advantage of the man of genius over other men, which alone repays him for the suffering that increases in proportion to the clearness of consciousness, and for the desert loneliness among men of a different race,—all this rests on the fact that the in-itself of life, the will, existence itself, is, as we shall see farther on, a constant sorrow, partly miserable, partly terrible; while, on the contrary, as idea alone, purely contemplated, or copied by art, free from pain, it presents to us a drama full of significance. This purely knowable side of the world, and the copy of it in any art, is the element of the artist. He is chained to the contemplation of the play, the objectification of will; he remains beside it, does not get tired of contemplating it and representing it in copies; and meanwhile he bears himself the cost of the production of that play, *i.e.*, he himself is the will which objectifies itself, and remains in constant suffering. That pure, true, and deep knowledge of the inner nature of the world becomes now for him an end in itself: he stops there. Therefore it does not become to him a quieter of the will, as, we shall see in the next book, it does in the case of the saint who has attained to resignation; it does not deliver him for ever from life, but only at moments, and is therefore not for him a path out of life, but only an occasional consolation in it, till his power, increased by this contemplation and at last tired of the play, lays hold on the real. The St. Cecilia of Raphael may be regarded as a representation of this transition. To the real, then, we now turn in the following book.

Fourth Book

THE WORLD AS WILL

SECOND ASPECT

THE ASSERTION AND DENIAL OF THE WILL TO LIVE, WHEN SELF-CONSCIOUSNESS HAS BEEN ATTAINED

Tempore quo cognitio simul advenit, amor e medio supersurrexit.—
Oupnek'hat, Studio Anquetil Duperron, vol. ii. p. 216.

§ 54. The first three books will, it is hoped, have con-
veyed the distinct and certain knowledge that the world as
idea is the complete mirror of the will, in which it knows
itself in ascending grades of distinctness and completeness,
the highest of which is man, whose nature, however, receives its complete expression only through the whole connected series of his actions. The self-conscious connection
of these actions is made possible by reason, which enables a
man constantly to survey the whole in the abstract.

The will, which, considered purely in itself, is without
knowledge, and is merely a blind incessant impulse, as we
see it appear in unorganised and vegetable nature and their
laws, and also in the vegetative part of our own life, receives through the addition of the world as idea, which is
developed in subjection to it, the knowledge of its own willing and of what it is that it wills. And this is nothing else
than the world as idea, life, precisely as it exists. Therefore
we called the phenomenal world the mirror of the will, its
objectivity. And since what the will wills is always life,
just because life is nothing but the representation of that
willing for the idea, it is all one and a mere pleonism if,
instead of simply saying "the will," we say, "the will to
live."

Will is the thing-in-itself, the inner content, the essence
of the world. Life, the visible world, the phenomenon, is
only the mirror of the will. Therefore life accompanies the
will as inseparably as the shadow accompanies the body;
and if will exists, so will life, the world, exist. Life is,
therefore, assured to the will to live; and so long as we are
filled with the will to live we need have no fear for our
existence, even in the presence of death. It is true we see the
individual come into being and pass away; but the indi-

vidual is only phenomenal, exists only for the knowledge which is bound to the principle of sufficient reason, to the *principium individuationis*. Certainly, for this kind of knowledge, the individual receives his life as a gift, rises out of nothing, then suffers the loss of this gift through death, and returns again to nothing. But we desire to consider life philosophically, *i.e.*, according to its Ideas, and in this sphere we shall find that neither the will, the thing-in-itself in all phenomena, nor the subject of knowing, that which perceives all phenomena, is affected at all by birth or by death. Birth and death belong merely to the phenomenon of will, thus to life; and it is essential to this to exhibit itself in individuals which come into being and pass away, as fleeting phenomena appearing in the form of time—phenomena of that which in itself knows no time, but must exhibit itself precisely in the way we have said, in order to objectify its peculiar nature. Birth and death belong in like manner to life, and hold the balance as reciprocal conditions of each other, or, if one likes the expression, as poles of the whole phenomenon of life. The wisest of all mythologies, the Indian, expresses this by giving to the very god that symbolises destruction, death (as Brahma, the most sinful and the lowest god of the Trimurti, symbolises generation, coming into being, and Vishnu maintaining or preserving), by giving, I say, to Siva as an attribute not only the necklace of skulls, but also the lingam, the symbol of generation, which appears here as the counterpart of death, thus signifying that generation and death are essentially correlatives, which reciprocally neutralise and annul each other. It was precisely the same sentiment that led the Greeks and Romans to adorn their costly sarcophagi, just as we see them now, with feasts, dances, marriages, the chase, fights of wild beasts, bacchanalians, &c.; thus with representations of the full ardour of life, which they place before us not only in such revels and sports, but also in sensual groups, and even go so far as to represent the sexual intercourse of satyrs and goats. Clearly the aim was to point in the most impressive manner away from the death of the mourned individual to the immortal life of nature, and thus to indicate, though without abstract knowledge, that the whole of nature is the phenomenon and also the fulfilment of the will to live. The form of this phenomenon is time, space, and causality, and by means of these individuation, which carries with it that the individual must come into being and pass away. But this no more affects the will to live, of whose manifestation the individual is, as it were, only a particular example or specimen, than the death of an individual injures the whole of nature. For it is not the individual, but only the species that Nature cares for, and for the preservation of which she so earnestly strives, providing for it with the utmost prodigality through the vast surplus of the seed and the great strength of the fructifying impulse. The individual, on the contrary, neither has nor can have any value for Nature, for her kingdom is infinite time and infinite space, and in these infinite multiplicity of possible individuals. Therefore she is always ready to let the individual fall, and hence it is not only exposed to destruction in a thousand ways by the most insignificant accident, but originally destined for it, and conducted towards it by Nature herself from the moment it has served its end of maintaining the species. Thus Nature naïvely expresses the great truth that only the Ideas, not the individuals, have, properly speaking, reality, *i.e.,* are complete objectivity of the will. Now, since man is Nature itself, and indeed Nature at the highest grade of its self-consciousness, but Nature is only the objectified will to live, the man who has comprehended and retained this point of view may well console himself, when contemplating his own death and that of his friends, by turning his eyes to the immortal life of Nature, which he himself is. This is the significance of Siva with the lingam, and of those ancient sarcophagi with their pictures of glowing life, which say to the mourning beholder, *Natura non contristatur.*

Above all things, we must distinctly recognise that the form of the phenomenon of will, the form of life or reality, is really only the *present*, not the future nor the past. The latter are only in the conception, exist only in the connection of knowledge, so far as it follows the principle of sufficient reason. No man has ever lived in the past, and none will live in the future; the *present* alone is the form of all life, and is its sure possession which can never be taken from it. The present always exists, together with its content. Both remain fixed without wavering, like the rainbow on the waterfall. For life is firm and certain in the will, and the present is firm and certain in life. Certainly, if we reflect on the thousands of years that are past, of the millions of men who lived in them, we ask, What were they? what has become of them? But, on the other hand, we need only recall our own past life and renew its scenes vividly in our imagination, and then ask again, What was all this? what has become of it? As it is with it, so is it with the life of those millions. Or should we suppose that the past could receive a new existence because it has been sealed by death? Our own past, the most recent part of it, and even yesterday, is now no more than an empty dream of the fancy, and such is the past of all those millions. What was? What is? The will, of which life is the mirror, and knowledge free from will, which beholds it clearly in that mirror. Whoever has not yet recognised this, or will not recognise it, must add to the question asked above as to the fate of past generations of men this question also: Why he, the questioner, is so fortunate as to be conscious of this costly, fleeting, and only real present, while those hundreds of generations of men, even the heroes and philosophers of those ages, have sunk into the night of the past, and have thus become nothing; but he, his insignificant ego, actually exists?

or more shortly, though somewhat strangely: Why this now, his now, *is* just now and *was* not long ago? Since he asks such strange questions, he regards his existence and his time as independent of each other, and the former as projected into the latter. He assumes indeed two nows—one which belongs to the object, the other which belongs to the subject, and marvels at the happy accident of their coincidence. But in truth, only the point of contact of the object, the form of which is time, with the subject, which has no mode of the principle of sufficient reason as its form, constitutes the present, as is shown in the essay on the principle of sufficient reason. Now all object is the will so far as it has become idea, and the subject is the necessary correlative of the object. But real objects are only in the present; the past and the future contain only conceptions and fancies, therefore the present is the essential form of the phenomenon of the will, and inseparable from it. The present alone is that which always exists and remains immovable. That which, empirically apprehended, is the most transitory of all, presents itself to the metaphysical vision, which sees beyond the forms of empirical perception, as that which alone endures, the *nunc stans* of the schoolmen. The source and the supporter of its content is the will to live or the thing-in-itself,—which we are. That which constantly becomes and passes away, in that it has either already been or is still to be, belongs to the phenomenon as such on account of its forms, which make coming into being and passing away possible. Accordingly, we must think:—*Quid fuit?*—*Quod est. Quid erit?*—*Quod fuit;* and take it in the strict meaning of the words; thus understand not *simile* but *idem.* For life is certain to the will, and the present is certain to life. Thus it is that every one can say, "I am once for all lord of the present, and through all eternity it will accompany me as my shadow: therefore I do not wonder where it has come from, and how it happens that it is exactly now." We might compare time to a constantly revolving sphere; the half that was always sinking would be the past, that which was always rising would be the future; but the indivisible point at the top, where the tangent touches, would be the extensionless present. As the tangent does not revolve with the sphere, neither does the present, the point of contact of the object, 'he form of which is time, with the subject, which has no form, because it does not belong to the knowable, but is the condition of all that is knowable. Or, time is like an unceasing stream, and the present a rock on which the stream breaks itself, but does not carry away with it. The will, as thing-in-itself, is just as little subordinate to the principle of sufficient reason as the subject of knowledge, which, finally, in a certain regard is the will itself or its expression. And as life, its own phenomenon, is assured to the will, so is the present, the single form of real life. Therefore we have not to investigate the past before life, nor the future after death: we have rather to know the *present*, the one form in which the will manifests itself. It will not escape from the will, but neither will the will escape from it. If, therefore, life as it is satisfies, whoever affirms it in every way may regard it with confidence as endless, and banish the fear of death as an illusion that inspires him with the foolish dread that he can ever be robbed of the present, and foreshadows a time in which there is no present; an illusion with regard to time analogous to the illusion with regard to space through which every one imagines the position on the globe he happens to occupy as above, and all other places as below. In the same way every one links the present to his own individuality, and imagines that all present is extinguished with it; that then past and future might be without a present. But as on the surface of the globe every place is above, so the form of all life is the *present*, and to fear death because it robs us of the present, is just as foolish as to fear that we may slip down from the round globe upon which we have now the good fortune to occupy the upper surface. The present is the form essential to the objectification of the will. It cuts time, which extends infinitely in both directions, as a mathematical point, and stands immovably fixed, like an everlasting mid-day with no cool evening, as the actual sun burns without intermission, while it only seems to sink into the bosom of night. Therefore, if a man fears death as his annihilation, it is just as if he were to think that the sun cries out at evening, "Woe is me! for I go down into eternal night." And conversely, whoever is oppressed with the burden of life, whoever desires life and affirms it, but abhors its torments, and especially can no longer endure the hard lot that has fallen to himself, such a man has no deliverance to hope for from death, and cannot right himself by suicide. The cool shades of Orcus allure him only with the false appearance of a haven of rest. The earth rolls from day into night, the individual dies, but the sun itself shines without intermission, an eternal noon. Life is assured to the will to live; the form of life is an endless present, no matter how the individuals, the phenomena of the Idea, arise and pass away in time, like fleeting dreams. Thus even already suicide appears to us as a vain and therefore a foolish action; when we have carried our investigation further it will appear to us in a still less favourable light.

But this that we have brought to clearest consciousness, that although the particular phenomenon of the will has a temporal beginning and end, the will itself as thing-in-itself is not affected by it, nor yet the correlative of all object, the knowing but never known subject, and that life is always assured to the will to live—this is not to be numbered with the doctrines of immortality. For permanence has no more to do with the will or with the pure subject of knowing, the eternal eye of the world, than transitoriness, for both are predicates that are only valid in time, and the will and the pure subject of knowing lie outside time. Therefore the egoism of the individual (this particular phenomenon of will enlightened by the subject of knowing) can extract as little nourishment and consolation for his wish to endure through endless time from the view we have expressed, as he could from the knowledge that after his death the rest of the eternal world would continue to exist, which is just the expression of the same view considered objectively, and therefore temporally. For every individual is transitory only as phenomenon, but as thing-in-itself is timeless, and therefore endless. But it is also only as phenomenon that an individual is distinguished from the other things of the world; as thing-in-itself he is the will which appears in all, and death destroys the illusion which separates his consciousness from that of the rest: this is immortality. His exemption from death, which belongs to him only as thing-in-itself, is for the phenomenon one with the immortality of the rest of the external world. Hence also, it arises that although the inward and merely felt consciousness of that which we have raised to distinct knowledge is indeed, as we have said, sufficient to prevent the thought of death from poisoning the life of the rational being, because this consciousness is the basis of that love of life which maintains everything living, and enables it to live on at ease as if there were no such thing as death, so long as it is face to face with life, and turns its attention to it, yet it will not prevent the individual from being seized with the fear of death, and trying in every way to escape from it, when it presents itself to him in some particular real case, or even only in his imagination, and he is compelled to contemplate it. For just as, so long as his knowledge was directed to life as such, he was obliged to recognise immortality in it, so when death is brought before his eyes, he is obliged to recognise it as that which it is, the temporal end of the particular temporal phenomenon. What we fear in death is by no means the pain, for it lies clearly on this side of death, and, moreover, we often take refuge in death from pain, just as, on the contrary, we sometimes endure the most fearful suffering merely to escape death for a while, although it would be quick and easy. Thus we distinguish pain and death as two entirely different evils. What we fear in death is the end of the individual which it openly professes itself to be, and since the individual is a particular objectification of the will to live itself, its whole nature struggles against death. Now when feeling thus exposes us helpless, reason can yet step in and for the most part overcome its adverse influence, for it places us upon a higher standpoint, from which we no longer contemplate the particular but the whole. Therefore a philosophical knowledge of the nature of the world, which extended to the point we have now reached in this work but went no farther, could even at this point of view overcome the terror of death in the measure in which reflection had power over direct feeling in the given individual. A man who had thoroughly assimilated the truths we have already advanced, but had not come to know, either from his own experience or from a deeper insight, that constant suffering is essential to life, who found satisfaction and all that he wished in life, and could calmly and deliberately desire that his life, as he had hitherto known it, should endure for ever or repeat itself ever anew, and whose love of life was so great that he willingly and gladly accepted all the hardships and miseries to which it is exposed for the sake of its pleasures,—such a man would stand "with firm-knit bones on the well-rounded, enduring earth," and would have nothing to fear. Armed with the knowledge we have given him, he would await with indifference the death that hastens towards him on the wings of time. He would regard it as a false illusion, an impotent spectre, which frightens the weak but has no power over him who knows that he is himself the will of which the

whole world is the objectification or copy, and that therefore he is always certain of life, and also of the present, the
peculiar and only form of the phenomenon of the will.
He could not be terrified by an endles past or future in
which he would not be, for this he would regard as the
empty delusion of the web of Mâyâ. Thus he would no
more fear death than the sun fears the night. In the "Bhagavad-Gita" Krishna thus raises the mind of his young pupil
Arjuna, when, seized with compunction at the sight of the
arrayed hosts (somewhat as Xerxes was), he loses heart and
desires to give up the battle in order to avert the death of
so many thousands. Krishna leads him to this point of view,
and the death of those thousands can no longer restrain
him; he gives the sign for battle. This point of view is also
expressed by Goethe's Prometheus, especially when he says—

> "Here sit I, form mankind
> In my own image,
> A race like to myself,
> To suffer and to weep,
> Rejoice, enjoy,
> And heed thee not,
> As I."

That the will asserts itself means, that while in its objectivity, *i.e.*, in the world and life, its own nature is completely and distinctly given it as idea, this knowledge does
not by any means check its volition; but this very life, so
known, is willed as such by the will with knowledge, consciously and deliberately, just as up to this point it willed it
as blind effort without knowledge. The opposite of this, the
denial of the will to live, shows itself if, when that knowledge is attained, volition ends, because the particular known
phenomena no longer act as *motives* for willing, but the
whole knowledge of the nature of the world, the mirror of
the will, which has grown up through the comprehension
of the *Ideas*, becomes a *quieter* of the will; and thus free,
the will suppresses itself. These quite unfamiliar conceptions

are difficult to understand when expressed in this general way, but it is hoped they will become clear through the exposition we shall give presently, with special reference to action, of the phenomena in which, on the one hand, the assertion in its different grades, and, on the other hand, the denial, expresses itself. For both proceed from knowledge, yet not from abstract knowledge, which is expressed in words, but from living knowledge, which is expressed in action and behaviour alone, and is independent of the dogmas which at the same time occupy the reason as abstract knowledge. To exhibit them both, and bring them to distinct knowledge of the reason, can alone be my aim, and not to prescribe or recommend the one or the other, which would be as foolish as it would be useless; for the will in itself is absolutely free and entirely self-determining, and for it there is no law. But before we go on to the exposition referred to, we must first explain and more exactly define this *freedom* and its relation to necessity. And also, with regard to the life, the assertion and denial of which is our problem, we must insert a few general remarks connected with the will and its objects. Through all this we shall facilitate the apprehension of the inmost nature of the knowledge we are aiming at, of the ethical significance of methods of action.

§ 55. That the will as such is *free*, follows from the fact that, according to our view, it is the thing-in-itself, the content of all phenomena. The phenomena, on the other hand, we recognise as absolutely subordinate to the principle of sufficient reason in its four forms. And since we know that necessity is throughout identical with following from given grounds, and that these are convertible conceptions, all that belongs to the phenomenon, *i.e.*, all that is object for the knowing subject as individual, is in one aspect reason, and in another aspect consequent; and in this last capacity is determined with absolute necessity, and can, therefore, in no respect be other than it is. The whole content of Nature, the collective sum of its phenomena, is thus throughout necessary, and the necessity of every part, of every phenomenon, of every event, can always be proved, because it must be possible to find the reason from which it follows as a consequent. This admits of no exception: it follows from the unrestricted validity of the principle of sufficient reason. In another aspect, however, the same world is for us, in all its phenomena, objectivity of will. And the will, since it is not phenomenon, is not idea or object, but thing-in-itself, and is not subordinate to the principle of sufficient reason, the form of all object; thus is not determined as a consequent through any reason, knows no necessity, *i.e.*, is *free*. The concept of freedom is thus properly a negative concept, for its content is merely the denial of necessity, *i.e.*, the relation of consequent to its reason, according to the principle of sufficient reason. Now here lies before us in its most distinct form the solution of that great contradiction, the union of freedom with necessity, which has so often been discussed in recent times, yet, so far as I know, never clearly and adequately. Everything is as phenomenon, as object, absolutely necessary: *in itself* it is will, which is perfectly free to all eternity. The phenomenon, the object, is necessarily and unalterably determined in that chain of causes and effects which admits of no interruption. But the existence in general of this object, and its specific nature, *i.e.*, the Idea which reveals itself in it, or, in other words, its character, is a direct manifestation of will. Thus, in conformity with the freedom of this will, the object might not be at all, or it might be originally and essentially something quite different from what it is, in which case, however, the whole chain of which it is a link, and which is itself a manifestation of the same will, would be quite different also. But once there and existing, it has entered the chain of causes and effects, is always necessarily determined in it, and can, therefore, neither become something else, *i.e.*, change itself, nor yet escape from the chain, *i.e.*, vanish. Man, like every other part of Nature, is objectivity of the will; therefore all that has been said holds good of him. As everything in Nature has its forces and qualities, which react in a definite way when definitely affected, and constitute its character, man also has his *character*, from which the motives call forth his actions with necessity. In this manner of conduct his empirical character reveals itself, but in this again his intelligible character, the will in itself, whose determined phenomenon he is. But man is the most complete phenomenon of will, and, as we explained in the Second Book, he had to be enlightened with so high a degree of knowledge in order to maintain himself in existence, that in it a perfectly adequate copy or repetition of the nature of the world under the form of the idea became possible: this is the comprehension of the Ideas, the pure mirror of the world, as we learnt in the Third Book. Thus in man the will can attain to full self-consciousness, to distinct and exhaustive knowledge of its own nature, as it mirrors itself in the whole world. We saw in the preceding book that art springs from the actual presence of this degree of knowledge; and at the end of our whole work it will further appear that, through the same knowledge, in that the will relates it to itself, a suppression and self-denial of the will in its most perfect manifestation is possible. So that the freedom which otherwise, as belonging to the thing-in-itself, can never show itself in the phenomenon, in such a case does also appear in it, and, by abolishing the nature which lies at the foundation of the phenomenon, while the latter itself still continues to exist in time, it brings about a contradiction of the phenomenon with itself, and in this way exhibits the phenomena of holiness and self-renunciation. But all this can only be fully understood at the end of this book. What has just been said merely affords a preliminary and general indication of how man is distinguished from all the other phenomena of will by the fact that freedom, *i.e.*, independence of the principle of sufficient reason, which only belongs to the will as thing-in-itself, and contradicts the phenomenon, may yet possibly, in his case, appear in the phenomenon also, where, however, it necessarily exhibits itself as a contradiction of the phenomenon with itself. In this sense, not only the will in itself, but man also may certainly be called free, and thus distinguished from all other beings. But how this is to be understood can only become clear through all that is to follow, and for the present we must turn away from it altogether. For, in the first place, we must beware of the error that the action of the individual definite man is subject to no necessity, *i.e.*, that the power of the motive is less certain than the power of the cause, or the following of the conclusion from the premises. The freedom of the will as thing-in-itself, if, as has been said, we abstract from the entirely exceptional case mentioned above, by no means extends directly to its phenomenon, not even in the case in which this reaches the highest grade of its visibility, and thus does not extend to the rational animal endowed with individual character, *i.e.*, the person. The person is never free although he is the phenomenon of a free will; for he is already the determined phenomenon of the free volition of this will, and, because he enters the form of every object, the principle of sufficient reason, he develops indeed the unity of that will in a multiplicity of actions, but on account of the timeless unity of that volition in itself, this multiplicity exhibits in itself the regular conformity to law of a force of nature. Since, however, it is that free volition that becomes visible in the person and the whole of his conduct, relating itself to him as the concept to the definition, every individual action of the person is to be ascribed to the free will, and directly proclaims itself as such in consciousness. Therefore, as was said in the Second Book, every one regards himself *a priori* (*i.e.*, here in this original feeling) as free in his individual actions, in the sense that in every given case every action is possible for him, and he only recognises *a posteriori* from experience and reflection upon experience that his actions take place with absolute necessity from the coincidence of his character with his motives. Hence it arises that every uncultured man, following his feeling, ardently defends complete freedom in particular actions, while the great thinkers of all ages, and indeed the more profound systems of religion, have denied it. But whoever has come to see clearly that the whole nature of man is will, and he himself only a phenomenon of this will, and that such a phenomenon has, even from the subject itself, the principle of suf-· ficient reason as its necessary form, which here appears as the law of motivation,—such a man will regard it as just as absurd to doubt the inevitable nature of an action when the motive is presented to a given character, as to doubt that the three angles of any triangle are together equal to two right angles.

Apart from the fact that the will as the true thing-in-itself is actually original and independent, and that the feeling of its originality and absoluteness must accompany its acts in self-consciousness, though here they are already determined, there arises the illusion of an empirical freedom of the will (instead of the transcendental freedom which alone is to be attributed to it), and thus a freedom of its particular actions, from the attitude of the intellect towards the will. The intellect knows the conclusions of the will only *a posteriori* and empirically; therefore when a choice is presented, it has no data as to how the will is to decide. For the intelligible character, by virtue of which, when motives are given, only *one* decision is possible and is therefore necessary, does not come within the knowledge of the intellect, but merely the empirical character is known to it through the succession of its particular acts. Therefore it seems to the intellect that in a given case two opposite decisions are possible for the will. But this is just the same thing as if we were to say of a perpendicular beam that has lost its balance, and is hesitating which way to fall, "It can fall either to the right hand or the left." This *can* has merely a subjective significance, and really means "as far as the data known to us are concerned." Objectively, the direction of the fall is necessarily determined as soon as the equilibrium is lost. Accordingly, the decision of one's own will is undetermined only to the beholder, one's own intellect, and thus merely relatively and subjectively for the subject of knowing. In itself and objectively, on the other hand, in every choice presented to it, its decision is at once determined and necessary. But this determination only comes into consciousness through the decision that follows upon it. Indeed, we receive an empirical proof of this when any difficult and important choice lies before us, but only under a condition which is not yet present, but merely hoped for, so that in the meanwhile we can do nothing, but must remain passive. Now we consider how we shall decide when the circumstances occur that will give us a free activity and choice. Generally the foresight of rational deliberation recommends one decision, while direct inclination leans rather to the other. So long as we are compelled to remain passive, the side of reason seems to wish to keep the upperhand; but we see beforehand how strongly the other side will influence us when the opportunity for action arises. Till then we are eagerly concerned to place the motives on both sides in the clearest light, by calm meditation on the *pro et contra*, so that every motive may exert its full influence upon the will when the time arrives, and it may not be misled by a mistake on the part of the intellect to decide otherwise than it would have done if all the motives had their due influence upon it. But this distinct unfolding of the motives on both sides is all that the intellect can do to assist the choice. It awaits the real decision just as passively and with the same intense curiosity as if it were that of a foreign will. Therefore from its point of view both decisions must seem to it equally possible; and this is just the illusion of the empirical freedom of the will. Certainly the decision enters the sphere of the intellect altogether empirically, as the final conclusion of the matter; but yet it proceeded from the inner nature, the intelligible character, of the individual will in its conflict with given motives, and therefore with complete necessity. The intellect can do nothing more than bring out clearly and fully the nature of the motives; it cannot determine the will itself; for the will is quite inaccessible to it, and, as we have seen, cannot be investigated.

The assertion of an empirical freedom of the will, a *liberum arbitrium indifferentiœ*, agrees precisely with the doctrine that places the inner nature of man in a *soul*, which is originally a *knowing*, and indeed really an abstract *thinking* nature, and only in consequence of this a *willing* nature —a doctrine which thus regards the will as of a secondary or derivative nature, instead of knowledge which is really so. The will indeed came to be regarded as an act of thought, and to be identified with the judgment, especially by Descartes and Spinoza. According to this doctrine every man must become what he is only through his knowledge; he must enter the world as a moral cipher come to know the things in it, and thereupon determine to be this or that, to act thus or thus, and may also through new knowledge achieve a new course of action, that is to say, become another person. Further, he must first know a thing to be *good*, and in consequence of this will it, instead of first *willing* it, and in consequence of this calling it *good*. According to my fundamental point of view, all this is a reversal of the true relation. Will is first and original;

knowledge is merely added to it as an instrument belonging to the phenomenon of will. Therefore every man is what he is through his will, and his character is original, for willing is the basis of his nature. Through the knowledge which is added to it he comes to know in the course of experience *what he is, i.e.,* he learns his character. Thus he *knows* himself in consequence of and in accordance with the nature of his will, instead of *willing* in consequence of and in accordance with his knowing. According to the latter view, he would only require to consider how he would like best to be, and he would be it; that is its doctrine of the freedom of the will. Thus it consists really in this, that a man is his own work guided by the light of knowledge. I, on the contrary, say that he is his own work before all knowledge, and knowledge is merely added to it to enlighten it. Therefore he cannot resolve to be this or that, nor can he become other than he is; but he *is* once for all, and he knows in the course of experience *what* he is. According to one doctrine he *wills* what he knows, and according to the other he *knows* what he wills.

The motives which determine the manifestation of the character or conduct influence it through the medium of knowledge. But knowledge is changeable, and often vacillates between truth and error, yet, as a rule, is rectified more and more in the course of life, though certainly in very different degrees. Therefore the conduct of a man may be observedly altered without justifying us in concluding that his character has been changed. What the man really and in general wills, the striving of his inmost nature, and the end he pursues in accordance with it, this we can never change by influence upon him from without by instruction, otherwise we could transform him. Seneca says admirably, *velle non discitur;* whereby he preferred truth to his Stoic philosophers, who taught διδακτην ειναι την αρετην (*doceri posse virtutem*). From without the will can only be affected by

motives. But these can never change the will itself; for
they have power over it only under the presupposition that it
is precisely such as it is. All that they can do is thus to alter
the direction of its effort, *i.e.,* bring it about that it shall
seek in another way than it has hitherto done that which it
invariably seeks. Therefore instructions, improved knowledge, in other words, influence from without, may indeed
teach the will that it erred in the means it employed, and
can therefore bring it about that the end after which it
strives once for all according to its inner nature shall be
pursued on an entirely different path and in an entirely different object from what has hitherto been the case. But it
can never bring about that the will shall will something
actually different from what it has hitherto willed; this
remains unchangeable, for the will is simply this willing
itself, which would have to be abolished. The former, however, the possible modification of knowledge, and through
knowledge of conduct, extends so far that the will seeks to
attain its unalterable end, for example, Mohammed's paradise, at one time in the real world, at another time in a
world of imagination, adapting the means to each, and thus
in the first case applying prudence, might, and fraud, and
in the second case, abstinence, justice, alms, and pilgrimages
to Mecca. But its effort itself has not therefore changed,
still less the will itself. Thus, although its action certainly
shows itself very different at different times, its willing has
yet remained precisely the same. *Velle non discitur.*

For motives to act, it is necessary not only that they
should be present, but that they should be known; for, according to a very good expression of the schoolmen, which
we referred to once before, *causa finalis movet non secundum suum esse reale; sed secundum esse cognitum.* For
example, in order that the relation may appear that exists
in a given man between egoism and sympathy, it is not sufficient that he should possess wealth and see others in want,

but he must also know what he can do with his wealth, both for himself and for others: not only must the suffering of others be presented to him, but he must know both what suffering and also what pleasure is. Perhaps, on a first occasion, he did not know all this so well as on a second; and if, on a similar occasion, he acts differently, this arises simply from the fact that the circumstances were really different, as regards the part of them that depends on his knowing them, although they seem to be the same. As ignorance of actually existing circumstances robs them of their influence, so, on the other hand, entirely imaginary circumstances may act as if they were real, not only in the case of a particular deception, but also in general and continuously. For example, if a man is firmly persuaded that every good action will be repaid him a hundredfold in a future life, such a conviction affects him in precisely the same way as a good bill of exchange at a very long date, and he can give from mere egoism, as from another point of view he would take from egoism. He has not changed himself: *velle non discitur*. It is on account of this great influence of knowledge upon action, while the will remains unchangeable, that the character develops and its different features appear only little by little. Therefore it shows itself different at every period of life, and an impetuous, wild youth may be succeeded by a staid, sober, manly age. Especially what is bad in the character will always come out more strongly with time, yet sometimes it occurs that passions which a man gave way to in his youth are afterwards voluntarily restrained, simply because the motives opposed to them have only then come into knowledge. Hence, also, we are all innocent to begin with, and this merely means that neither we nor others know the evil of our own nature; it only appears with the motives, and only in time do the motives appear in knowledge. Finally we come to know ourselves as quite different from what *a priori* we supposed ourselves to be, and then we are often terrified at ourselves.

The influence which knowledge, as the medium of motives, exerts, not indeed upon the will itself, but upon its appearance in actions, is also the source of the principal distinction between the action of men and that of brutes, for their methods of knowledge are different. The brute has only knowledge of perception, the man, through reason, has also abstract ideas, conceptions. Now, although man and brute are with equal necessity determined by their motives, yet man, as distinguished from the brute, has a complete *choice*, which has often been regarded as a freedom of the will in particular actions, although it is nothing but the possibility of a thoroughly-fought-out battle between several motives, the strongest of which then determines it with necessity. For this the motives must have assumed the form of abstract thoughts, because it is really only by means of these that deliberation, *i.e.*, a weighing of opposite reasons for action, is possible. In the case of the brute there can only be a choice between perceptible motives presented to it, so that the choice is limited to the narrow sphere of its present sensuous perception. Therefore the necessity of the determination of the will by the motive, which is like that of the effect by the cause, can be exhibited perceptibly and directly only in the case of the brutes, because here the spectator has the motives just as directly before his eyes as their effect; while in the case of man the motives are almost always abstract ideas, which are not communicated to the spectator, and even for the actor himself the necessity of their effect is hidden behind their conflict. For only *in abstracto* can several ideas, as judgments and chains of conclusions, lie beside each other in consciousness, and then, free from all determination of time, work against each other till the stronger overcomes the rest and determines the will. This is the complete *choice* or power of deliberation which man has as distinguished from the brutes, and on account of which freedom of the will has been attributed to him, in the belief that his willing is a mere result of the operations of his intellect, without a definite tendency which serves as its basis; while, in truth, the motives only work on the foundation and under the presupposition of his definite tendency, which in his case is individual *i.e.*, a character. A fuller exposition of this power of deliberation, and the difference between human and brute choice which is introduced by it, will be found in the "Two Fundamental Problems of Ethics" (1st edition, p. 35, *et seq.*; 2d edition, p. 34, *et seq.*), to which I therefore refer. For the rest, this power of deliberation which man possesses is one of those things that makes his existence so much more miserable than that of the brute. For in general our greatest sufferings do not lie in the present as ideas of perception or as immediate feelings; but in the reason, as abstract conceptions, painful thoughts, from which the brute, which lives only in the present, and therefore in enviable carelessness, is entirely free.

It seems to have been the dependence, which we have shown, of the human power of deliberation upon the faculty of abstract thinking, and thus also of judging and drawing conclusions also, that led both Descartes and Spinoza to identify the decisions of the will with the faculty of asserting and denying (the faculty of judgment). From this Descartes deduced the doctrine that the will which, according to him, is indifferently free, is the source of sin, and also of all theoretical error. And Spinoza, on the other hand, concluded that the will is necessarily determined by the motives, as the judgment is by the reasons.[1] The latter doctrine is in a sense true, but it appears as a true conclusion from false premises.

The distinction we have established between the ways in which the brutes and man are respectively moved by motives

[1] Cart. Medit. 4.—Spin. Eth., pt. ii. prop. 48 et 49, cæt.

exerts a very wide influence upon the nature of both, and has most to do with the complete and obvious differences of their existence. While an idea of perception is in every case the motive which determines the brute, the man strives to exclude this kind of motivation altogether, and to determine himself entirely by abstract ideas. Thus he uses his prerogative of reason to the greatest possible advantage. Independent of the present, he neither chooses nor avoids the passing pleasure or pain, but reflects on the consequences of both. In most cases, setting aside quite insignificant actions, we are determined by abstract, thought motives, not present impressions. Therefore all particular privation for the moment is for us comparatively light, but all renunciation is terribly hard; for the former only concerns the fleeting present, but the latter concerns the future, and includes in itself innumerable privations, of which it is the equivalent. The causes of our pain, as of our pleasure, lie for the most part, not in the real present, but merely in abstract thoughts. It is these which are often unbearable to us—inflict torments in comparison with which all the sufferings of the animal world are very small; for even our own physical pain is not felt at all when they are present. Indeed, in the case of keen mental suffering, we even inflict physical suffering on ourselves merely to distract our attention from the former to the latter. This is why, in great mental anguish, men tear their hair, beat their breasts, lacerate their faces, or roll on the floor, for all these are in reality only violent means of diverting the mind from an unbearable thought. Just because mental pain, being much greater, makes us insensible to physical pain, suicide is very easy to the person who is in despair, or who is consumed by morbid depression, even though formerly, in comfortable circumstances, he recoiled at the thought of it. In the same way care and passion (thus the play of thought) wear out the body oftener and more than physical hardships. And in accordance with this Epictetus rightly says: *Ταρασσει τους ανθρωπους ου τα πραγματα, αλλα τα περι των πραγματων δογματα* (*Perturbant homines non res ipsæ, sed de rebus decreta*) (V.); and Seneca: *Plura sunt quæ nos terrent, quam quæ premunt, et sæpius opinione quam re laboramus* (Ep. 5). Eulenspiegel also admirably bantered human nature, for going uphill he laughed, and going downhill he wept. Indeed, children who have hurt themselves often cry, not at the pain, but at the thought of the pain which is awakened when some one condoles with them. Such great differences in conduct and in life arise from the diversity between the methods of knowledge of the brutes and man. Further, the appearance of the distinct and decided individual character, the principal distinction between man and the brute, which has scarcely more than the character of the species, is conditioned by the choice between several motives, which is only possible through abstract conceptions. For only after a choice has been made are the resolutions, which vary in different individuals, an indication of the individual character which is different in each; while the action of the brute depends only upon the presence or absence of the impression, supposing this impression to be in general a motive for its species. And, finally, in the case of man, only the resolve, and not the mere wish, is a valid indication of his character both for himself and for others; but the resolve becomes for himself, as for others, a certain fact only through the deed. The wish is merely the necessary consequence of the present impression, whether of the outward stimulus, or the inward passing mood; and is therefore as immediately necessary and devoid of consideration as the action of the brutes. Therefore, like the action of the brutes, it merely expresses the character of the species, not that of the individual, *i.e.,* it indicates merely what *man in general*, not what the individual who experiences the wish, is capable of doing. The deed alone,—because as human action it always requires a certain deliberation, and because as a rule a man has command of his reason, is considerate, *i.e.*, decides in accordance with considered and abstract motives,—is the expression of the intelligible maxims of his conduct, the result of his inmost willing, and is related as a letter to the word that stands for his empirical character, itself merely the temporal expression of his intelligible character. In a healthy mind, therefore, only deeds oppress the conscience, not wishes and thoughts; for it is only our deeds that hold up to us the mirror of our will. The deed that is entirely unconsidered and is really committed in blind passion, is to a certain extent an intermediate thing between the mere wish and the resolve. Therefore, by true repentance, which, however, shows itself as action also, it can be obliterated, as a falsely drawn line, from that picture of our will which our course of life is. I may insert the remark here, as a very good comparison, that the relation between wish and deed has a purely accidental but accurate analogy with that between the accumulation and discharge of electricity.

As the result of the whole of this discussion of the freedom of the will and what relates to it, we find that although the will may, in itself and apart from the phenomenon, be called free and even omnipotent, yet in its particular phenomena enlightened by knowledge, as in men and brutes, it is determined by motives to which the special character regularly and necessarily responds, and always in the same way. We see that because of the possession on his part of abstract or rational knowledge, man, as distinguished from the brutes, has a *choice*, which only makes him the scene of the conflict of his motives, without withdrawing him from their control. This choice is therefore certainly the condition of the possibility of the complete expression of the individual character, but is by no means to be regarded as freedom of the particular volition, *i.e.*, independence of the law of causality, the necessity of which extends to man as to every other phenomenon. Thus the difference between human volition and that of the brutes, which is introduced by reason or knowledge through concepts, extends to the point we have indicated, and no farther. But, what is quite a different thing, there may arise a phenomenon of the human will which is quite impossible in the brute creation, if man altogether lays aside the knowledge of particular things as such which is subordinate to the principle of sufficient reason, and by means of his knowledge of the Ideas sees through the *principium individuationis*. Then an actual appearance of the real freedom of the will as a thing-in-itself is possible, by which the phenomenon comes into a sort of contradiction with itself, as is indicated by the word self-renunciation; and, finally, the "in-itself" of its nature suppresses itself. But this, the one, real, and direct expression of the freedom of the will in itself in the phenomenon, cannot be distinctly explained here, but will form the subject of the concluding part of our work.

Now that we have shown clearly in these pages the unalterable nature of the empirical character, which is just the unfolding of the intelligible character that lies outside time, together with the necessity with which actions follow upon its contact with motives, we hasten to anticipate an argument which may very easily be drawn from this in the interest of bad dispositions. Our character is to be regarded as the temporal unfolding of an extra-temporal, and therefore indivisible and unalterable, act of will, or an intelligible character. This necessarily determines all that is essential in our conduct in life, *i.e.*, its ethical content, which must express itself in accordance with it in its phenomenal appearance, the empirical character; while only what is unessential in this, the outward form of our course of life, depends upon the forms in which the motives present themselves. It might, therefore, be inferred that it is a waste of trouble to endeavour to improve one's character, and that it

is wiser to submit to the inevitable, and gratify every inclination at once, even if it is bad. But this is precisely the
same thing as the theory of an inevitable fate which is called
αργος λογος, and in more recent times Turkish faith. Its
true refutation, as it is supposed to have been given by
Chrysippus, is explained by Cicero in his book *De Fato*, ch.
12, 13.

Though everything may be regarded as irrevocably predetermined by fate, yet it is so only through the medium of
the chain of causes; therefore in no case can it be determined that an effect shall appear without its cause. Thus it
is not simply the event that is predetermined, but the event
as the consequence of preceding causes; so that fate does
not decide the consequence alone, but also the means as the
consequence of which it is destined to appear. Accordingly,
if some means is not present, it is certain that the consequence also will not be present: each is always present in
accordance with the determination of fate, but this is never
known to us till afterwards.

As events always take place according to fate, *i.e.*, according to the infinite concatenation of causes, so our actions
always take place according to our intelligible character.
But just as we do not know the former beforehand, so no
a priori insight is given us into the latter, but we only come
to know ourselves as we come to know other persons *a posteriori* through experience. If the intelligible character involved that we could only form a good resolution after a
long conflict with a bad disposition, this conflict would have
to come first and be waited for. Reflection on the unalterable nature of the character, on the unity of the source
from which all our actions flow, must not mislead us into
claiming the decision of the character in favour of one side
or the other; it is in the resolve that follows that we shall
see what manner of men we are, and mirror ourselves in our
actions. This is the explanation of the satisfaction or the

anguish of soul with which we look back on the course of our past life. Both are experienced, not because these past deeds have still an existence; they are past, they have been, and now are no more; but their great importance for us lies in their significance, lies in the fact that these deeds are the expression of the character, the mirror of the will, in which we look and recognise our inmost self, the kernel of our will. Because we experience this not before, but only after, it behoves us to strive and fight in time, in order that the picture we produce by our deeds may be such that the contemplation of it may calm us as much as possible, instead of harassing us. The significance of this consolation or anguish of soul will, as we have said, be inquired into farther on; but to this place there belongs the inquiry which follows, and which stands by itself.

Besides the intelligible and the empirical character, we must mention a third which is different from them both, the *acquired character*, which one only receives in life through contact with the world, and which is referred to when one is praised as a man of character or censured as being without character. Certainly one might suppose that, since the empirical character, as the phenomenon of the intelligible, is unalterable, and, like every natural phenomenon, is consistent with itself, man would always have to appear like himself and consistent, and would therefore have no need to acquire a character artificially by experience and reflection. But the case is otherwise, and although a man is always the same, yet he does not always understand himself, but often mistakes himself, till he has in some degree acquired real self-knowledge. The empirical character, as a mere natural tendency, is in itself irrational; nay, more, its expressions are disturbed by reason, all the more so the more intellect and power of thought the man has; for these always keep before him what becomes *man in general* as the character of the species, and what is possible for him both in will and in deed. This makes it the more difficult for him to see how much his individuality enables him to will and to accomplish. He finds in himself the germs of all the various human pursuits and powers, but the difference of degree in which they exist in his individuality is not clear to him in the absence of experience; and if he now applies himself to the pursuits which alone correspond to his character, he yet feels, especially at particular moments and in particular moods, the inclination to directly opposite pursuits which cannot be combined with them, but must be entirely suppressed if he desires to follow the former undisturbed. For as our physical path upon earth is always merely a line, not an extended surface, so in life, if we desire to grasp and possess one thing, we must renounce and leave innumerable others on the right hand and on the left. If we cannot make up our minds to this, but, like children at the fair, snatch at everything that attracts us in passing, we are making the perverse endeavour to change the line of our path into an extended surface; we run in a zigzag, skip about like a will-o'-the-wisp, and attain to nothing. Or, to use another comparison, as, according to Hobbes' philosophy of law, every one has an original right to everything but an exclusive right to nothing, yet can obtain an exclusive right to particular things by renouncing his right to all the rest, while others, on their part, do likewise with regard to what he has chosen; so is it in life, in which some definite pursuit, whether it be pleasure, honour, wealth, science, art, or virtue, can only be followed with seriousness and success when all claims that are foreign to it are given up, when everything else is renounced. Accordingly, the mere will and the mere ability are not sufficient, but a man must also *know* what he wills, and *know* what he can do; only then will he show character, and only then can he accomplish something right. Until he attains to that, notwithstanding the natural consistency of the empirical character, he is without character.

And although, on the whole, he must remain true to him-self, and fulfil his course, led by his dæmon, yet his path will not be a straight line, but wavering and uneven. He will hesitate, deviate, turn back, lay up for himself re-pentance and pain. And all this is because, in great and small, he sees before him all that is possible and attainable for man in general, but does not know what part of all this is alone suitable for him, can be accomplished by him, and is alone enjoyable by him. He will, therefore, envy many men on account of a position and circumstances which are yet only suitable to their characters and not to his, and in which he would feel unhappy, if indeed he found them en-durable at all. For as a fish is only at home in water, a bird in the air, a mole in the earth, so every man is only at home in the atmosphere suitable to him. For example, not all men can breathe the air of court life. From deficiency of proper insight into all this, many a man will make all kinds of abortive attemps, will do violence to his character in particu-lars, and yet, on the whole, will have to yield to it again; and what he thus painfully attains will give him no pleasure; what he thus learns will remain dead; even in an ethical regard, a deed that is too noble for his character, that has not sprung from pure, direct impulse, but from a con-cept, a dogma, will lose all merit even in his own eyes, through subsequent egoistical repentance. *Velle non discitur.* We only become conscious of the inflexibility of another person's character through experience, and till then we childishly believe that it is possible, by means of rational ideas, by prayers and entreaties, by example and noble-mindedness, ever to persuade any one to leave his own way, o change his course of conduct, to depart from his mode of thinking, or even to extend his capacities: so is it also with ourselves. We must first learn from experience what we desire and what we can do. Till then we know it not, we are without character, and must often be driven back to our own way by hard blows from without. But if we have finally learnt it, then we have attained to what in the world is called character, the *acquired character*. This is accordingly nothing but the most perfect knowledge possible of our own individuality. It is the abstract, and consequently distinct, knowledge of the unalterable qualities of our own empirical character, and of the measure and direction of our mental and physical powers, and thus of the whole strength and weakness of our own individuality. This places us in a position to carry out deliberately and methodically the rôle which belongs to our own person, and to fill up the gaps which caprices or weaknesses produce in it, under the guidance of fixed conceptions.

§ 56. This freedom, this omnipotence, as the expression of which the whole visible world exists and progressively develops in accordance with the laws which belong to the form of knowledge, can now, at the point at which in its most perfect manifestation it has attained to the completely adequate knowledge of its own nature, express itself anew in two ways. Either it wills here, at the summit of mental endowment and self-consciousness, simply what it willed before blindly and unconsciously, and if so, knowledge always remains its *motive* in the whole as in the particular case. Or, conversely, this knowledge becomes for it a *quieter*, which appeases and suppresses all willing. This is that assertion and denial of the will to live which was stated above in general terms. As, in the reference of individual conduct, a general, not a particular manifestation of will, it does not disturb and modify the development of the character, nor does it find its expression in particular actions; but, either by an ever more marked appearance of the whole method of action it has followed hitherto, or conversely by the entire suppression of it, it expresses in a living form the maxims which the will has freely adopted in accordance with the knowledge it has now attained to. By the explanations we have just given of freedom, necessity, and character, we have somewhat facilitated and prepared the way for the clearer development of all this, which is the principal subject of this last book. But we shall have done so still more when we have turned our attention to life itself, the willing or not willing of which is the great question, and have endeavoured to find out generally what the will itself, which is everywhere the inmost nature of this life, will really attain by its assertion—in what way and to what extent this assertion satisfies or can satisfy the will; in short, what is generally and mainly to be regarded as its position in this its own world, which in every relation belongs to it.

First of all, I wish the reader to recall the passage with which we closed the Second Book,—a passage occasioned by the question, which met us then, as to the end and aim of the will. Instead of the answer to this question, it appeared clearly before us how, in all the grades of its manifestation, from the lowest to the highest, the will dispenses altogether with a final goal and aim. It always strives, for striving is its sole nature, which no attained goal can put an end to. Therefore it is not susceptible of any final satisfaction, but can only be restrained by hindrances, while in itself it goes on for ever. We see this in the simplest of all natural phenomena, gravity, which does not cease to strive and press towards a mathematical centre to reach which would be the annihilation both of itself and matter, and would not cease even if the whole universe were already rolled into one ball. We see it in the other simple natural phenomena. A solid tends towards fluidity either by melting or dissolving, for only so will its chemical forces be free; rigidity is the imprisonment in which it is held by cold. The fluid tends towards the gaseous state, into which it passes at once as soon as all pressure is removed from it. No body is without relationship, i.e., without tendency or without desire and longing, as Jakob Böhm would say. Electricity transmits its inner self-repulsion to infinity, though the mass of the earth absorbs the effect. Galvanism is certainly, so long as the pile is working, an aimless, unceasingly repeated act of repulsion and attraction. The existence of the plant is just such a restless, never satisfied striving, a ceaseless tendency through ever-ascending forms, till the end, the seed, becomes a new starting-point; and this repeated *ad infinitum*—nowhere an end, nowhere a final satisfaction, nowhere a resting-place. It will also be remembered, from the Second Book, that the multitude of natural forces and organised forms everywhere strive with each other for the matter in which they desire to appear, for each of them only possesses what it has wrested from the others; and thus a constant internecine war is waged, from which, for the most part, arises the resistance through which that striving, which constitutes the inner nature of everything, is at all points hindered; struggles in vain, yet, from its nature, cannot leave off; toils on laboriously till this phenomenon dies, when others eagerly seize its place and its matter.

We have long since recognised this striving, which constitutes the kernel and in-itself of everything, as identical with that which in us, where it manifests itself most distinctly in the light of the fullest consciousness, is called *will*. Its hindrance through an obstacle which places itself between it and its temporary aim we call *suffering*, and, on the other hand, its attainment of the end satisfaction, well-being, happiness. We may also transfer this terminology to the phenomena of the unconscious world, for though weaker in degree, they are identical in nature. Then we see them involved in constant suffering, and without any continuing happiness. For all effort springs from defect—from discontent with one's estate—is thus suffering so long as it is not satisfied; but no satisfaction is lasting, rather it is always merely the starting-point of a new effort. The striving we see everywhere hindered in many ways, everywhere in conflict, and therefore always under the form of suffering. Thus, if there is no final end of striving, there is no measure and end of suffering.

But what we only discover in unconscious Nature by sharpened observation, and with an effort, presents itself distinctly to us in the intelligent world in the life of animals, whose constant suffering is easily proved. But without lingering over these intermediate grades, we shall turn to the life of man, in which all this appears with the greatest distinctness, illuminated by the clearest knowledge; for as the phenomenon of will becomes more complete, the suffering also becomes more and more apparent. In the plant here is as yet no sensibility, and therefore no pain. A certain very small degree of suffering is experienced by the lowest species of animal life—infusoria and radiata; even in insects the capacity to feel and suffer is still limited. It first appears in a high degree with the complete nervous system of vertebrate animals, and always in a higher degree the more intelligence devolops. Thus, in proportion as knowledge attains to distinctness, as consciousness ascends, pain also increases, and therefore reaches its highest degree in man. And then, again, the more distinctly a man knows, the more intelligent he is, the more pain he has; the man who is gifted with genius suffers most of all. In this sense, that is, with reference to the degree of knowledge in general, not mere abstract rational knowledge, I understand and use here that saying of the Preacher: *Qui auget scientiam, auget et dolorem.* That philosophical painter or painting philosopher, Tischbein, has very beautifully expressed the accurate relation between the degree of consciousness and that of suffering by exhibiting it in a visible and clear form in a drawing. The upper half of his drawing represents women whose children have been stolen, and who in different groups and attitudes, express in many ways deep maternal pain, anguish, and despair. The lower half of the drawing represents sheep whose lambs have been taken away. They are arranged and grouped in precisely the same way; so that every human head, every human attitude of the upper half, has below a brute head and attitude corresponding to it. Thus we see distinctly how the pain which is possible in the dull brute consciousness is related to the violent grief, which only becomes possible through distinctness of knowledge and clearness of consciousness.

We desire to consider in this way, in *human existence*, the inner and essential destiny of will. Every one will easily recognise that same destiny expressed in various degrees in the life of the brutes, only more weakly, and may also convince himself to his own satisfaction, from the suffering animal world, *how essential to all life is suffering*.

§ 57. At every grade that is enlightened by knowledge, the will appears as an individual. The human individual finds himself as finite in infinite space and time, and consequently as a vanishing quantity compared with them. He is projected into them, and, on account of their unlimited nature, he has always a merely relative, never absolute *when* and *where* of his existence; for his place and duration are finite parts of what is infinite and boundless. His real existence is only in the present, whose unchecked flight into the past is a constant transition into death, a constant dying. For his past life, apart from its possible consequences for the present, and the testimony regarding the will that is expressed in it, is now entirely done with, dead, and no longer anything; and, therefore, it must be, as a matter of reason, indifferent to him whether the content of that past was pain or pleasure. But the present is always passing through his hands into the past; the future is quite uncertain and always short. Thus his existence, even when we consider only its formal side, is a constant hurrying of the present into the dead past, a constant dying. But if we look at it from the physical side; it is clear that, as our walking is admittedly merely a constantly prevented falling, the life of our body is only a constantly prevented dying, an ever-postponed death: finally, in the same way, the activity of our mind is a constantly deferred ennui. Every breath we draw wards off the death that is constantly intruding upon us. In this way we fight with it every moment, and again, at longer intervals, through every meal we eat, every sleep we take, every time we warm ourselves, &c. In the end, death must conquer, for we became subject to him through birth, and he only plays for a little while with his prey before he swallows it up. We pursue our life, however, with great interest and much solicitude as long as possible, as we blow out a soap-bubble as long and as large as possible, although we know perfectly well that it will burst.

We saw that the inner being of unconscious nature is a constant striving without end and without rest. And this appears to us much more distinctly when we consider the nature of brutes and man. Willing and striving is its whole being, which may be very well compared to an unquenchable thirst. But the basis of all willing is need, deficiency, and thus pain. Consequently, the nature of brutes and man is subject to pain originally and through its very being. If, on the other hand, it lacks objects of desire, because it is at once deprived of them by a too easy satisfaction, a terrible void and ennui comes over it, i.e., its being and existence itself becomes an unbearable burden to it. Thus its life swings like a pendulum backwards and forwards between pain and ennui. This has also had to express itself very oddly in this way; after man had transferred all pain and torments to hell, there then remained nothing over for heaven but ennui.

But the constant striving which constitutes the inner nature of every manifestation of will obtains its primary and most general foundation at the higher grades of objectification, from the fact that here the will manifests itself as a living body, with the iron command to nourish it; and what gives strength to this command is just that this body is nothing but the objectified will to live itself. Man, as the most complete objectification of that will, is in like measure also the most necessitous of all beings: he is through and through concrete willing and needing; he is a concretion of a thousand necessities. With these he stands upon the earth, left to himself, uncertain about everything except his own need and misery. Consequently the care for the maintenance of that existence under exacting demands, which are renewed every day, occupies, as a rule, the whole of human life. To this is directly related the second claim, that of the propagation of the species. At the same time he is threatened from all sides by the most different kinds of dangers, from which it requires constant watchfulness to escape. With cautious steps and casting anxious glances round him he pursues his path, for a thousand accidents and a thousand enemies lie in wait for him. Thus he went while yet a savage, thus he goes in civilised life; there is no security for him.

The life of the great majority is only a constant struggle for this existence itself, with the certainty of losing it at last. But what enables them to endure this wearisome battle is not so much the love of life as the fear of death, which yet stands in the background as inevitable, and may come upon them at any moment. Life itself is a sea, full of rocks and whirlpools, which man avoids with the greatest care and solicitude, although he knows that even if he succeeds in getting through with all his efforts and skill, he yet by doing so comes nearer at every step to the greatest, the total, inevitable, and irremediable shipwreck, death; nay, even steers right upon it: this is the final goal of the laborious voyage, and worse for him than all the rocks from which he has escaped.

Now it is well worth observing that, on the one hand, the suffering and misery of life may easily increase to such an extent that death itself, in the flight from which the whole of life consists, becomes desirable, and we hasten towards it voluntarily; and again, on the other hand, that as soon as want and suffering permit rest to a man, ennui is at once so near that he necessarily requires diversion. The striving after existence is what occupies all living things and maintains them in motion. But when existence is assured, then they know not what to do with it; thus the second thing that sets them in motion is the effort to get free from the burden of existence, to make it cease to be felt, "to kill time," *i.e.*, to escape from ennui. Accordingly we see that almost all men who are secure from want and care, now that at last they have thrown off all other burdens, become a burden to themselves, and regard as a gain every hour they succeed in getting through, and thus every diminution of the very life which, till then, they have employed all their powers to maintain as long as possible. Ennui is by no means an evil to be lightly esteemed; in the end it depicts on the countenance real despair. It makes beings who love each other so little as men do, seek each other eagerly, and thus becomes the source of social intercourse. Moreover, even from motives of policy, public precautions are everywhere taken against it, as against other universal calamities. For this evil may drive men to the greatest excesses, just as much as its opposite extreme, famine: the people require *panem et circenses*. The strict penitentiary system of Philadelphia makes use of ennui alone as a means of punishment, through solitary confinement and idleness, and it is found so terrible that it has even led prisoners to commit suicide. As want is the constant scourge of the people, so ennui is that of the fashionable world. In middle-class life ennui is represented by the Sunday, and want by the six week-days.

Thus between desiring and attaining all human life flows on throughout. The wish is, in its nature, pain; the attain-

ment soon begets satiety: the end was only apparent; possession takes away the charm; the wish, the need, presents itself
under a new form; when it does not, then follows desolate-
ness, emptiness, ennui, against which the conflict is just as
painful as against want.

That wish and satisfaction should follow each other
neither too quickly nor too slowly reduces the suffering,
which both occasion to the smallest amount, and constitutes
the happiest life. For that which we might otherwise call the
most beautiful part of life, its purest joy, if it were only
because it lifts us out of real existence and transforms us
into disinterested spectators of it—that is, pure knowledge,
which is foreign to all willing, the pleasure of the beautiful,
the true delight in art—this is granted only to a very few,
because it demands rare talents, and to these few, only as a
passing dream. And then, even these few, on account of
their higher intellectual power, are made susceptible of far
greater suffering than duller minds can ever feel, and are
also placed in lonely isolation by a nature which is obviously
different from that of others; thus here also accounts are
squared. But to the great majority of men purely intellectual pleasures are not accessible. They are almost quite incapable of the joys which lie in pure knowledge. They are
entirely given up to willing. If, therefore, anything is to
win their sympathy, to be *interesting* to them, it must (as
is implied in the meaning of the word) in some way excite
their *will*, even if it is only through a distant and merely
problematical relation to it; the will must not be left altogether out of the question, for their existence lies far more
in willing than in knowing,—action and reaction is their
one element. We may find in trifles and everyday occur-
rences the naïve expressions of this quality. Thus, for example, at any place worth seeing they may visit, they write
their names, in order thus to react, to affect the place since
it does not affect them. Again, when they see a strange, rare

animal, they cannot easily confine themselves to merely observing it; they must rouse it, tease it, play with it, merely
to experience action and reaction; but this need for excitement of the will manifests itself very specially in the discovery and support of card-playing, which is quite peculiarly the expression of the miserable side of humanity.

But whatever nature and fortune may have done, whoever a man be and whatever he may possess, the pain which
is essential to life cannot be thrown off. The ceaseless efforts to banish suffering accomplish no more than to make
it change its form. It is essentially deficiency, want, care for
the maintenance of life. If we succeed, which is very difficult, in removing pain in this form, it immediately
assumes a thousand others, varying according to age and
circumstances, such as lust, passionate love, jealousy, envy,
hatred, anxiety, ambition, covetousness, sickness, &c, &c.
If at last it can find entrance in no other form it comes in
the sad, grey garments of tediousness and ennui, against
which we then strive in various ways. If finally we succeed
in driving this away, we shall hardly do so without letting
pain enter in one of its earlier forms, and the dance begin
again from the beginning; for all human life is tossed
backwards and forwards between pain and ennui. Depress-
ing as this view of life is, I will draw attention, by the way,
to an aspect of it from which consolation may be drawn,
and perhaps even a stoical indifference to one's own present
ills may be attained. For our impatience at these arises for
the most part from the fact that we regard them as brought
about by a chain of causes which might easily be different.
We do not generally grieve over ills which are directly
necessary and quite universal; for example, the necessity of
age and of death, and many daily inconveniences. It is
rather the consideration of the accidental nature of the circumstances that brought some sorrow just to us, that gives
it its sting. But if we have recognised that pain, as such, is

inevitable and essential to life, and that nothing depends upon chance but its mere fashion, the form under which it presents itself, that thus our present sorrow fills a place that, without it, would at once be occupied by another which now is excluded by it, and that therefore fate can affect us little in what is essential; such a reflection, if it were to become a living conviction, might produce a considerable degree of stoical equanimity, and very much lessen the anxious care for our own well-being. But, in fact, such a powerful control of reason over directly felt suffering seldom or never occurs.

Besides, through this view of the inevitableness of pain, of the supplanting of one pain by another, and the introduction of a new pain through the passing away of that which preceded it, one might be led to the paradoxical but not absurd hypothesis, that in every individual the measure of the pain essential to him was determined once for all by his nature, a measure which could neither remain empty, nor be more than filled, however much the form of the suffering might change. Thus his suffering and well-being would by no means be determined from without, but only through that measure, that natural disposition, which indeed might experience certain additions and diminutions from the physical condition at different times, but yet, on the whole, would remain the same. This hypothesis is supported not only by the well-known experience that great suffering makes all lesser ills cease to be felt, and conversely that freedom from great suffering makes even the most trifling inconveniences torment us and put us out of humour; but experience also teaches that if a great misfortune, at the mere thought of which we shuddered, actually befalls us, as soon as we have overcome the first pain of it, our disposition remains for the most part unchanged; and, conversely, that after the attainment of some happiness we have long desired, we do not feel ourselves on the whole and permanently very much better off and more agreeably situated than before. Only the moment at which these changes occur affects us with unusual strength, as deep sorrow or exulting joy, but both soon pass away, for they are based upon illusion. For they do not spring from the immediately present pleasure or pain, but only from the opening up of a new future which is anticipated in them. Only by borrowing from the future could pain or pleasure be heightened so abnormally, and consequently not enduringly. It would follow, from the hypothesis advanced, that a large part of the feeling of suffering and of well-being would be subjective and determined *a priori*, as is the case with knowing; and we may add the following remarks as evidence in favour of it. Human cheerfulness or dejection are manifestly not determined by external circumstances, such as wealth and position, for we see at least as many glad faces among the poor as among the rich. Further, the motives which induce suicide are so very different, that we can assign no motive that is so great as to bring it about, even with great probability, in every character, and few that would be so small that the like of them had never caused it. Now, although the degree of our serenity or sadness is not at all times the same, yet, in consequence of this view, we shall not attribute it to the change of outward circumstances, but to that of the inner condition, the physical state. For when an actual, though only temporary, increase of our serenity, even to the extent of joyfulness, takes place, it usually appears without any external occasion. It is true that we often see our pain arise only from some definite external relation, and are visibly oppressed and saddened by this only. Then we believe that if only this were taken away, the greatest contentment would necessarily ensue. But this is illusion. The measure of our pain and our happiness is on the whole, according to our hypothesis, subjectively determined for each point of time, and the motive for sadness is related to that, just as a blister which draws to a head all the bad humours otherwise distributed is related to the body. The pain which is at that period of time essential to our nature, and therefore cannot be shaken off, would, without the definite external cause of our suffering, be divided at a hundred points, and appear in the form of a hundred little annoyances and cares about things which we now entirely overlook, because our capacity for pain is already filled by that chief evil which has concentrated in a point all the suffering otherwise dispersed. This corresponds also to the observation that if a great and pressing care is lifted from our breast by its fortunate issue, another immediately takes its place, the whole material of which was already there before, yet could not come into consciousness as care because there was no capacity left for it, and therefore this material of care remained indistinct and unobserved in a cloudy form on the farthest horizon of consciousness. But now that there is room, this prepared material at once comes forward and occupies the throne of the reigning care of the day (πρυτανευουσα). And if it is very much lighter in its matter than the material of the care which has vanished, it knows how to blow itself out so as apparently to equal it in size, and thus, as the chief care of the day, completely fills the throne.

Excessive joy and very keen suffering always occur in the same person, for they condition each other reciprocally, and are also in common conditioned by great activity of the mind. Both are produced, as we have just seen, not by what is really present, but by the anticipation of the future. But since pain is essential to life, and its degree is also determined by the nature of the subject, sudden changes, because they are always external, cannot really alter its degree. Thus an error and delusion always lies at the foundation of immoderate joy or grief, and consequently both these excessive strainings of the mind can be avoided by knowledge.

Every immoderate joy (*exultatio, insolens lœtitia*) always rests on the delusion that one has found in life what can never be found there—lasting satisfaction of the harassing desires and cares, which are constantly breeding new ones. From every particular delusion of this kind one must inevitably be brought back later, and then when it vanishes must pay for it with pain as bitter as the joy its entrance caused was keen. So far, then, it is precisely like a height from which one can come down only by a fall. Therefore one ought to avoid them; and every sudden excessive grief is just a fall from some such height, the vanishing of such a delusion, and so conditioned by it. Consequently we might avoid them both if we had sufficient control over ourselves to survey things always with perfect clearness as a whole and in their connection, and steadfastly to guard against really lending them the colours which we wish they had. The principal effort of the Stoical ethics was to free the mind from all such delusion and its consequences, and to give it instead an equanimity that could not be disturbed. It is this insight that inspires Horace in the well-known ode—

> "*Æquam memento rebus in arduïs*
> *Servare mentem, non secus in bonis*
> *Ab insolenti temperatam*
> *Lœtitia.*"

For the most part, however, we close our minds against the knowledge, which may be compared to a bitter medicine, that suffering is essential to life, and therefore does not flow in upon us from without, but that every one carries about with him its perennial source in his own heart. We rather seek constantly for an external particular cause, as it were, a pretext for the pain which never leaves us, just as the free man makes himself an idol, in order to have a master. For we unweariedly strive from wish to wish; and although every satisfaction, however much it promised, when attained fails to satisfy us, but for the most part comes presently to be an error of which we are ashamed, yet we do not see that we draw water with the sieve of the Danaides, but ever hasten to new desires. Thus it either goes on for ever, or, what is more rare and presupposes a certain strength of character, till we reach a wish which is not satisfied and yet cannot be given up. In that case we have, as it were, found what we sought, something that we can always blame, instead of our own nature, as the source of our suffering. And thus, although we are now at variance with our fate, we are reconciled to our existence, for the knowledge is again put far from us that suffering is essential to this existence itself, and true satisfaction impossible. The result of this form of development is a somewhat melancholy disposition, the constant endurance of a single great pain, and the contempt for all lesser sorrows or joys that proceeds from it; consequently an already nobler phenomenon than that constant seizing upon ever-new forms of illusion, which is much more common.

§ 58. All satisfaction, or what is commonly called happiness, is always really and essentially only *negative,* and never positive. It is not an original gratification coming to us of itself, but must always be the satisfaction of a wish. The wish, *i.e.,* some want, is the condition which precedes every pleasure. But with the satisfaction the wish and therefore the pleasure cease. Thus the satisfaction or the pleasing can never be more than the deliverance from a pain, from a want; for such is not only every actual, open sorrow, but every desire, the importunity of which disturbs our peace, and, indeed, the deadening ennui also that makes life a burden to us. It is, however, so hard to attain or achieve anything; difficulties and troubles without end are opposed to every purpose, and at every step hindrances accumulate. But when finally everything is overcome and attained, nothing can ever be gained but deliverance from some sorrow or desire, so that we find ourselves just in the same position as we occupied before this sorrow or desire appeared. All that is even directly given us is merely the want, *i.e.*, the pain. The satisfaction and the pleasure we can only know indirectly through the remembrance of the preceding suffering and want, which ceases with its appearance. Hence it arises that we are not properly conscious of the blessings and advantages we actually possess, nor do we prize them, but think of them merely as a matter of course, for they gratify us only negatively by restraining suffering. Only when we have lost them do we become sensible of their value; for the want, the privation, the sorrow, is the positive, communicating itself directly to us. Thus also we are pleased by the remembrance of past need, sickness, want, and such like, because this is the only means of enjoying the present blessings. And, further, it cannot be denied that in this respect, and from this standpoint of egoism, which is the form of the will to live, the sight or the description of the sufferings of others affords us satisfaction and pleasure in precisely the way Lucretius beautifully and frankly expresses it in the beginning of the Second Book—

> "*Suave, mari magno, turbantibus æquora ventis,*
> *E terra magnum alterius spectare laborem:*
> *Non, quia vexari quemquam est jucunda voluptas;*
> *Sed, quibus ipse malis careas, quia cernere suave est.*"

That all happiness is only of a negative not a positive nature, that just on this account it cannot be lasting satisfaction and gratification, but merely delivers us from some pain or want which must be followed either by a new pain, or by languor, empty longing, and ennui; this finds support in art, that true mirror of the world and life, and especially in poetry. Every epic and dramatic poem can only represent a struggle, an effort, and fight for happiness, never enduring and complete happiness itself. It conducts its heroes through a thousand difficulties and dangers to the goal; as soon as this is reached, it hastens to let the curtain fall; for now there would remain nothing for it to do but to show that the glittering goal in which the hero expected to find happiness had only disappointed him, and that after its attainment he was no better off than before. Because a genuine enduring happiness is not possible, it cannot be the subject of art. Certainly the aim of the idyll is the description of such a happiness, but one also sees that the idyll as such cannot continue. The poet always finds that it either becomes epical in his hands, and in this case it is a very insignificant epic, made up of trifling sorrows, trifling delights, and trifling efforts—this is the commonest case—or else it becomes a merely descriptive poem, describing the beauty of nature, *i.e.*, pure knowing free from will, which certainly, as a matter of fact, is the only pure happiness, which is neither preceded by suffering or want, nor necessarily followed by repentance, sorrow, emptiness, or satiety; but this happiness cannot fill the whole life, but is only possible at moments. What we see in poetry we find again in music; in the melodies of which we have recognised the universal expression of the inmost history of the self-conscious will, the most secret life, longing, suffering, and delight; the ebb and flow of the human heart. Melody is always a deviation from the keynote through a thousand capricious wanderings, even to the most painful discord, and then a final return to the keynote which expresses the satisfaction and appeasing of the will, but with which nothing more can then be done, and the continuance of which any longer would only be a wearisome and unmeaning monotony corresponding to ennui.

All that we intend to bring out clearly through these investigations, the impossibility of attaining lasting satisfaction and the negative nature of all happiness, finds its explanation in what is shown at the conclusion of the Second Book: that the will, of which human life, like every phenomenon, is the objectification, is a striving without aim or end. We find the stamp of this endlessness imprinted upon all the parts of its whole manifestation, from its most universal form, endless time and space, up to the most perfect of all phenomena, the life and efforts of man. We may theoretically assume three extremes of human life, and treat them as elements of actual human life. First, the powerful will, the strong passions (Radscha-Guna). It appears in great historical characters; it is described in the epic and the drama. But it can also show itself in the little world, for the size of the objects is measured here by the degree in which they influence the will, not according to their external relations. Secondly, pure knowing, the comprehension of the Ideas, conditioned by the freeing of knowledge from the service of will: the life of genius (Satwa-Guna). Thirdly and lastly, the greatest lethargy of the will, and also of the knowledge attaching to it, empty longing, life-benumbing languor (Tama-Guna). The life of the individual, far from becoming permanently fixed in one of these extremes, seldom touches any of them, and is for the most part only a weak and wavering approach to one or the other side, a needy desiring of trifling objects, constantly recurring, and so escaping ennui. It is really incredible how meaningless and void of significance when looked at from without, how dull and unenlightened by intellect when felt from within, is the course of the life of the great majority of men. It is a weary longing and complaining, a dreamlike staggering through the four ages of life to death, accompanied by a series of trivial thoughts. Such men are like clockwork, which is wound up, and goes it knows not why; and every time a man is begotten and born, the clock of human life is wound up anew, to repeat the same old piece it has played innumerable times before, passage after passage, measure after measure, with insignificant variations. Every individual, every human being and his course of life, is but another short dream of the endless spirit of nature, of the persistent will to live; is only another fleeting form, which it carelessly sketches on its infinite page, space and time; allows to remain for a time so short that it vanishes into nothing in comparison with these, and then obliterates to make new room. And yet, and here lies the serious side of life, every one of these fleeting forms, these empty fancies, must be paid for by the whole will to live, in all its activity, with many and deep sufferings, and finally with a bitter death, long feared and coming at last. This is why the sight of a corpse makes us suddenly so serious.

The life of every individual, if we survey it as a whole and in general, and only lay stress upon its most significant features, is really always a tragedy, but gone through in detail, it has the character of a comedy. For the deeds and vexations of the day, the restless irritation of the moment, the desires and fears of the week, the mishaps of every hour, are all through chance, which is ever bent upon some jest, scenes of a comedy. But the never-satisfied wishes, the frustrated efforts, the hopes unmercifully crushed by fate, the unfortunate errors of the whole life, with increasing suffering and death at the end, are always a tragedy. Thus, as if fate would add derision to the misery of our existence, our life must contain all the woes of tragedy, and yet we cannot even assert the dignity of tragic characters, but in the broad detail of life must inevitably be the foolish characters of a comedy.

§ 59. If we have so far convinced ourselves *a priori*, by the most general consideration, by investigation of the primary and elemental features of human life, that in its whole plan it is capable of no true blessedness, but is in its very nature suffering in various forms, and throughout a state of misery, we might now awaken this conviction much more vividly within us if, proceeding more *a posteriori*, we were to turn to more definite instances, call up pictures to the fancy, and illustrate by examples the unspeakable misery which experience and history present, wherever one may look and in whatever direction one may seek. But the chapter would have no end, and would carry us far from the standpoint of the universal, which is essential to philosophy; and, moreover, such a description might easily be taken for a mere declamation on human misery, such as has often been given, and, as such, might be charged with one-sidedness, because it started from particular facts. From such a reproach and suspicion our perfectly cold and philosophical investigation of the inevitable suffering which is founded in the nature of life is free, for it starts from the universal and is conducted *a priori*. But confirmation *a posteriori* is everywhere easily obtained. Every one who has awakened from the first dream of youth, who has considered his own experience and that of others, who has studied himself in life, in the history of the past and of his own time, and finally in the works of the great poets, will, if his judgment is not paralysed by some indelibly imprinted prejudice, certainly arrive at the conclusion that this human world is the kingdom of chance and error, which rule without mercy in great things and in small, and along with which folly and wickedness also wield the scourge. Hence it arises that everything better only struggles through with difficulty; what is noble and wise seldom attains to expression, becomes effective and claims attention, but the absurd and the perverse in the sphere of thought, the dull and tasteless in the sphere of art, the wicked and deceitful in the sphere of action, really assert a supremacy, only disturbed by short interruptions. On the other hand, everything that is excellent is always a mere exception, one case in millions, and therefore, if it presents itself in a lasting work, this, when it has outlived the enmity of its contemporaries, exists in isolation, is preserved like a meteoric stone, sprung from an order of things different from that which prevails here. But as far as the life of the individual is concerned, every biography is the history of suffering, for every life is, as a rule, a continual series of great and small misfortunes, which each one conceals as much as possible, because he knows that others can seldom feel sympathy or compassion, but almost always satisfaction at the sight of the woes from which they are themselves for the moment exempt. But perhaps at the end of life, if a man is sincere and in full possession of his faculties, he will never wish to have it to live over again, but rather than this, he will much prefer absolute annihilation. The essential content of the famous soliloquy in "Hamlet" is briefly this: Our state is so wretched that absolute annihilation would be decidedly preferable. If suicide really offered us this, so that the alternative "to be or not to be," in the full sense of the word, was placed before us, then it would be unconditionally to be chosen as "a consummation devoutly to be wished." But there is something in us which tells us that this is not the case: suicide is not the end; death is not absolute annihilation. In like manner, what was said by the father of history [1] has not since him been contradicted, that no man has ever lived who has not wished more than once that he had not to live the following day. According to this, the brevity of life, which is so constantly lamented, may be the best quality it possesses. If, finally, we should bring clearly to a man's sight the terrible sufferings and miseries to which his life is constantly exposed, he would be seized with horror; and if we were to conduct the confirmed optimist through the hospitals, infirmaries, and surgical operating-rooms, through the prisons, torture-chambers, and slave-kennels, over battle-fields and places of execution; if we were to open to him all the dark abodes of misery, where it hides itself from the glance of cold curiosity, and, finally, allow him to glance into the starving dungeon of Ugolino, he, too, would understand at last the nature of this "best of

[1] Herodot. vii. 46.

possible worlds." For whence did Dante take the materials for his hell but from this our actual world? And yet he made a very proper hell of it. And when, on the other hand, he came to the task of describing heaven and its delights, he had an insurmountable difficulty before him, for our world affords no materials at all for this. Therefore there remained nothing for him to do but, instead of describing the joys of paradise, to repeat to us the instruction given him there by his ancestor, by Beatrice, and by various saints. But from this it is sufficiently clear what manner of world it is. Certainly human life, like all bad ware, is covered over with a false lustre: what suffers always conceals itself; on the other hand, whatever pomp or splendour any one can get, he makes a show of openly, and the more inner contentment deserts him, the more he desires to exist as fortunate in the opinion of others: to such an extent does folly go, and the opinion of others is a chief aim of the efforts of every one, although the utter nothingness of it is expressed in the fact that in almost all languages vanity, *vanitas*, originally signifies emptiness and nothingness. But under all this false show, the miseries of life can so increase —and this happens every day—that the death which hitherto has been feared above all things is eagerly seized upon. Indeed, if fate will show its whole malice, even this refuge is denied to the sufferer, and, in the hands of enraged enemies, he may remain exposed to terrible and slow tortures without remedy. In vain the sufferer then calls on his gods for help; he remains exposed to his fate without grace. But this irremediableness is only the mirror of the invincible nature of his will, of which his person is the objectivity. As little as an external power can change or suppress this will, so little can a foreign power deliver it from the miseries which proceed from the life which is the phenomenal appearance of that will. In the principal matter, as in everything else, a man is always thrown back upon himself. In vain does he make to himself gods in order to get from them by prayers and flattery what can only be accomplished by his own will-power. The Old Testament made the world and man the work of a god, but the New Testament saw that, in order to teach that holiness and salvation from the sorrows of this world can only come from the world itself, it was necessary that this god should become man. It is and remains the will of man upon which everything depends for him. Fanatics, martyrs, saints of every faith and name, have voluntarily and gladly endured every torture, because in them the will to live had suppressed itself; and then even the slow destruction of its phenomenon was welcome to them. But I do not wish to anticipate the later exposition. For the rest, I cannot here avoid the statement that, to me, *optimism*, when it is not merely the thoughtless talk of such as harbour nothing but words under their low foreheads, appears not merely as an absurd, but also as a really *wicked* way of thinking, as a bitter mockery of the unspeakable suffering of humanity. Let no one think that Christianity is favourable to optimism; for, on the contrary, in the Gospels world and evil are used as almost synonymous.

§ 60. We have now completed the two expositions it was necessary to insert; the exposition of the freedom of the will in itself together with the necessity of its phenomenon, and the exposition of its lot in the world which reflects its own nature, and upon the knowledge of which it has to assert or deny itself. Therefore we can now proceed to bring out more clearly the nature of this assertion and denial itself, which was referred to and explained in a merely general way above. This we shall do by exhibiting the conduct in which alone it finds its expression, and considering it in its inner significance.

The *assertion of the will* is the continuous willing itself, undisturbed by any knowledge, as it fills the life of man in general. For even the body of a man is the objectivity of the will, as it appears at this grade and in this individual. And thus his willing which develops itself in time is, as it were, a paraphrase of his body, an elucidation of the significance of the whole and its parts; it is another way of exhibiting the same thing-in-itself, of which the body is already the phenomenon. Therefore, instead of saying assertion of the will, we may say assertion of the body. The fundamental theme or subject of all the multifarious acts of will is the satisfaction of the wants which are inseparable from the existence of the body in health, they already have their expression in it, and may be referred to the maintenance of the individual and the propagation of the species. But indirectly the most different kinds of motives obtain in this way power over the will, and bring about the most multifarious acts of will. Each of these is only an example, an instance, of the will which here manifests itself generally. Of what nature this example may be, what form the motive may have and impart to it, is not essential; the important point here is that something is willed in general and the degree of intensity with which it is so willed. The will can only become visible in the motives, as the eye only manifests its power of seeing in the light. The motive in general stands before the will in protean forms. It constantly promises complete satisfaction, the quenching of the thirst of will. But whenever it is attained it at once appears in another form, and thus influences the will anew, always according to the degree of the intensity of this will and its relation to knowledge which are revealed as empirical character, in these very examples and instances.

From the first appearance of consciousness, a man finds himself a willing being, and as a rule, his knowledge remains in constant relation to his will. He first seeks to know thoroughly the objects of his desire, and then the means of attaining them. Now he knows what he has to do, and, as a rule, he does not strive after other knowledge. He moves and acts; his consciousness keeps him always working directly and actively towards the aims of his will; his thought is concerned with the choice of motives. Such is life for almost all men; they wish they know what they wish, and they strive after it, with sufficient success to keep them from despair, and sufficient failure to keep them from ennui and its consequences. From this proceeds a certain serenity, or at least indifference, which cannot be affected by wealth or poverty; for the rich and the poor do not enjoy what they have, for this, as we have shown, acts in a purely negative way, but what they hope to attain to by their efforts. They press forward with much earnestness, and indeed with an air of importance; thus children also pursue their play. It is always an exception if such a life suffers interruption from the fact that either the æsthetic demand for contemplation or the ethical demand for renunciation proceed from a knowledge which is independent of the service of the will, and directed to the nature of the world in general. Most men are pursued by want all through life, without ever being allowed to come to their senses. On the other hand, the will is often inflamed to a degree that far transcends the assertion of the body, and then violent emotions and powerful passions show themselves, in which the individual not only asserts his own existence, but denies and seeks to suppress that of others when it stands in his way.

The maintenance of the body through its own powers is so small a degree of the assertion of will, that if it voluntarily remains at this degree, we might assume that, with the death of this body, the will also which appeared in it would be extinguished. But even the satisfaction of the sexual passions goes beyond the assertion of one's own existence, which fills so short a time, and asserts life for an indefinite time after the death of the individual. Nature, always true and consistent, here even naïve, exhibits to us openly the inner significance of the act of generation. Our own consciousness, the intensity of the impulse, teaches us that in this act the most decided *assertion of the will to live* expresses itself, pure and without further addition (any denial of other individuals); and now, as the consequence of this act, a new life appears in time and the causal series, *i.e.*, in nature; the begotten appears before the begetter, different as regards the phenomenon, but in himself, *i.e.*, according to the Idea, identical with him. Therefore it is this act through which every species of living creature binds itself to a whole and is perpetuated. Generation is, with reference to the begetter, only the expression, the symptom, of his decided assertion of the will to live: with reference to the begotten, it is not the cause of the will which appears in him, for the will in itself knows neither cause nor effect, but, like all causes, it is merely the occasional cause of the phenomenal appearance of this will at this time in this place. As thing-in-itself, the will of the begetter and that of the begotten are not different, for only the phenomenon, not the thing-in-itself, is subordinate to the *principium individuationis*. With that assertion beyond our own body and extending to the production of a new body, suffering and death, as belonging to the phenomenon of life, have also been asserted anew, and the possibility of salvation, introduced by the completest capability of knowledge, has for this time been shown to be fruitless. Here lies the profound reason of the shame connected with the process of generation. This view is mythically expressed in the dogma of Christian theology that we are all partakers in Adam's first transgression (which is clearly just the satisfaction of sexual passion), and through it are guilty of suffering and death. In this theology goes beyond the consideration of things according to the principle of sufficient reason, and recognises the Idea of man, the unity of which is re-established out of its dispersion into innumerable individuals through the bond of generation which holds them all together. Accordingly it regards every individual as on one side identical with Adam, the representative of the assertion of life, and, so far, as subject to sin (original sin), suffering and death; on the other side, the knowledge of the Idea of man enables it to regard every individual as identical with the saviour, the representative of the denial of the will to live, and, so far as a partaker of his sacrifice of himself, saved through his merits, and delivered from the bands of sin and death, *i.e.*, the world (Rom. v. 12-21).

Another mythical exposition of our view of sexual pleasure as the assertion of the will to live beyond the individual life, as an attainment to life which is brought about for the first time by this means, or as it were a renewed assignment of life, is the Greek myth of Proserpine, who might return from the lower world so long as she had not tasted its fruit, but who became subject to it altogether through eating the pomegranate. This meaning appears very clearly in Goethe's incomparable presentation of this myth, especially when, as soon as she has tasted the pomegranate, the invisible chorus of the Fates—

> "Thou art ours!
> Fasting shouldest thou return:
> And the bite of the apple makes thee ours!"

The sexual impulse also proves itself the decided and strongest assertion of life by the fact that to man in a state of nature, as to the brutes, it is the final end, the highest goal of life. Self-maintenance is his first effort, and as soon as he has made provision for that, he only strives after the propagation of the species: as a merely natural being he can attempt no more. Nature also, the inner being of which is the will to live itself, impels with all her power both man and the brute towards propagation. Then it has attained its end with the individual, and is quite indifferent to its death, for, as the will to live, it cares only for the preservation of the species, the individual is nothing to it. Because the will to live expresses itself most strongly in the sexual impulse, the inner being of nature, the old poets and philosophers— Hesiod and Parmenides—said very significantly that Eros is the first, the creator, the principle from which all things proceed.

The genital organs are, far more than any other external member of the body, subject merely to the will, and not at all to knowledge. Indeed, the will shows itself here almost as independent of knowledge, as in those parts which, acting merely in consequence of stimuli, are subservient to vegetative life and reproduction, in which the will works blindly as in unconscious Nature. For generation is only reproduction passing over to a new individual, as it were reproduction at the second power, as death is only excretion at the second power. According to all this, the genitals are properly the *focus* of will, and consequently the opposite pole of the brain, the representative of knowledge, *i.e.*, the other side of the world, the world as idea. The former are the life-sustaining principle ensuring endless life to time. In this respect they were worshipped by the Greeks in the *phallus*, and by the Hindus in the *lingam*, which are thus the symbol of the assertion of the will. Knowledge, on the other hand, affords the possibility of the suppression of willing, of salvation through freedom, of conquest and annihilation of the world.

We already considered fully at the beginning of this Fourth Book how the will to live in its assertion must regard its relation to death. We saw that death does not trouble it, because it exists as something included in life itself and belonging to it. Its opposite, generation, completely counterbalances it; and, in spite of the death of the individual, ensures and guarantees life to the will to live through all time. To express this the Hindus made the *lingam* an attribute of Siva, the god of death. We also fully explained there how he who with full consciousness occupies the standpoint of the decided assertion of life awaits death without fear. We shall therefore say nothing more about this here. Without clear consciousness most men occupy this standpoint and continually assert life. The world exists as the mirror of this assertion, with innumerable individuals in infinite time and space, in infinite suffering, between generation and death without end. Yet from no side is a complaint to be further raised about this; for the will conducts the great tragedy and comedy at its own expense, and is also its own spectator. The world is just what it is, because the will, whose manifestation it is, is what it is, because it so wills. The justification of suffering is, that in this phenomenon also the will asserts itself; and this assertion is justified and balanced by the fact that the will bears the suffering. Here we get a glimpse of *eternal justice* in the whole: we shall recognise it later more definitely and distinctly, and also in the particular. But first we must consider temporal or human justice.[1]

§ 61. It may be remembered from the Second Book that in the whole of nature, at all the grades of the objectification of will, there was a necessary and constant conflict between the individuals of all species; and in this way was expressed the inner contradiction of the will to live with itself. At the highest grade of the objectification, this phenomenon, like all others, will exhibit itself with greater distinctness, and will therefore be more easily explained. With this aim we shall next attempt to trace the source of *egoism* as the starting-point of all conflict.

We have called time and space the *principium individuationis,* because only through them and in them is multiplicity of the homogeneous possible. They are the essential forms of natural knowledge, *i.e.,* knowledge springing from the will. Therefore the will everywhere manifests itself in the multiplicity of individuals. But this multiplicity

[1] Cf. Ch. xlv. of the Supplement.

does not concern the will as thing-in-itself, but only its phenomena. The will itself is present, whole and undivided, in every one of these, and beholds around it the innumerably repeated image of its own nature; but this nature itself, the actually real, it finds directly only in its inner self. Therefore every one desires everything for himself, desires to possess, or at least to control, everything, and whatever opposes it it would like to destroy. To this is added, in the case of such beings as have knowledge, that the individual is the supporter of the knowing subject, and the knowing subject is the supporter of the world, *i.e.*, that the whole of Nature outside the knowing subject, and thus all other individuals, exist only in its idea; it is only conscious of them as its idea, thus merely indirectly as something which is dependent on its own nature and existence; for with its consciousness the world necessarily disappears for it, *i.e.*, its being and non-being become synonymous and indistinguishable. Every knowing individual is thus in truth, and finds itself as the whole will to live, or the inner being of the world itself, and also as the complemental condition of the world as idea, consequently as a microcosm which is of equal value with the macrocosm. Nature itself, which is everywhere and always truthful, gives him this knowledge, originally and independently of all reflection, with simple and direct certainty. Now from these two necessary properties we have given the fact may be explained that every individual, though vanishing altogether and diminished to nothing in the boundless world, yet makes itself the centre of the world, has regard for its own existence and well-being before everything else; indeed, from the natural standpoint, is ready to sacrifice everything else for this—is ready to annihilate the world in order to maintain its own self, this drop in the ocean, a little longer. This disposition is *egoism*, which is essential to everything in Nature. Yet it is just through egoism that the inner conflict of the will with itself attains to such a terrible revelation; for this egoism has its continuance and being in that opposition of the microcosm and macrocosm, or in the fact that the objectification of will has the *principium individuationis* for its form, through which the will manifests itself in the same way in innumerable individuals, and indeed entire and completely in both aspects (will and idea) in each. Thus, while each individual is given to itself directly as the whole will and the whole subject of ideas, other individuals are only given it as ideas. Therefore its own being, and the maintenance of it, is of more importance to it than that of all others together. Every one looks upon his own death as upon the end of the world, while he accepts the death of his acquaintances as a matter of comparative indifference, if he is not in some way affected by it. In the consciousness that has reached the highest grade, that of man, egoism, as well as knowledge, pain, and pleasure, must have reached its highest grade also, and the conflict of individuals which is conditioned by it must appear in its most terrible form. And indeed we see this everywhere before our eyes, in small things as in great. Now we see its terrible side in the lives of great tyrants and miscreants, and in world-desolating wars; now its absurd side, in which it is the theme of comedy, and very specially appears as self-conceit and vanity. Rochefoucault understood this better than any one else, and presented it in the abstract. We see it both in the history of the world and in our own experience. But it appears most distinctly of all when any mob of men is set free from all law and order; then there shows itself at once in the distinctest form the *bellum omnium contra omnes*, which Hobbes has so admirably described in the first chapter *De Cive*. We see not only how every one tries to seize from the other what he wants himself, but how often one will destroy the whole happiness or life of another for the sake of an insignificant addition to his own happiness. This is the highest expression of egoism, the manifestations of which in this regard are only surpassed by those of actual wickedness which seeks, quite disinterestedly, the hurt and suffering of others, without any advantage to itself.

A chief source of that suffering which we found above to be essential and inevitable to all life is, when it really appears in a definite form, that *Eris,* the conflict of all individuals, the expression of the contradiction, with which the will to live is affected in its inner self, and which attains a visible form through the *principium individuationis.* Wild-beast fights are the most cruel means of showing this directly and vividly. In this original discord lies an unquenchable source of suffering, in spite of the precautions that have been taken against it, and which we shall now consider more closely.

§ 62. It has already been explained that the first and simplest assertion of the will to live is only the assertion of one's own body, *i.e.,* the exhibition of the will through acts in time, so far as the body, in its form and design, exhibits the same will in space, and no further. This assertion shows itself as maintenance of the body, by means of the application of its own powers. To it is directly related the satisfaction of the sexual impulse; indeed this belongs to it, because the genitals belong to the body. Therefore *voluntary* renunciation of the satisfaction of that impulse based upon no *motive,* is already a denial of the will to live, is a voluntary self-suppression of it, upon the entrance of knowledge which acts as a *quieter.* Accordingly such denial of one's own body exhibits itself as a contradiction by the will of its own phenomenon. For although here also the body objectifies in the genitals the will to perpetuate the species, yet this is not willed. Just on this account, because it is a denial or suppression of the will to live, such a renunciation is a hard and painful self-conquest. But since the will exhibits that *self-assertion* of one's own body in innumerable individuals beside each other, it very easily extends in one individual, on account of the egoism peculiar to them all, beyond this asertion to the *denial* of the same will appearing in another individual. The will of the first breaks through the limits of the assertion of will of another, because the individual either destroys or injures this other body itself, or else because it compels the powers of the other body to serve *its own* will, instead of the will which manifests itself in that other body. Thus if, from the will manifesting itself as another body, it withdraws the powers of this body, and so increases the power serving its own will beyond that of its own body, it consequently asserts its own will beyond its own body by means of the negation of the will appearing in another body. This breaking through the limits of the assertion of will of another has always been distinctly recognised, and its concept denoted by the word *wrong*. For both sides recognise the fact instantly, not, indeed, as we do here in distinct abstraction, but as feeling. He who suffers wrong feels the transgression into the sphere of the assertion of his own body, through the denial of it by another individual, as a direct and mental pain which is entirely separated and different from the accompanying physical suffering experienced from the act or the vexation at the loss. To the doer of wrong, on the other hand, the knowledge presents itself that he is in himself the same will which appears in that body also, and which asserts itself with such vehemence in the one phenomenon that, transgressing the limits of its own body and its powers, it extends to the denial of this very will in another phenomenon, and so, regarded as will in itself, it strives against itself by this vehemence and rends itself. Moreover, this knowledge presents itself to him instantly, not *in abstracto*, but as an obscure feeling; and this is called remorse, or, more accurately in this case, the feeling of *wrong committed*.

Wrong, the conception of which we have thus analysed

in its most general and abstract form, expresses itself in the concrete most completely, peculiarly, and palpably in cannibalism. This is its most distinct and evident type, the terrible picture of the greatest conflict of the will with itself at the highest grade of its objectification, which is man. Next to this, it expresses itself most distinctly in murder; and therefore the committal of murder is followed instantly and with fearful distinctness by remorse, the abstract and dry significance of which we have just given, which inflicts a wound on our peace of mind that a lifetime cannot heal. For our horror at the murder committed, as also our shrinking from the committal of it, corresponds to that infinite clinging to life with which everything living, as phenomenon of the will to live, is penetrated. Mutilation, or mere injury of another body, indeed every blow, is to be regarded as in its nature the same as murder, and differing from it only in degree. Further, wrong shows itself in the subjugation of another individual, in forcing him into slavery, and, finally, in the seizure of another's goods, which, so far as these goods are regarded as the fruit of his labour, is just the same thing as making him a slave, and is related to this as mere injury is to murder.

§ 63. We have recognised *temporal justice*, which has its seat in the state, as requiting and punishing, and have seen that this only becomes justice through a reference to the *future*. For without this reference all punishing and requiting would be an outrage without justification, and indeed merely the addition of another evil to that which has already occurred, without meaning or significance. But it is quite otherwise with *eternal justice*, which was referred to before, and which rules not the state but the world, is not dependent upon human institutions, is not subject to chance and deception, is not uncertain, wavering, and erring, but infallible, fixed, and sure. The conception of requital implies that of time; therefore *eternal justice* cannot be re-

quital. Thus it cannot, like temporal justice, admit of respite
and delay, and require time in order to triumph, equalising
the evil deed by the evil consequences only by means of
time. The punishment must here be so bound up with the
offence that both are one.

Now that such an eternal justice really lies in the nature
of the world will soon become completely evident to whoever has grasped the whole of the thought which we have
hitherto been developing.

The world, in all the multiplicity of its parts and forms,
is the manifestation, the objectivity, of the one will to live.
Existence itself, and the kind of existence, both as a collective whole and in every part, proceeds from the will alone.
The will is free, the will is almighty. The will appears in
everything, just as it determines itself in itself and outside
time. The world is only the mirror of this willing; and all
finitude, all suffering, all miseries, which it contains, belong
to the expression of that which the will wills, are as they
are because the will so wills. Accordingly with perfect right
every being supports existence in general, and also the existence of its species and its peculiar individuality, entirely
as it is and in circumstances as they are, in a world such as
it is, swayed by chance and error, transient, ephemeral, and
constantly suffering; and in all that it experiences, or indeed
can experience, it always gets its due. For the will belongs
to it; and as the will is, so is the world. Only this world
itself can bear the responsibility of its own existence and
nature—no other; for by what means could another have
assumed it? Do we desire to know what men, morally considered, are worth as a whole and in general, we have only
to consider their fate as a whole and in general. This is
want, wretchedness, affliction, misery, and death. Eternal
justice reigns; if they were not, as a whole, worthless, their
fate, as a whole, would not be so sad. In this sense we may
say, the world itself is the judgment of the world. If we

could lay all the misery of the world in one scale of the balance, and all the guilt of the world in the other, the needle would certainly point to the centre.

Certainly, however, the world does not exhibit itself to the knowledge of the individual as such, developed for the service of the will, as it finally reveals itself to the inquirer as the objectivity of the one and only will to live, which he himself is. But the sight of the uncultured individual is clouded, as the Hindus say, by the veil of Mâyâ. He sees not the thing-in-itself but the phenomenon in time and space, the *principium individuationis*, and in the other forms of the principle of sufficient reason. And in this form of his limited knowledge he sees not the inner nature of things, which is one, but its phenomena as separated, disunited, innumerable, very different, and indeed opposed. For to him pleasure appears as one thing and pain as quite another thing: one man as a tormentor and a murderer, another as a martyr and a victim; wickedness as one thing and evil as another. He sees one man live in joy, abundance, and pleasure, and even at his door another die miserably of want and cold. Then he asks, Where is the retribution? And he himself, in the vehement pressure of will which is his origin and his nature, seizes upon the pleasures and enjoyments of life, firmly embraces them, and knows not that by this very act of his will he seizes and hugs all those pains and sorrows at the sight of which he shudders. He sees the ills and he sees the wickedness in the world, but far from knowing that both of these are but different sides of the manifestation of the one will to live, he regards them as very different, and indeed quite opposed, and often seeks to escape by wickedness, *i.e.*, by causing the suffering of another, from ills, from the suffering of his own individuality, for he is involved in the *principium individuationis*, deluded by the veil of Mâyâ. Just as a sailor sits in a boat trusting to his frail barque in a stormy sea, unbounded in every direction,

rising and falling with the howling mountainous waves;
so in the midst of a world of sorrows the individual man sits
quietly, supported by and trusting to the *principium individuationis*, or the way in which the individual knows things
as phenomena. The boundless world, everywhere full of
suffering in the infinite past, in the infinite future, is strange
to him, indeed is to him but a fable; his ephemeral person,
his extensionless present, his momentary satisfaction, this
alone has reality for him; and he does all to maintain this,
so long as his eyes are not opened by a better knowledge.
Till then, there lives only in the inmost depths of his consciousness a very obscure presentiment that all that is after
all not really so strange to him, but has a connection with
him, from which the *principium individuationis* cannot pro-
tect him. From this presentiment arises that ineradicable *awe*
common to all men (and indeed perhaps even to the most
sensible of the brutes) which suddenly seizes them if by any
chance they become puzzled about the *principium individuationis*, because the principle of sufficient reason in some one
of its forms seems to admit of an exception. For example, if
it seems as if some change took place without a cause, or some
one who is dead appears again, or if in any other way the
past or the future becomes present or the distant becomes
near. The fearful terror at anything of the kind is founded
on the fact that they suddenly become puzzled about the
forms of knowledge of the phenomenon, which alone separate their own individuality from the rest of the world.
But even this separation lies only in the phenomenon, and
not in the thing-in-itself; and on this rests eternal justice.
In fact, all temporal happiness stands, and all prudence proceeds, upon ground that is undermined. They defend the
person from accidents and supply its pleasures; but the person is merely phenomenon, and its difference from other
individuals, and exemption from the sufferings which they
endure, rests merely in the form of the phenomenon, the

principium individuationis. According to the true nature of things, every one has all the suffering of the world as his own, and indeed has to regard all merely possible suffering as for him actual, so long as he is the fixed will to live, *i.e.*, asserts life with all his power. For the knowledge that sees through the *principium individuationis*, a happy life in time, the gift of chance or won by prudence, amid the sorrows of innumerable others, is only the dream of a beggar in which he is a king, but from which he must awake and learn from experience that only a fleeting illusion had separated him from the suffering of his life.

Eternal justice withdraws itself from the vision that is involved in the knowledge which follows the principle of sufficient reason in the *principium individuationis;* such vision misses it altogether unless it vindicates it in some way by fictions. It sees the bad, after misdeeds and cruelties of every kind, live in happiness and leave the world unpunished. It sees the oppressed drag out a life full of suffering to the end without an avenger, a requiter appearing. But that man only will grasp and comprehend eternal justice who raises himself above the knowledge that proceeds under the guidance of the principle of sufficient reason, bound to the particular thing, and recognises the Ideas, sees through the *principium individuationis*, and becomes conscious that the forms of the phenomenon do not apply to the thing-in-itself. Moreover, he alone, by virtue of the same knowledge, can understand the true nature of virtue, as it will soon disclose itself to us in connection with the present inquiry, although for the practice of virtue this knowledge in the abstract is by no means demanded. Thus it becomes clear to whoever has attained to the knowledge referred to, that because the will is the in-itself of all phenomena, the misery which is awarded to others and that which he experiences himself, the bad and the evil, always concerns only that one inner being which is everywhere the same, although the phenomena in which the one and the other exhibits itself exists as quite different individuals, and are widely separated by time and space. He sees that the difference between him who inflicts the suffering and him who must bear it is only the phenomenon, and does not concern the thing-in-itself, for this is the will living in both, which here, deceived by the knowledge which is bound to its service, does not recognise itself, and seeking an increased happiness in *one* of its phenomena, produces great suffering in *another*, and thus, in the pressure of excitement, buries its teeth in its own flesh, not knowing that it always injures only itself, revealing in this form, through the medium of individuality, the conflict with itself which it bears in its inner nature. The inflicter of suffering and the sufferer are one. The former errs in that he believes he is not a partaker in the suffering; the latter, in that he believes he is not a partaker in the guilt. If the eyes of both were opened, the inflicter of suffering would see that he lives in all that suffers pain in the wide world, and which, if endowed with reason, in vain asks why it was called into existence for such great suffering, its desert of which it does not understand. And the sufferer would see that all the wickedness which is or ever was committed in the world proceeds from that will which constitutes *his* own nature also, appears also in *him*, and that through this phenomenon and its assertion he has taken upon himself all the sufferings which proceed from such a will and bears them as his due, so long as he is this will. From this knowledge speaks the profound poet Calderon in "Life a Dream"—

> "For the greatest crime of man
> Is that he ever was born."

Why should it not be a crime, since, according to an eternal law, death follows upon it? Calderon has merely expressed in these lines the Christian dogma of original sin.

The living knowledge of eternal justice, of the balance that inseparably binds together the *malum culpæ* with the *malum pœnæ*, demands the complete transcending of individuality and the principle of its possibility. Therefore it will always remain unattainable to the majority of men, as will also be the case with the pure and distinct knowledge of the nature of all virtue, which is akin to it, and which we are about to explain. Accordingly the wise ancestors of the Hindu people have directly expressed it in the Vedas, which are only allowed to the three regenerate castes, or in their esoteric teaching, so far at any rate as conception and language comprehend it, and their method of exposition, which always remains pictorial and even rhapsodical, admits; but in the religion of the people, or exoteric teaching, they only communicate it by means of myths. The direct exposition we find in the Vedas, the fruit of the highest human knowledge and wisdom, the kernel of which has at last reached us in the Upanishads as the greatest gift of this century. It is expressed in various ways, but especially by making all the beings in the world, living and lifeless, pass successively before the view of the student, and pronouncing over every one of them that word which has become a formula, and as such has been called the Mahavakya: Tatoumes,—more correctly, Tat twam asi,—which means, "This thou art."[1] But for the people, that great truth, so far as in their limited condition they could comprehend it, was translated into the form of knowlege which follows the principle of sufficient reason. This form of knowledge is indeed, from its nature, quite incapable of apprehending that truth pure and in itself, and even stands in contradiction to it, yet in the form of a myth it received a substitute for it which was sufficient as a guide for conduct. For the myth enables the method of knowledge, in accordance with the principle of sufficient reason, to comprehend by figura-

[1] Oupnek'hat, vol. i. p. 60 et seq.

tive representation the ethical significance of conduct, which itself is ever foreign to it. This is the aim of all systems of religion, for as a whole they are the mythical clothing of the truth which is unattainable to the uncultured human intellect. In this sense this myth might, in Kant's language, be called a postulate of the practical reason; but regarded as such, it has the great advantage that it contains absolutely no elements but such as lie before our eyes in the course of actual experience, and can therefore support all its conceptions with perceptions. What is here referred to is the myth of the transmigration of souls. It teaches that all sufferings which in life one inflicts upon other beings must be expiated in a subsequent life in this world, through precisely the same sufferings; and this extends so far, that he who only kills a brute must, some time in endless time, be born as the same kind of brute and suffer the same death. It teaches that wicked conduct involves a future life in this world in suffering and despised creatures, and, accordingly, that one will then be born again in lower castes, or as a woman, or as a brute, as Pariah or Tschandala, as a leper, or as a crocodile, and so forth. All the pains which the myth threatens it supports with perceptions from actual life, through suffering creatures which do not know how they have merited their misery, and it does not require to call in the assistance of any other hell. As a reward, on the other hand, it promises rebirth, in better, nobler forms, as Brahmans, wise men or saints. The highest reward, which awaits the noblest deeds and the completest resignation, which is also given to the woman who in seven successive lives has voluntarily died on the funeral pile of her husband, and not less to the man whose pure mouth has never uttered a single lie,—this reward the myth can only express negatively in the language of this world by the promise, which is so often repeated, that they shall never be born again, *Non adsumes iterum existentiam apparentem;* or, as the Buddhists, who recognise neither Vedas nor castes, express it, "Thou shalt attain to Nirvâna," *i.e.*, to a state in which four things no longer exist—birth, age, sickness, and death.

Never has a myth entered, and never will one enter, more closely into the philosophical truth which is attainable to so few than this primitive doctrine of the noblest and most ancient nation. Broken up as this nation now is into many parts, this myth yet reigns as the universal belief of the people, and has the most decided influence upon life to-day, as four thousand years ago. Therefore Pythagoras and Plato have seized with admiration on that *ne plus ultra* of mythical representation, received it from India or Egypt, honoured it, made use of it, and, we know not how far, even believed it. We, on the contrary, now send the Brahmans English clergymen and evangelical linen-weavers to set them right out of sympathy, and to show them that they are created out of nothing, and ought thankfully to rejoice in the fact. But it is just the same as if we fired a bullet against a cliff. In India our religions will never take root. The ancient wisdom of the human race will not be displaced by what happened in Galilee. On the contrary, Indian philosophy streams back to Europe, and will produce a fundamental change in our knowledge and thought.

§ 65. In all the preceding investigations of human action, we have been leading up to the final investigation, and have to a considerable extent lightened the task of raising to abstract and philosophical clearness, and exhibiting as a branch of our central thought that special ethical significance of action which in life is with perfect understanding denoted by the words *good* and *bad*.

First, however, I wish to trace back to their real meaning those conceptions of *good* and *bad* which have been treated by the philosophical writers of the day, very extraordinarily, as simple conceptions, and thus incapable of analysis; so that

the reader may not remain involved in the senseless delusion that they contain more than is actually the case, and
express in and for themselves all that is here necessary.
I am in a position to do this because in ethics I am no more
disposed to take refuge behind the word *good* than formerly
behind the words *beautiful* and *true*, in order that by the
adding a "ness," which at the present day is supposed to have
a special σεμνοτης, and therefore to be of assistance in various cases, and by assuming an air of solemnity, I might induce the belief that by uttering three such words I had done
more than denote three very wide and abstract, and consequently empty conceptions, of very different origin and significance. Who is there, indeed, who has made himself ac-
quainted with the books of our own day to whom these three
words, admirable as are the things to which they originally
refer, have not become an aversion after he has seen for
the thousandth time how those who are least capable of
thinking believe that they have only to utter these three
words with open mouth and the air of an intelligent sheep,
in order to have spoken the greatest wisdom?

The explanation of the concept *true* has already been
given in the essay on the principle of sufficient reason, chap.
v § 29 *et seq.* The content of the concept *beautiful* found
for the first time its proper explanation throung the whole
of the Third Book of the present work. We now wish to
discover the significance of the concept *good*, which can be
done with very little trouble. This concept is essentially
relative, and signifies *the conformity of an object to any
definite effort of the will.* Accordingly everything that corresponds to the will in any of its expressions and fulfils its
end is thought through the concept *good*, however different
such things may be in other respects. Thus we speak of good
eating, good roads, good weather, good weapons, good
omens, and so on; in short, we call everything good that
is just as we wish it to be; and therefore that may be good

in the eyes of one man which is just the reverse in those of another. The conception of the good divides itself into two sub-species—that of the direct and present satisfaction of any volition, and that of its indirect satisfaction which has reference to the future, *i.e.*, the agreeable, and the useful. The conception of the opposite, so long as we are speaking of unconscious existence, is expressed by the word *bad*, more rarely and abstractly by the word *evil*, which thus denotes everything that does not correspond to any effort of the will. Like all other things that can come into relation to the will, men who are favourable to the ends which happen to be desired who further and befriend them, are called good in the same sense, and always with that relative limitation, which shows itself, for example, in the expression, "I find this good, but you don't." Those, however, who are naturally disposed not to hinder the endeavours of others, but rather to assist them, and who are thus consistently helpful, benevolent, friendly, and charitable, are called *good* men, on account of this relation of their conduct to the will of others in general. In the case of conscious beings (brutes and men) the contrary conception is denoted in German, and, within the last hundred years or so, in French also, by a different word from that which is used in speaking of unconscious existence; in German, *böse;* in French, *méchant;* while in almost all other languages this distinction does not exist; and κακος, *malus, cattivo, bad*, are used of men, as of lifeless things, which are opposed to the ends of a definite individual will. Thus, having started entirely from the passive element to the good, the inquiry could only proceed later to the active element, and investigate the conduct of the man who is called good, no longer with reference to others, but to himself; specially setting itself the task of explaining both the purely objective respect which such conduct produces in others, and the peculiar contentment with himself which it clearly produces in the man himself, since he purchases it with sacrifices of another kind; and also, on the other hand, the inner pain which accompanies the bad disposition, whatever outward advantages it brings to him who entertains it. It was from this source that the ethical systems, both the philosophical and those which are supported by systems of religion, took their rise. Both seek constantly in some way or other to connect happiness with virtue, the former either by means of the principle of contradiction or that of sufficient reason, and thus to make happiness either identical with or the consequence of virtue, always sophistically; the latter, by asserting the existence of other worlds than that which alone can be known to experience. In our system, on the contrary, virtue will show itself, not as a striving after happiness, that is, well-being and life, but as an effort in quite an opposite direction.

It follows from what has been said above, that the *good* is, according to its concept, των πρως τι; thus every good is essentially relative, for its being consists in its relation to a desiring will. *Absolute good* is, therefore, a contradiction in terms; highest good, *summum bonum*, really signifies the same thing—a final satisfaction of the will, after which no new desire could arise,—a last motive, the attainment of which would afford enduring satisfaction of the will. But, according to the investigations which have already been conducted in this Fourth Book, such a consummation is not even thinkable. The will can just as little cease from willing altogether on account of some particular satisfaction, as time can end or begin; for it there is no such thing as a permanent fulfilment which shall completely and for ever satisfy its craving. It is the vessel of the Danaides; for it there is no highest good, no absolute good, but always a merely temporary good. If, however, we wish to give an honorary position, as it were emeritus, to an old expression, which from custom we do not like to discard altogether, **ντε** may, metaphorically and figuratively, call the complete self-effacement and denial of the will, the true absence of will, which alone for ever stills and silences its struggle, alone gives that contentment which can never again be disturbed, alone redeems the world, and which we shall now soon consider at the close of our whole investigation—the absolute good, the *summum bonum*—and regard it as the only radical cure of the disease of which all other means are only palliations or anodynes. In this sense the Greek *τελος* and also *finis bonorum* correspond to the thing still better. So much for the words *good* and *bad;* now for the thing itself.

If a man is always disposed to do *wrong* whenever the opportunity presents itself, and there is no external power to restrain him, we call him *bad*. According to our doctrine of wrong, this means that such a man does not merely assert the will to live as it appears in his own body, but in this assertion goes so far that he denies the will which appears in other individuals. This is shown by the fact that he desires their powers for the service of his own will, and seeks to destroy their existence when they stand in the way of its efforts. The ultimate source of this is a high degree of egoism, the nature of which has been already explained. Two things are here apparent. In the first place, that in such a man an excessively vehement will to live expresses itself, extending far beyond the assertion of his own body; and, in the second place, that his knowledge, entirely given up to the principle of sufficient reason and involved in the *principium individuationis,* cannot get beyond the difference which this latter principle establishes between his own person and every one else. Therefore he seeks his own well-being alone, completely indifferent to that of all others, whose existence is to him altogether foreign and divided from his own by a wide gulf, and who are indeed regarded by him as mere masks with no reality behind them. And these two qualities are the constituent elements of the bad character.

This great intensity of will is in itself and directly a
constant source of suffering. In the first place, because all
volition as such arises from want; that is, suffering. (Therefore, as will be remembered, from the Third Book, the momentary cessation of all volition, which takes place whenever we give ourselves up to æsthetic contemplation, as pure
will-less subject of knowledge, the correlative of the Idea,
is one of the principal elements in our pleasure in the beautiful.) Secondly, because, through the causal connection of
things, most of our desires must remain unfulfilled, and the
will is oftener crossed than satisfied, and therefore much
intense volition carries with it much intense suffering. For
all suffering is simply unfulfilled and crossed volition; and
even the pain of the body when it is injured or destroyed is
as such only possible through the fact that the body is nothing but the will itself become object. Now on this account,
because much intense suffering is inseparable from much
intense volition, very bad men bear the stamp of inward
suffering in the very expression of the countenance; even
when they have attained every external happiness, they always look unhappy so long as they are not transported by
some momentary ecstasy and are not dissembling. From this
inward torment, which is absolutely and directly essential to
them, there finally proceeds that delight in the suffering of
others which does not spring from mere egoism, but is disinterested, and which constitutes *wickedness* proper, rising
to the pitch of *cruelty*. For this the suffering of others is not
a means for the attainment of the ends of its own will, but
an end in itself. The more definite explanation of this
phenomenon is as follows:—Since man is a manifestation
of will illuminated by the clearest knowledge, he is always
contrasting the actual and felt satisfaction of his will with
the merely possible satisfaction of it which knowledge presents to him. Hence arises envy: every privation is infinitely
increased by the enjoyment of others, and relieved by the

knowledge that others also suffer the same privation. Those ills which are common to all and inseparable from human life trouble us little, just as those which belong to the climate, to the whole country. The recollection of greater sufferings than our own stills our pain; the sight of the sufferings of others soothes our own. If, now, a man is filled with an exceptionally intense pressure of will,—if with burning eagerness he seeks to accumulate everything to slake the thirst of his egoism, and thus experiences, as he inevitably must, that all satisfaction is merely apparent, that the attained end never fulfils the promise of the desired object, the final appeasing of the fierce pressure of will, but that when fulfilled the wish only changes its form, and now torments him in a new one; and indeed that if at last all wishes are exhausted, the pressure of will itself remains without any conscious motive, and makes itself known to him with fearful pain as a feeling of terrible desolation and emptiness; if from all this, which in the case of the ordinary degrees of volition is only felt in a small measure, and only produces the ordinary degree of melancholy, in the case of him who is a manifestation of will reaching the point of extraordinary wickedness, there necessarily springs an excessive inward misery, an eternal unrest, an incurable pain; he seeks indirectly the alleviation which directly is denied him,—seeks to mitigate his own suffering by the sight of the suffering of others, which at the same time he recognises as an expression of his power. The suffering of others now becomes for him an end in itself, and is a spectacle in which he delights; and thus arises the phenomenon of pure cruelty, blood-thirstiness, which history exhibits so often in the Neros and Domitians, in the African Deis, in Robespierre, and the like.

The desire of revenge is closely related to wickedness. It recompenses evil with evil, not with reference to the future, which is the character of punishment, but merely on account of what has happened, what is past, as such, thus disinterestedly, not as a means, but as an end, in order to revel in the torment which the avenger himself has inflicted on the offender. What distinguishes revenge from pure wickedness, and to some extent excuses it, is an appearance of justice. For if the same act, which is now revenge, were to be done legally, that is, according to a previously determined and known rule, and in a society which had sanctioned this rule, it would be punishment, and thus justice.

Besides the suffering which has been described, and which is inseparable from wickedness, because it springs from the same root, excessive vehemence of will, another specific pain quite different from this is connected with wickedness, which is felt in the case of every bad action, whether it be merely injustice proceeding from egoism or pure wickedness, and according to the length of its duration is called *the sting of conscience* or *remorse*. Now, whoever remembers and has present in his mind the content of the preceding portion of this Fourth Book, and especially the truth explained at the beginning of it, that life itself is always assured to the will to live, as its mere copy or mirror, and also the exposition of eternal justice, will find that the sting of conscience can have no other meaning than the following, *i.e.*, its content, abstractly expressed, is what follows, in which two parts are distinguished, which again, however, entirely coincide, and must be thought as completely united.

However closely the veil of Mâyâ may envelop the mind of the bad man, *i.e.*, however firmly he may be involved in the *principium individuationis*, according to which he regards his person as absolutely different and separated by a wide gulf from all others, a knowledge to which he clings with all his might, as it alone suits and supports his egoism, so that knowledge is almost always corrupted by will, yet there arises in the inmost depths of his consciousness the secret presentiment that such an order of things is only

phenomenal, and that their real constitution is quite different. He has a dim foreboding that, however much time and
space may separate him from other individuals and the innumerable miseries which they suffer, and even suffer
through him, and may represent them as quite foreign to
him, yet in themselves, and apart from the idea and its
forms, it is the one will to live appearing in them all, which
here failing to recognise itself, turns its weapons against
itself, and, by seeking increased happiness in one of its
phenomena, imposes the greatest suffering upon another.
He dimly sees that he, the bad man, is himself this whole
will; that consequently he is not only the inflicter of pain
but also the endurer of it, from whose suffering he is only
separated and exempted by an illusive dream, the form of
which is space and time, which, however, vanishes away;
that he must in reality pay for the pleasure with the pain,
and that all suffering which he only knows as possible
really concerns him as the will to live, inasmuch as the
possible and actual, the near and the distant in time and
space, are only different for the knowledge of the individual, only by means of the *principium individuationis,* not
in themselves. This is the truth which mythically, *i.e.,*
adapted to the principle of sufficient reason, and so translated into the form of the phenomenal, is expressed in the
transmigration of souls. Yet it has its purest expression free
from all foreign admixture, in that obscurely felt yet inconsolable misery called remorse. But this springs also from
a second immediate knowledge, which is closely bound to
the first—the knowledge of the strength with which the
will to live asserts itself in the wicked individual, which
extends far beyond his own individual phenomenon, to the
absolute denial of the same will appearing in other individuals. Consequently the inward horror of the wicked man
at his own deed, which he himself tries to conceal, contains,
besides that presentment of the nothingness, the mere illu-

siveness of the *principium individuationis*, and of the distinction established by it between him and others; also the knowledge of the vehemence of his own will, the intensity with which he has seized upon life and attached himself closely to it, even that life whose terrible side he sees before him in the misery of those who are oppressed by him, and with which he is yet so firmly united, that just on this account the greatest atrocity proceeds from him himself, as a means for the fuller assertion of his own will. He recognises himself as the concentrated manifestation of the will to live, feels to what degree he is given up to life, and with it also to innumerable sufferings which are essential to it, for it has infinite time and infinite space to abolish the distinction between the possible and the actual, and to change all the sufferings which as yet are merely *known* to him into sufferings he has *experienced*. The millions of years of constant rebirth certainly exist, like the whole past and future, only in conception; occupied time, the form of the phenomenon of the will, is only the present, and for the individual time is ever new: it seems to him always as if he had newly come into being. For life is inseparable from the will to live, and the only form of life is the present. Death (the repetition of the comparison must be excused) is like the setting of the sun, which is only apparently swallowed up by the night, but in reality, itself the source of all light, burns without intermission, brings new days to new worlds, is always rising and always setting. Beginning and end only concern the individual through time, the form of the phenomenon for the idea. Outside time lies only the will, Kant's thing-in-itself, and its adequate objectification, the Idea of Plato. Therefore suicide affords no escape; what every one in his inmost consciousness *wills*, that must he *be*; and what every one *is*, that he *wills*. Thus, besides the merely felt knowledge of the illusiveness and nothingness of the forms of the idea which separate individuals, it is the self-knowledge of one's own will and its degree that gives the sting to conscience. The course of life draws the image of the empirical character, whose original is the intelligible character, and horrifies the wicked man by this image. He is horrified all the same whether the image is depicted in large characters, so that the world shares his horror, or in such small ones that he alone sees it, for it only concerns him directly. The past would be a matter of indifference, and could not pain the conscience if the character did not feel itself free from all time and unalterable by it, so long as it does not deny itself. Therefore things which are long past still weigh on the conscience. The prayer, "Lead me not into temptation," means, "Let me not see what manner of person I am." In the might with which the bad man asserts life, and which exhibits itself to him in the sufferings which he inflicts on others, he measures how far he is from the surrender and denial of that will, the only possible deliverance from the world and its miseries. He sees how far he belongs to it, and how firmly he is bound to it; the *known* suffering of others has no power to move him; he is given up to life and *felt* suffering. It remains hidden whether this will ever break and overcome the vehemence of his will.

This exposition of the significance and inner nature of the *bad*, which as mere feeling, *i.e.*, not as distinct, abstract knowledge, is the content of *remorse*, will gain distinctness and completeness by the similar consideration of the *good* as a quality of human will, and finally of absolute resignation and holiness, which proceeds from it when it has attained its highest grade. For opposites always throw light upon each other, and the day at once reveals both itself and the night, as Spinoza admirably remarks.

§ 66. A theory of morals without proof, that is, mere moralising, can effect nothing, because it does not act as a motive. A theory of morals which does act as a motive can do so only by working on self-love. But what springs from this source has no moral worth. It follows from this that no genuine virtue can be produced through moral theory or abstract knowledge in general, but that such virtue must spring from that intuitive knowledge which recognises in the individuality of others the same nature as in our own.

For virtue certainly proceeds from knowledge, but not from the abstract knowledge that can be communicated through words. If it were so, virtue could be taught, and by here expressing in abstract language its nature and the knowledge which lies at its foundation, we should make every one who comprehends this even ethically better. But this is by no means the case. On the contrary, ethical discourses and preaching will just as little produce a virtuous man as all the systems of æsthetics from Aristotle downwards have succeeded in producing a poet. For the real inner nature of virtue the concept is unfruitful, just as it is in art, and it is only in a completely subordinate position that it can be of use as a tool in the elaboration and preserving of what has been ascertained and inferred by other means. *Velle non discitur.* Abstract dogmas are, in fact, without influence upon virtue, *i.e.*, upon the goodness of the disposition. False dogmas do not disturb it; true ones will scarcely assist it. It would, in fact, be a bad look-out if the cardinal fact in the life of man, his ethical worth, that worth which counts for eternity, were dependent upon anything the attainment of which is so much a matter of chance as is the case with dogmas, religious doctrines, and philosophical theories. For morality dogmas have this value only: The man who has become virtuous from knowledge of another kind, which is presently to be considered, possesses in them a scheme or formula according to which he accounts to his own reason, for the most part fictitiously, for his non-egoistical action, the nature of which it, *i.e.*, he himself, does not comprehend, and with which account he has accustomed it to be content.

Upon conduct, outward action, dogmas may certainly exercise a powerful influence, as also custom and example (the last because the ordinary man does not trust his judgment, of the weakness of which he is conscious, but only follows his own or some one else's experience), but the disposition is not altered in this way.[1] All abstract knowledge gives only motives; but, as was shown above, motives can only alter the direction of the will, not the will itself. All communicable knowledge, however, can only affect the will as a motive. Thus when dogmas lead it, what the man really and in general wills remains still the same. He has only received different thoughts as to the ways in which it is to be attained, and imaginary motives guide him just like real ones. Therefore, for example, it is all one, as regards his ethical worth, whether he gives large gifts to the poor, firmly persuaded that he will receive everything tenfold in a future life, or expends the same sum on the improvement of an estate which will yield interest, certainly late, but all the more surely and largely. And he who for the sake of orthodoxy commits the heretic to the flames is as much a murderer as the bandit who does it for gain; and indeed, as regards inward circumstances, so also was he who slaughtered the Turks in the Holy Land, if, like the burner of heretics, he really did so because he thought that he would thereby gain a place in heaven. For these are careful only for themselves, for their own egoism, just like the bandit, from whom they are only distinguished by the absurdity of their means. From without, as has been said, the will can only be reached through motives, and these only alter the

[1] The Church would say that these are merely *opera operata*, which do not avail unless grace gives the faith which leads to the new birth. But of this farther on.

way in which it expresses itself, never the will itself. *Velle non discitur.*

In the case of good deeds, however, the doer of which appeals to dogmas, we must always distinguish whether these dogmas really are the motives which lead to the good deeds, or whether, as was said above, they are merely the illusive account of them with which he seeks to satisfy his own reason with regard to a good deed which really flows from quite a different source, a deed which he does because he is good, though he does not understand how to explain it rightly, and yet wishes to think something with regard to it. But this distinction is very hard to make, because it lies in the heart of a man. Therefore, we can scarcely ever pass a correct moral judgment on the action of others, and very seldom on our own. The deeds and conduct of an individual and of a nation may be very much modified through dogmas, example, and custom. But in themselves all deeds (*opera operata*) are merely empty forms, and only the disposition which leads to them gives them moral significance. This disposition, however, may be quite the same when its outward manifestation is very different. With an equal degree of wickedness, one man may die on the wheel, and another in the bosom of his family. It may be the same grade of wickedness which expresses itself in one nation in the coarse characteristics of murder and cannibalism, and in another finely and softly in miniature, in court intrigues, oppressions, and delicate plots of every kind; the inner nature remains the same. It is conceivable that a perfect state, or perhaps indeed a complete and firmly believed doctrine of rewards and punishments after death, might prevent every crime; politically much would be gained thereby; morally, nothing; only the expression of the will in life would be restricted.

Thus genuine goodness of disposition, disinterested virtue, and pure nobility do not proceed from abstract knowledge. Yet they do proceed from knowledge; but it is a direct intuitive knowledge, which can neither be reasoned away, nor arrived at by reasoning, a knowledge which, just because it is not abstract, cannot be communicated, but must arise in each for himself, which therefore finds its real and adequate expression not in words, but only in deeds, in conduct, in the course of the life of man. We who here seek the theory of virtue, and have therefore also to express abstractly the nature of the knowledge which lies at its foundation, will yet be unable to convey that knowledge itself in this expression. We can only give the concept of this knowledge, and thus always start from action in which alone it becomes visible, and refer to action as its only adequate expression. We can only explain and interpret action, *i.e.*, express abstractly what really takes place in it.

§ 67. We have seen how justice proceeds from the penetration of the *principium individuationis* in a less degree, and how from its penetration in a higher degree there arises goodness of disposition proper, which shows itself as pure, *i.e.*, disinterested love towards others. When now the latter becomes perfect, it places other individuals and their fate completely on the level with itself and its own fate. Further than this it cannot go, for there exists no reason for preferring the individuality of another to its own. Yet the number of other individuals whose whole happiness or life is in danger may outweigh the regard for one's own particular well-being. In such a case, the character that has attained to the highest goodness and perfect nobility will entirely sacrifice its own well-being and even its life, for the well-being of many others. So died Codrus, and Leonidas, and Regulus, and Decius Mus, and Arnold von Winkelried; so dies every one who voluntarily and consciously faces certain death for his friends or his country. And they also stand on the same level who voluntarily submit to suffering and death for maintaining what conduces and rightly

belongs to the welfare of all mankind; that is, for maintaining universal and important truths and destroying great
errors. So died Socrates and Giordano Bruno, and so many a
hero of the truth suffered death at the stake at the hands
of the priests.

Now, however, I must remind the reader, with reference
to the paradox stated above, that we found before that suffering is essential to life as a whole, and inseparable from
it. And that we saw that every wish proceeds from a need,
from a want, from suffering, and that therefore every satisfaction is only the removal of a pain, and brings no positive
happiness; that the joys certainly lie to the wish, presenting
themselves as a positive good, but in truth they have only a
negative nature, and are only the end of an evil. Therefore
what goodness, love, and nobleness do for others, is always
merely an alleviation of their suffering, and consequently
all that can influence them to good deeds and works of love,
is simply the *knowledge of the suffering of others*, which is
directly understood from their own suffering and placed
on a level with it. But it follows from this that pure love
(αγαπη, *caritas*) is in its nature sympathy; whether the suffering it mitigates, to which every unsatisfied wish belongs,
be great or small. Therefore we shall have no hesitation,
in direct contradiction to Kant, who will only recognise all
true goodness and all virtue to be such, if it has proceeded
from abstract reflection, and indeed from the conception of
duty and of the categorical imperative, and explains felt
sympathy as weakness, and by no means virtue, we shall
have no hesitation, I say, in direct contradiction to Kant, in
saying: the mere concept is for genuine virtue just as unfruitful as it is for genuine art: all true and pure love is
sympathy, and all love which is not sympathy is selfishness.
Combinations of the two frequently occur. Indeed genuine
friendship is always a mixture of selfishness and sympathy;
the former lies in the pleasure experienced in the presence

of the friend, whose individuality corresponds to our own, and this almost always constitutes the greatest part; sympathy shows itself in the sincere participation in his joy and grief, and the disinterested sacrifices made in respect of the latter. As a confirmation of our paradoxical proposition it may be observed that the tone and words of the language and caresses of pure love, entirely coincide with the tones of sympathy; and we may also remark in passing that in Italian sympathy and true love are denoted by the same word *pietà*.

I now take up the thread of our discussion of the ethical significance of action, in order to show how, from the same source from which all goodness, love, virtue, and nobility of character spring, there finally arises that which I call the denial of the will to live.

We saw before that hatred and wickedness are conditioned by egoism, and egoism rests on the entanglement of knowledge in the *principium individuationis*. Thus we found that the penetration of that *principium individuationis* is the source and the nature of justice, and when it is carried further, even to its fullest extent, it is the source and nature of love and nobility of character. For this penetration alone, by abolishing the distinction between our own individuality and that of others, renders possible and explains perfect goodness of disposition, extending to disinterested love and the most generous self-sacrifice for others.

If, however, this penetration of the *principium individuationis*, this direct knowledge of the identity of will in all its manifestations, is present in a high degree of distinctness, it will at once show an influence upon the will which extends still further. If that veil of Mâyâ, the *principium individuationis*, is lifted from the eyes of a man to such an extent that he no longer makes the egotistical distinction between his person and that of others, but takes as much interest in the sufferings of other individuals as in his own, and therefore is not only benevolent in the highest degree, but even ready to sacrifice his own individuality whenever such a sacrifice will save a number of other persons, then it clearly follows that such a man, who recognises in all beings his own inmost and true self, must also regard the infinite suffering of all suffering beings as his own, and take on himself the pain of the whole world. No suffering is any longer strange to him. All the miseries of others which he sees and is so seldom able to alleviate, all the miseries he knows directly, and even those which he only knows as possible, work upon his mind like his own. It is no longer the changing joy and sorrow of his own person that he has in view, as is the case with him who is still involved in egoism; but, since he sees through the *principium individuationis*, all lies equally near him. He knows the whole, comprehends its nature, and finds that it consists in a constant passing away, vain striving, inward conflict, and continual suffering. He sees wherever he looks suffering humanity, the suffering brute creation, and a world that passes away. But all this now lies as near him as his own person lies to the egoist. Why should he now, with such knowledge of the world, assert this very life through constant acts of will, and thereby bind himself ever more closely to it, press it ever more firmly to himself? Thus he who is still involved in the *principium individuationis*, in egoism, only knows particular things and their relation to his own person, and these constantly become new *motives* of his volition. But, on the other hand, that knowledge of the whole, of the nature of the thing-in-itself which has been described, becomes a *quieter* of all and every volition. The will now turns away from life; it now shudders at the pleasures in which it recognises the assertion of life. Man now attains to the state of voluntary renunciation, resignation, true indifference, and perfect will-lessness. If at times, in the hard experience of our own suffering, or in the vivid recognition of that of others, the knowledge of the vanity and bitterness of life draws nigh to us also who are still wrapt in the veil of Mâyâ, and we would like to destroy the sting of the desires, close the entrance against all suffering, and purify and sanctify ourselves by complete and final renunciation; yet the illusion of the phenomenon soon entangles us again, and its motives influence the will anew; we cannot tear ourselves free. The allurement of hope, the flattery of the present, the sweetness of pleasure, the well-being which falls to our lot, amid the lamentations of a suffering world governed by chance and error, draws us back to it and rivets our bonds anew. Therefore Jesus says: "It is easier for a camel to go through the eye of a needle, than for a rich man to enter into the kingdom of God."

If we compare life to a course or path through which we must unceasingly run—a path of red-hot coals, with a few cool places here and there; then he who is entangled in delusion is consoled by the cool places, on which he now stands, or which he sees near him, and sets out to run through the course. But he who sees through the *principium individuationis*, and recognises the real nature of the thing-in-itself, and thus the whole, is no longer susceptible of such consolation; he sees himself in all places at once, and withdraws. His will turns round, no longer asserts its own nature, which is reflected in the phenomenon, but denies it. The phenomenon by which this change is marked, is the transition from virtue to asceticism. That is to say, it no longer suffices for such a man to love others as himself, and to do as much for them as for himself; but there arises within him a horror of the nature of which his own phenomenal existence is an expression, the will to live, the kernel and inner nature of that world which is recognised as full of misery. He therefore disowns this nature which appears in him, and is already expressed through his body, and his action gives the lie to his phenomenal existence, and appears in open contradiction to it. Essentially nothing else but a manifestation of will, he ceases to will anything, guards against attaching his will to anything, and seeks to confirm in himself the greatest indifference to everything. His body, healthy and strong, expresses through the genitals, the sexual impulse; but he denies the will and gives the lie to the body; he desires no sensual gratification under any condition. Voluntary and complete chastity is the first step in asceticism or the denial of the will to live. It thereby denies the assertion of the will which extends beyond the individual life, and gives the assurance that with the life of this body, the will, whose manifestation it is, ceases. Nature, always true and naïve, declares that if this maxim became universal, the human race would die out; and I think I may assume, in accordance with what was said in the Second Book about the connection of all manifestations of will, that with its highest manifestation, the weaker reflection of it would also pass away, as the twilight vanishes along with the full light. With the entire abolition of knowledge, the rest of the world would of itself vanish into nothing; for without a subject there is no object. I should like here to refer to a passage in the Vedas, where it is said: "As in this world hungry infants press round their mother; so do all beings await the holy oblation." (Asiatic Researches, vol. viii.; Colebrooke, On the Vedas, Abstract of the Sama-Veda; also in Colebrooke's Miscellaneous Essays, vol. i. p. 79.) Sacrifice means resignation generally, and the rest of nature must look for its salvation to man who is at once the priest and the sacrifice. Indeed it deserves to be noticed as very remarkable, that this thought has also been expressed by the admirable and unfathomably profound Angelus Silesius, in the little poem entitled, "Man brings all to God"; it runs, "Man! all loves thee; around thee great is the throng. All things flee to thee that they may attain to God." But a yet greater mystic, Meister Eckhard, whose wonderful writings are at last accessible (1857) through the edition of Franz Pfeiffer, says the same thing (p. 459) quite in the sense explained here: "I bear witness to the saying of Christ, 'I, if I be lifted up from the earth, will draw all things unto me' (John xii, 32). So shall the good man draw all things up to God, to the source whence they first came. The Masters certify to us that all creatures are made for the sake of man. This is proved in all created things, by the fact that the one makes use of the other; the ox makes use of the grass, the fish of the water, the bird of the air, the wild beast of the forest. Thus, all created things become of use to the good man. A good man brings to God the one created thing in the other." He means to say, that man makes use of the brutes in this life because, in and with himself, he saves them also. It also seems to me that that difficult passage in the Bible, Rom. viii. 21-24, must be interpreted in this sense.

In Buddhism also, there is no lack of expressions of this truth. For example, when Buddha, still as Bodisatwa, has his horse saddled for the last time, for his flight into the wilderness from his father's house, he says these lines to the horse: "Long hast thou existed in life and in death, but now thou shalt cease from carrying and drawing. Bear me but this once more, O Kantakana, away from here, and when I have attained to the Law (have become Buddha) I will not forget thee" (Foe Koue Ki, trad. p. Abel Rémusat, p. 233).

Asceticism then shows itself further in voluntary and intentional poverty, which not only arises *per accidens*, because the possessions are given away to mitigate the sufferings of others, but is here an end in itself, is meant to serve as a constant mortification of will, so that the satisfaction of the wishes, the sweet of life, shall not again arouse the will, against which self-knowledge has conceived a horror. He who has attained to this point, still always feels, as a living body, as concrete manifestation of will, the natural disposition for every kind of volition; but he intentionally suppresses it, for he compels himself to refrain from doing all that he would like to do, and to do all that he would like not to do, even if this has no further end than that of serving as a mortification of will. Since he himself denies the will which appears in his own person, he will not resist if another does the same, *i.e.*, inflicts wrongs upon him. Therefore every suffering coming to him from without, through chance or the wickedness of others, is welcome to him, every injury, ignominy, and insult; he receives them gladly as the opportunity of learning with certainty that he no longer asserts the will, but gladly sides with every enemy of the manifestation of will which is his own person. Therefore he bears such ignominy and suffering with inexhaustible patience and meekness, returns good for evil without ostentation, and allows the fire of anger to rise within him just as little as that of the desires. And he mortifies not only the will itself, but also its visible form, its objectivity, the body. He nourishes it sparingly, lest its excessive vigour and prosperity should animate and excite more strongly the will, of which it is merely the expression and the mirror. So he practises fasting, and even resorts to chastisement and self-inflicted torture, in order that, by constant privation and suffering, he may more and more break down and destroy the will, which he recognises and abhors as the source of his own suffering existence and that of the world. If at last death comes, which puts an end to this manifestation of that will, whose existence here has long since perished through free-denial of itself, with the exception of the weak residue of it which appears as the life of this body; it is most welcome, and is gladly received as a longed-for deliverance. Here it is not, as in the case of others, merely the manifestation which ends with death; but the inner nature itself is abolished, which here existed only in the manifestation, and that in a very weak degree; this last slight bond is now broken. For him who thus ends, the world has ended also.

And what I have here described with feeble tongue and only in general terms, is no philosophical fable, invented by myself, and only of to-day; no, it was the enviable life of so many saints and beautiful souls among Christians, and still more among Hindus and Buddhists, and also among the believers of other religions. However different were the dogmas impressed on their reason, the same inward, direct, intuitive knowledge from which alone all virtue and holiness proceed, expressed itself in precisely the same way in the conduct of life. For here also the great distinction between intuitive and abstract knowledge shows itself; a distinction which is of such importance and universal application in our whole investigation, and which has hitherto been too little attended to. There is a wide gulf between the two, which can only be crossed by the aid of philosophy, as regards the knowledge of the nature of the world. Intuitively or *in concreto*, every man is really conscious of all philosophical truths, but to bring them to abstract knowledge, to reflection, is the work of philosophy, which neither ought nor is able to do more than this.

Thus it may be that the inner nature of holiness, self-renunciation, mortification of our own will, asceticism, is here for the first time expressed abstractly, and free from all mythical elements, as *denial of the will to live,* appearing after the complete knowledge of its own nature has become a quieter of all volition. On the other hand, it has been known directly and realised in practice by saints and ascetics, who had all the same inward knowledge, though they used very different language with regard to it, according to the dogmas which their reason had accepted, and in consequence of which an Indian, a Christian, or a Lama saint must each give a very different account of his conduct, which is, however, of no importance as regards the fact. A saint may be full of the absurdest superstition, or, on the contrary, he may be a philosopher, it is all the same. His conduct alone certifies that he is a saint, for, in a moral regard, it proceeds from knowledge of the world and its nature, which is not abstractly but intuitively and directly apprehended, and is only expressed by him in any dogma for the satisfaction of his reason. It is therefore just as little needful that a saint should be a philosopher as that a philosopher should be a saint; just as it is not necessary that a perfectly beautiful man should be a great sculptor, or that a great sculptor should himself be a beautiful man. In general, it is a strange demand upon a moralist that he should teach no other virtue than that which he himself possesses. To repeat the whole nature of the world abstractly, universally, and distinctly in concepts, and thus to store up, as it were, a reflected image of it in permanent concepts always at the command of the reason; this and nothing else is philosophy.

But the description I have given above of the denial of the will to live, of the conduct of a beautiful soul, of a resigned and voluntarily expiating saint, is merely abstract and general, and therefore cold. As the knowledge from which the denial of the will proceeds is intuitive and not abstract, it finds its most perfect expression, not in abstract conceptions, but in deeds and conduct. Therefore, in order to understand fully what we philosophically express as denial of the will to live, one must come to know examples of it in experience and actual life. Certainly they are not to be met with in daily experience: *Nam omnia præclara tam difficilia quam rara sunt,* Spinoza admirably says. Therefore, unless by a specially happy fate we are made eye-witnesses, we have to content ourselves with descriptions of the lives of such men. Indian literature, as we see from the little that we as yet know through translations, is very rich in descriptions of the lives of saints, penitents, Samanas or ascetics, Sannyâsis or mendicants, and whatever else they may be called. The history of the world will, and indeed must, keep silence about the man whose conduct is the best and only adequate illustration of this important point of our investigation, for the material of the history of the world is quite different, and indeed opposed to this. It is not the denial of the will to live, but its assertion and its manifestation in innumerable individuals in which its conflict with itself at the highest grade of its objectification appears with perfect distinctness, and brings before our eyes, now the ascendancy of the individual through prudence, now the might of the many through their mass, now the might of chance personified as fate, always the vanity and emptiness of the whole effort. We, however, do not follow here the course of phenomena in time, but, as philosophers, we seek to investigate the ethical significance of action, and take this as the only criterion of what for us is significant and important. Thus we will not be withheld by any fear of the constant numerical superiority of vulgarity and dulness from acknowledging that the greatest, most important, and most significant phenomenon that the world can show is not the conqueror of the world, but the subduer of it; is nothing but the quiet, unobserved life of a man who has attained to the knowledge in consequence of which he surrenders and denies that will to live which fills everything and strives and strains in all, and which first gains freedom here in him alone, so that his conduct becomes the exact opposite of that of other men. In this respect, therefore, for the philosopher, these accounts of the lives of holy, self-denying men, badly as they are generally written, and mixed as they are with superstition and nonsense, are, because of the significance of the material, immeasurably more instructive and important than even Plutarch and Livy.

It will further assist us much in obtaining a more definite and full knowledge of what we have expressed abstractly and generally, according to our method of exposition, as the denial of the will to live, if we consider the moral teaching that has been imparted with this intention, and by men who were full of this spirit; and this will also show how old our view is, though the pure philosophical expression of it may be quite new. The teaching of this kind which lies nearest to hand is Christianity, the ethics of which are entirely in the spirit indicated, and lead not only to the highest degrees of human love, but also to renunciation. The germ of this last side of it is certainly distinctly present in the writings of the Apostles, but it was only fully developed and expressed later. We find the Apostles enjoining the love of our neighbour as ourselves, benevolence, the requital of hatred with love and well-doing, patience, meekness, the endurance of all possible injuries without resistance, abstemiousness in nourishment to keep down lust, resistance to sensual desire, if possible, altogether. We already see here the first degrees of asceticism, or denial of the will proper. This last expression denotes that which in the Gospels is called denying ourselves and taking up the cross (Matt. xvi. 24, 25; Mark viii. 34, 35; Luke ix. 23, 24, xiv. 26, 27, 33). This tendency soon developed itself more and more, and was the origin of hermits, anchorites, and monasticism —an origin which in itself was pure and holy, but for that very reason unsuitable for the great majority of men; therefore what developed out of it could only be hypocrisy and wickedness, for *abusus optimi pessimus*. In more developed Christianity, we see that seed of asceticism unfold into the full flower in the writings of the Christian saints and mystics. These preach, besides the purest love, complete resignation, voluntary and absolute poverty, genuine calmness, perfect indifference to all worldly things, dying to our own will and being born again in God, entire forgetting of our own person, and sinking ourselves in the contemplation of God. A full exposition of this will be found in Fénélon's "Explication des Maximes des Saints sur la Vie Interieure."

But the spirit of this development of Christianity is certainly nowhere so fully and powerfully expressed as in the writings of the German mystics, in the works of Meister Eckhard, and in that justly famous book "Die Deutsche Theologie," of which Luther says in the introduction to it which he wrote, that with the exception of the Bible and St. Augustine, he had learnt more from it of what God, Christ, and man are than from any other book. The precepts and doctrines which are laid down there are the most perfect exposition, sprung from deep inward conviction of what I have presented as the denial of the will. Tauler's "Nachfolgung des armen Leben Christi," and also his "Medulla Animæ," are written in the same admirable spirit, though not quite equal in value to that work. In my opinion the teaching of these genuine Christian mystics, when compared with the teaching of the New Testament, is as alcohol to wine, or what becomes visible in the New Testament as through a veil and mist appears to us in the works of the mystics without cloak or disguise, in full clearness and distinctness. Finally, the New Testament might be regarded as the first initiation, the mystics as the second.

We find, however, that which we have called the denial of the will to live more fully developed, more variously expressed, and more vividly represented in the ancient Sanscrit writings than could be the case in the Christian Church and the Western world. That this important ethical view of life could here attain to a fuller development and a more distinct expression is perhaps principally to be ascribed to the fact that it was not confined by an element quite foreign to it, as Christianity is by the Jewish theology, to which its sublime author had necessarily to adopt and accommodate it, partly consciously, partly, it may be, unconsciously. Thus Christianity is made up of two very different constituent parts, and I should like to call the purely ethical part especially and indeed exclusively Christian, and distinguish it from the Jewish dogmatism with which it is combined. If, as has often been feared, and especially at the present time, that excellent and salutary religion should altogether decline, I should look for the reason of this simply in the fact that it does not consist of one single element, but of two originally different elements, which have only been combined through the accident of history. In such a case dissolution had to follow through the separation of these elements, arising from their different relationship to and reaction against the progressive spirit of the age. But even after this dissolution the purely ethical part must always remain uninjured, because it is indestructible. Our knowledge of Hindu literature is still very imperfect. Yet, as we find their ethical teaching variously and powerfully expressed in the Vedas, Puranas, poems, myths, legends of their saints, maxims and precepts, we see that it inculcates love of our neighbour with complete renunciation of self-love; love generally, not confined to mankind, but including all living creatures; benevolence, even to the giving away of the hard-won wages of daily toil; unlimited patience towards all who injure us; the requital of all wickedness, however base, with goodness and love; voluntary and glad endurance of all ignominy; abstinence from all animal food; perfect chastity and renunciation of all sensual pleasure for him who strives after true holiness; the surrender of all possessions, the forsaking of every dwelling-place and of all relatives; deep unbroken solitude, spent in silent contemplation, with voluntary penance and terrible slow self-torture for the absolute mortification of the will, torture which extends to voluntary death by starvation, or by men giving themselves up to crocodiles, or flinging themselves over the sacred precipice in the Himalayas, or being buried alive, or, finally, by flinging themselves under the wheels of the huge car of an idol drawn along amid the singing, shouting, and dancing of bayaderes. And even yet these precepts, whose origin reaches back more than four thousand years, are carried out in practice, in some cases even to the utmost extreme,[1] and this notwithstanding the fact that the Hindu nation has been broken up into so many parts. A religion which demands the greatest sacrifices, and which has yet remained so long in practice in a nation that embraces so many millions of persons, cannot be an arbitrarily invented superstition, but must have its foundation in the nature of man. But besides this, if we read the life of a Christian penitent or saint, and also that of a Hindu saint, we cannot sufficiently wonder at the harmony we find between them. In the case of such radically different dogmas, customs, and circumstances, the inward life and effort of both is the same. And the same harmony prevails in the maxims prescribed for both of them. For example, Tauler speaks of the absolute poverty which one ought to seek, and which consists in giving away and divesting oneself completely of everything from which one might draw comfort or worldly pleasure, clearly because all this constantly affords new nourishment to the will, which it is intended to destroy entirely. And as an Indian counterpart of this, we find in the precepts of Fo that the Saniassi, who ought to be without a dwelling and entirely without property, is further finally enjoined not to lay himself down often under the same tree, lest he should acquire a preference or inclination for it above other trees. The Christian mystic and the teacher of the Vedânta philosophy agree in this respect also, they both regard all outward works and religious exercises as superfluous for him who has attained to perfection. So much agreement in the case of such different ages and nations is a practical proof that what is expressed here is not, as optimistic dulness likes to assert, an eccentricity and perversity of the mind, but an

---

[1] At the procession of Jagganath in June, 1840, eleven Hindus threw themselves under the wheels, and were instantly killed. (Letter of an East Indian proprietor in the *Times* of 30th December, 1840.)

essential side of human nature, which only appears so rarely because of its excellence.

I have now indicated the sources from which there may be obtained a direct knowledge, drawn from life itself, of the phenomena in which the denial of the will to live exhibits itself. In some respects this is the most important point of our whole work; yet I have only explained it quite generally, for it is better to refer to those who speak from direct experience, than to increase the size of this book unduly by weak repetitions of what is said by them.

I only wish to add a little to the general indication of the nature of this state. We saw above that the wicked man, by the vehemence of his volition, suffers constant, consuming, inward pain, and finally, if all objects of volition are exhausted, quenches the fiery thirst of his self-will by the sight of the suffering of others. He, on the contrary, who has attained to the denial of the will to live, however poor, joyless, and full of privation his condition may appear when looked at externally, is yet filled with inward joy and the true peace of heaven. It is not the restless strain of life, the jubilant delight which has keen suffering as its preceding or succeeding condition, in the experience of the man who loves life; but it is a peace that cannot be shaken, a deep rest and inward serenity, a state which we cannot behold without the greatest longing when it is brought before our eyes or our imagination, because we at once recognise it as that which alone is right, infinitely surpassing everything else, upon which our better self cries within us the great *sapere aude*. Then we feel that every gratification of our wishes won from the world is merely like the alms which the beggar receives from life to-day that he may hunger again on the morrow; resignation, on the contrary, is like an inherited estate, it frees the owner for ever from all care.

It will be remembered from the Third Book that the æsthetic pleasure in the beautiful consists in great measure in the fact that in entering the state of pure contemplation we are lifted for the moment above all willing, *i.e.*, all wishes and cares: we become, as it were, freed from ourselves. We are no longer the individual whose knowledge is subordinated to the service of its constant willing, the correlative of the particular thing to which objects are motives, but the eternal subject of knowing purified from will, the correlative of the Platonic Idea. And we know that these moments in which, delivered from the ardent strain of will, we seem to rise out of the heavy atmosphere of arth, are the happiest which we experience. From this we can understand how blessed the life of a man must be whose will is silenced, not merely for a moment, as in the enjoyment of the beautiful, but for ever, indeed altogether extinguished, except as regards the last glimmering spark that retains the body in life, and will be extinguished with its death. Such a man, who, after many bitter struggles with his own nature, has finally conquered entirely, continues to exist only as a pure, knowing being, the undimmed mirror of the world. Nothing can trouble him more, nothing can move him, for he has cut all the thousand cords of will which hold us bound to the world, and, as desire, fear, envy, anger, drag us hither and thither in constant pain. He now looks back smiling and at rest on the delusions of this world, which once were able to move and agonise his spirit also, but which now stands before him as utterly indifferent to him, as the chess-men when the game is ended, or as, in the morning, the cast-off masquerading dress which worried and disquieted us in a night in Carnival. Life and its forms now pass before him as a fleeting illusion, as a light morning dream before half-waking eyes, the real world already shining through it so that it can no longer deceive; and like this morning dream, they finally vanish altogether without any violent transition.

We must not, however, suppose that when, by means of

the knowledge which acts as a quieter of will, the denial of the will to live has once appeared, it never wavers or vacillates, and that we can rest upon it as on an assured possession. Rather, it must ever anew be attained by a constant battle. For since the body is the will itself only in the form of objectivity or as manifestation in the world as idea, so long as the body lives, the whole will to live exists potentially, and constantly strives to become actual, and to burn again with all its ardour. Therefore that peace and blessedness in the life of holy men which we have described is only found as the flower which proceeds from the constant victory over the will, and the ground in which it grows is the constant battle with the will to live, for no one can have lasting peace upon earth. We therefore see the histories of the inner life of saints full of spiritual conflicts, temptations, and absence of grace, *i.e.*, the kind of knowledge which makes all motives ineffectual, and as an universal quieter silences all volition, gives the deepest peace and opens the door of freedom. Therefore also we see those who have once attained to the denial of the will to live strive with all their might to keep upon this path, by enforced renunciation of every kind, by penance and severity of life, and by selecting whatever is disagreeable to them, all in order to suppress the will, which is constantly springing up anew. Hence, finally, because they already know the value of salvation, their anxious carefulness to retain the hard-won blessing, their scruples of conscience about every innocent pleasure, or about every little excitement of their vanity, which here also dies last, the most immovable, the most active, and the most foolish of all the inclinations of man. By the term *asceticism*, which I have used so often, I mean in its narower sense this *intentional* breaking of the will by the refusal of what is agreeable and the selection of what is disagreeable, the voluntarily chosen life of penance and self-chastisement for the continual mortification of the will.

We see this practised by him who has attained to the de-nial of the will in order to enable him to persist in it; but suffering in general, as it is inflicted by fate, is a second way (δευτερος πλους [1]) of attaining to that denial. Indeed, we may assume that most men only attain to it in this way, and that it is the suffering which is personally experienced, not that which is merely known, which most frequently pro-duces complete resignation, often only at the approach of death. For only in the case of a few is the mere knowledge which, seeing through the *principium individuationis,* first produces perfect goodness of disposition and universal love of humanity, and finally enables them to regard all the suf-fering of the world as their own; only in the case of a few, I say, is this knowledge sufficient to bring about the denial of the will. Even with him who approaches this point, it is al-most invariably the case that the tolerable condition of his own body, the flattery of the moment, the delusion of hope, and the satisfaction of the will, which is ever presenting it-self anew, *i.e.,* lust, is a constant hindrance to the denial of the will, and a constant temptation to the renewed assertion of it. Therefore in this respect all these illusions have been personified as the devil. Thus in most cases the will must be broken by great personal suffering before its self-conquest appears. Then we see the man who has passed through all the increasing degrees of affliction with the most vehement resistance, and is finally brought to the verge of despair, suddenly retire into himself, know himself and the world, change his whole nature, rise above himself and all suffer-ing, as if purified and sanctified by it, in inviolable peace, blessedness, and sublimity, willingly renounce everything he previously desired with all his might, and joyfully embrace death. It is the refined silver of the denial of the will to live that suddenly comes forth from the purifying flame of suf-fering. It is salvation. Sometimes we see even those who

---

[1] On δευτερος πλους cf. Stob. Floril., vol. ii. p. 374.

were very wicked purified to this degree by great grief; they have become new beings and are completely changed. Therefore their former misdeeds trouble their consciences no more, yet they willingly atone for them by death, and gladly see the end of the manifestation of that will which is now foreign to them and abhorred by them.

The more intense the will is, the more glaring is the conflict of its manifestation, and thus the greater is the suffering. A world which was the manifestation of a far more intense will to live than this world manifests would produce so much the greater suffering; would thus be a hell.

All suffering, since it is a mortification and a call to resignation, has potentially a sanctifying power. This is the explanation of the fact that every great misfortune or deep pain inspires a certain awe. But the sufferer only really becomes an object of reverence when, surveying the course of his life as a chain of sorrows, or mourning some great and incurable misfortune, he does not really look at the special combination of circumstances which has plunged his own life into suffering, nor stops at the single great misfortune that has befallen him; for in so doing his knowledge still follows the principle of sufficient reason, and clings to the particular phenomenon; he still wills life only not under the conditions which have happened to him; but only then, I say, he is truly worthy of reverence when he raises his glance from the particular to the universal, when he regards his suffering as merely an example of the whole, and for him, since in a moral regard he partakes of genius, one case stands for a thousand, so that the whole of life conceived as essentially suffering brings him to resignation.

A very noble character we always imagine with a certain trace of quiet sadness, which is anything but a constant fretfulness at daily annoyances (this would be an ignoble trait, and lead us to fear a bad disposition), but is a consciousness derived from knowledge of the vanity of all possessions, of the suffering of all life, not merely of his own. But such knowledge may primarily be awakened by the personal experience of suffering, especially some one great sorrow, as a single unfulfilled wish brought Petrarch to that state of resigned sadness concerning the whole of life which appeals to us so pathetically in his works; for the Daphne he pursued had to flee from his hands in order to leave him, instead of herself, the immortal laurel. When through some such great and irrevocable denial of fate the will is to some extent broken, almost nothing else is desired, and the character shows itself mild, just, noble, and resigned. When, finally, grief has no definite object, but extends itself over the whole of life, then it is to a certain extent a going into itself, a withdrawal, a gradual disappearance of the will, whose visible manifestation, the body, it imperceptibly but surely undermines, so that a man feels a certain loosening of his bonds, a mild foretaste of that death which promises to be the abolition at once of the body and of the will. Therefore a secret pleasure accompanies this grief, and it is this, as I believe, which the most melancholy of all nations has called "the joy of grief." But here also lies the danger of *sentimentality*, both in life itself and in the representation of it in poetry; when a man is always mourning and lamenting without courageously rising to resignation. In this way we lose both earth and heaven, and retain merely a watery sentimentality. Only if suffering assumes the form of pure knowledge, and this, acting as a *quieter of the will*, brings about resignation, is it worthy of reverence. In this regard, however, we feel a certain respect at the sight of every great sufferer which is akin to the feeling excited by virtue and nobility of character, and also seems like a reproach of our own happy condition. We cannot help regarding every sorrow, both our own and those of others, as at least a potential advance towards virtue and holiness, and, on the contrary, pleasures and worldly satisfactions as a retrogression from them. This goes so far, that every man who endures a great bodily or mental suffering, indeed every one who merely performs some physical labour which demands the greatest exertion, in the sweat of his brow and with evident exhaustion, yet with patience and without murmuring, every such man I say, if we consider him with close attention, appears to us like a sick man who tries a painful cure, and who willingly, and even with satisfaction, endures the suffering it causes him, because he knows that the more he suffers the more the cause of his disease is affected, and that therefore the present suffering is the measure of his cure.

According to what has been said, the denial of the will to live, which is just what is called absolute, entire resignation, or holiness, always proceeds from that quieter of the will which the knowledge of its inner conflict and essential vanity, expressing themselves in the suffering of all living things, becomes. The difference, which we have represented as two paths, consists in whether that knowledge is called up by suffering which is merely and purely *known*, and is freely appropriated by means of the penetration of the *principium individuationis*, or by suffering which is directly *felt* by a man himself. True salvation, deliverance from life and suffering, cannot even be imagined without complete denial of the will. Till then, every one is simply this will itself, whose manifestation is an ephemeral existence, a constantly vain and empty striving, and the world full of suffering we have represented, to which all irrevocably and in like manner belong. For we found above that life is always assured to the will to live, and its one real form is the present, from which they can never escape, since birth and death reign in the phenomenal world. The Indian mythus expresses this by saying "they are born again." The great ethical difference of character means this, that the bad man is infinitely far from the attainment of the knowledge from which the denial of the will proceeds, and therefore he is in truth *actually* exposed to all the miseries which appear in life as *possible;* for even the present fortunate condition of his personality is merely a phenomenon produced by the *principium individuationis*, and a delusion of Mâyâ, the happy dream of a beggar. The sufferings which in the vehemence and ardour of his will he inflicts upon others are the measure of the suffering, the experience of which in his own person cannot break his will, and plainly lead it to the denial of itself. All true and pure love, on the other hand, and even all free justice, proceed from the penetration of the *principium individuationis*, which, if it appears with its full power, results in perfect sanctification and salvation, the phenomenon of which is the state of resignation described above, the unbroken peace which accompanies it, and the greatest delight in death.[1]

§ 69. Suicide, the actual doing away with the individual manifestation of will, differs most widely from the denial of the will to live, which is the single outstanding act of free will in the manifestation, and is therefore, as Asmus calls it, the transcendental change. This last has been fully considered in the course of our work. Far from being denial of the will, suicide is a phenomenon of strong assertion of will; for the essence of negation lies in this, that the joys of life are shunned, not its sorrows. The suicide wills life, and is only dissatisfied with the conditions under which it has presented itself to him. He therefore by no means surrenders the will to live, but only life, in that he destroys the individual manifestation. He wills life—wills the unrestricted existence and assertion of the body; but the complication of circumstances does not allow this, and there results for him great suffering. The very will to live finds itself so much hampered in this particular manifestation that it cannot put forth its energies. It therefore comes to such a de-

[1] Cf. Ch. xlviii. of the Supplement.

termination as is in conformity with its own nature, which lies outside the conditions of the principle of sufficient reason, and to which, therefore, all particular manifestations are alike indifferent, inasmuch as it itself remains unaffected by all appearing and passing away, and is the inner life of all things; for that firm inward assurance by reason of which we all live free from the constant dread of death, the assurance that a phenomenal existence can never be wanting to the will, supports our action even in the case of suicide. Thus the will to live appears just as much in suicide (Siva) as in the satisfaction of self-preservation (Vishnu) and in the sensual pleasure of procreation (Brahma). This is the inner meaning of the unity of the Trimurtis, which is embodied in its entirety in every human being, though in time it raises now one, now another, of its three heads. Suicide stands in the same relation to the denial of the will as the individual thing does to the Idea. The suicide denies only the individual, not the species. We have already seen that as life is always assured to the will to live, and as sorrow is inseparable from life, suicide, the wilful destruction of the single phenomenal existence, is a vain and foolish act; for the thing-in-itself remains unaffected by it, even as the rainbow endures however fast the drops which support it for the moment may change. But, more than this, it is also the masterpiece of Mâyâ, as the most flagrant example of the contradiction of the will to live with itself. As we found this contradiction in the case of the lowest manifestations of will, in the permanent struggle of all the forces of nature, and of all organic individuals for matter and time and space; and as we saw this antagonism come ever more to the front with terrible distinctness in the ascending grades of the objectification of the will, so at last in the highest grade, the Idea of man, it reaches the point at which, not only the individuals which express the same Idea extirpate each other, but even the same individual, declares war against itself. The vehemence with which it wills life, and revolts against what hinders it, namely, suffering, brings it to the point of destroying itself; so that the individual will, by its own act, puts an end to that body which is merely its particular visible expression, rather than permit suffering to break the will. Just because the suicide cannot give up willing, he gives up living. The will asserts itself here even in putting an end to its own manifestation, because it can no longer assert itself otherwise. As, however, it was just the suffering which it so shuns that was able, as mortification of the will, to bring it to the denial of itself, and hence to freedom, so in this respect the suicide is like a sick man, who, after a painful operation which would entirely cure him has been begun, will not allow it to be completed, but prefers to retain his disease. Suffering approaches and reveals itself as the possibility of the denial of will; but the will rejects it, in that it destroys the body, the manifestation of itself, in order that it may remain unbroken. This is the reason why almost all ethical teachers, whether philosophical or religious, condemn suicide, although they themselves can only give far-fetched sophistical reasons for their opinion. But if a human being was ever restrained from committing suicide by purely moral motives, the inmost meaning of this self-conquest (in whatever ideas his reason may have clothed it) was this: "I will not shun suffering, in order that it may help to put an end to the will to live, whose manifestation is so wretched, by so strengthening the knowledge of the real nature of the world which is already beginning to dawn upon me, that it may become the final quieter of my will, and may free me for ever."

§ 70. It might be supposed that the entire exposition (now terminated) of that which I call the denial of the will is irreconcilable with the earlier explanation of necessity, which belongs just as much to motivation as to every other form of the principle of sufficient reason, and according to which, motives, like all causes, are only occasional causes, upon which the character unfolds its nature and reveals it with the necessity of a natural law, on account of which we absolutely denied freedom as *liberum arbitrium indifferentiæ*. But far from suppressing this here, I would call it to mind. In truth, real freedom, *i.e.*, independence of the principle of sufficient reason, belongs to the will only as a thing-in-itself, not to its manifestation, whose essential form is everywhere the principle of sufficient reason, the element or sphere of necessity. But the one case in which that freedom can become directly visible in the manifestation is that in which it makes an end of what manifests itself, and because the mere manifestation, as a link in the chain of causes, the living body in time, which contains only phenomena, still continues to exist, the will which manifests itself through this phenomenon then stands in contradiction to it, for it denies what the phenomenon expresses. In such a case the organs of generation, for example, as the visible form of the sexual impulse, are there and in health; but yet, in the inmost consciousness, no sensual gratification is desired; and although the whole body is only the visible expression of the will to live, yet the motives which correspond to this will no longer act; indeed, the dissolution of the body, the end of the individual, and in this way the greatest check to the natural will, is welcome and desired. Now, the contradiction between our assertions of the necessity of the determination of the will by motives, in accordance with the character, on the one hand, and of the possibility of the entire suppression of the will whereby the motives become powerless, on the other hand, is only the repetition in the reflection of philosophy of this *real* contradiction which arises from the direct encroachment of the freedom of the will-in-itself, which knows no necessity, into the sphere of the necessity of its manifestation. But the key to the solution of these contradictions lies in the fact that the state in which the character is withdrawn from the power of motives does not proceed directly from the will, but from a changed form of knowledge. So long as the knowledge is merely that which is involved in the *principium individuationis* and exclusively follows the principle of sufficient reason, the strength of the motives is irresistible. But when the *principium individuationis* is seen through, when the Ideas, and indeed the inner nature of the thing-in-itself, as the same will in all, are directly recognised, and from this knowledge a universal quieter of volition arises, then the particular motives become ineffective, because the kind of knowledge which corresponds to them is obscured and thrown into the background by quite another kind. Therefore the character can never partially change, but must, with the consistency of a law of Nature, carry out in the particular the will which it manifests as a whole. But this whole, the character itself, may be completely suppressed or abolished through the change of knowledge referred to above. It is this suppression or abolition which Asmus, as quoted above, marvels at and denotes the "catholic, transcendental change"; and in the Christian Church it has very aptly been called the *new birth*, and the knowledge from which it springs, the *work of grace*. Therefore it is not a question of a change, but of an entire suppression of the character; and hence it arises that, however different the characters which experience the suppression may have been before it, after it they show a great similarity in their conduct, though every one still speaks very differently according to his conceptions and dogmas.

In this sense, then, the old philosophical doctrine of the freedom of the will, which has constantly been contested and constantly maintained, is not without ground, and the dogma of the Church of the work of grace and the new birth is not without meaning and significance. But we now unexpectedly see both united in one, and we can also now understand in what sense the excellent Malebranche could say, *"La liberté est un mystère,"* and was right. For precisely what the Christian mystics call *the work of grace* and *the new birth,* is for us the single direct expression of *the freedom of the will.* It only appears if the will, having attained to a knowledge of its own real nature, receives from this a *quieter,* by means of which the motives are deprived of their effect, which belongs to the province of another kind of knowledge, the objects of which are merely phenomena. The possibility of the freedom which thus expresses itself is the greatest prerogative of man, which is for ever wanting to the brute, because the condition of it is the deliberation of reason, which enables him to survey the whole of life independent of the impression of the present. The brute is entirely without the possibility of freedom, as, indeed, it is without the possibility of a proper or deliberate choice following upon a completed conflict of motives, which for this purpose would have to be abstract ideas. Therefore with the same necessity with which the stone falls to the earth, the hungry wolf buries its fangs in the flesh of its prey, without the possibility of the knowledge that it is itself the destroyed as well as the destroyer. *Necessity is the kingdom of nature; freedom is the kingdom of grace.*

Now because, as we have seen, that *self-suppression of the will* proceeds from knowledge, and all knowledge is involuntary, that denial of will also, that entrance into freedom, cannot be forcibly attained to by intention or design, but proceeds from the inmost relation of knowing and volition in the man, and therefore comes suddenly, as if spontaneously from without. This is why the Church has called it *the work of grace;* and that it still regards it as independent of the acceptance of grace corresponds to the fact that the effect of the quieter is finally a free act of will. And because, in consequence of such a work of grace, the whole nature of man is changed and reversed from its foundation, so that he no longer wills anything of all that he previously willed so intensely, so that it is as if a new man actually took the place of the old, the Church has called this consequence of the work of grace the *new birth*. For what it calls the *natural man*, to which it denies all capacity for good, is just the will to live, which must be denied if deliverance from an existence such as ours is to be attained. Behind our existence lies something else, which is only accessible to us if we have shaken off this world.

Having regard, not to the individuals according to the principle of sufficient reason, but to the Idea of man in its unity, Christian theology symbolises *nature*, the *assertion of the will to live* in Adam, whose sin, inherited by us, *i.e.*, our unity with him in the Idea, which is represented in time by the bond of procreation, makes us all partakers of suffering and eternal death. On the other hand, it symbolises *grace*, the *denial of the will, salvation*, in the incarnate God, who, as free from all sin, that is, from all willing of life, cannot, like us, have proceeded from the most pronounced assertion of the will, nor can he, like us, have a body which is through and through simply concrete will, manifestation of the will; but born of a pure virgin, he has only a phantom body. This last is the doctrine of the Docetæ, *i.e.*, certain Church Fathers, who in this respect are very consistent. It is especially taught by Apelles, against whom and his followers Tertullian wrote. But even Augustine comments thus on the passage, Rom. viii. 3, "God sent his Son in the likeness of sinful flesh": "*Non enim caro peccati erat, quæ non de carnali delectatione nata erat: sed tamen inerat ei similitudo carnis peccati, quia mortalis caro erat*" (*Liber 83, quæst. qu.* 66). He also teaches in his work entitled "*Opus Imperfectum*," i. 47, that inherited sin is both sin and punishment at once. It is already present in new-born children, but only shows itself if they grow up. Yet the origin of this sin

THE WORLD AS WILL

is to be referred to the will of the sinner. This sinner was Adam, but we all existed in him; Adam became miserable, and in him we have all become miserable. Certainly the doctrine of original sin (assertion of the will) and of salvation (denial of the will) is the great truth which constitutes the essence of Christianity, while most of what remains is only the clothing of it, the husk or accessories. Therefore Jesus Christ ought always to be conceived in the universal, as the symbol or personification of the denial of the will to live, but never as an individual, whether according to his mythical history given in the Gospels, or according to the probably true history which lies at the foundation of this. For neither the one nor the other will easily satisfy us entirely. It is merely the vehicle of that conception for the people, who always demand something actual. That in recent times Christianity has forgotten its true significance, and degenerated into dull optimism, does not concern us here.

It is further an original and evangelical doctrine of Christianity—which Augustine, with the consent of the leaders of the Church, defended against the platitudes of the Pelagians, and which it was the principal aim of Luther's endeavour to purify from error and re-establish, as he expressly declares in his book, *"De Servo Arbitrio,"*—the doctrine that *the will is not free,* but originally subject to the inclination to evil. Therefore according to this doctrine the deeds of the will are always sinful and imperfect, and can never fully satisfy justice; and, finally, these works can never save us, but faith alone, a faith which itself does not spring from resolution and free will, but from the work of grace, without our co-operation, comes to us as from without.

Not only the dogmas referred to before, but also this last genuine evangelical dogma belongs to those which at the present day an ignorant and dull opinion rejects as absurd or hides. For, in spite of Augustine and Luther, it adheres to the vulgar Pelagianism, which the rationalism of the day really is, and treats as antiquated those deeply significant dogmas which are peculiar and essential to Christianity in the strictest sense; while, on the other hand, it holds fast and regards as the principal matter only the dogma that originates in Judaism, and has been retained from it, and is merely historically connected with Christianity.

I have here introduced these dogmas of Christian theology, which in themselves are foreign to philosophy, merely for the purpose of showing that the ethical doctrine which proceeds from our whole investigation, and is in complete agreement and connection with all its parts, although new and unprecedented in its expression, is by no means so in its real nature, but fully agrees with the Christian dogmas properly so called, and indeed, as regards its essence, was contained and present in them. It also agrees quite as accurately with the doctrines and ethical teachings of the sacred books of India, which in their turn are presented in quite different forms. At the same time the calling to mind of the dogmas of the Christian Church serves to explain and illustrate the apparent contradiction between the necessity of all expressions of character when motives are presented (the kingdom of Nature) on the one hand, and the freedom of the will in itself, to deny itself, and abolish the character with all the necessity of the motives based upon it (the kingdom of grace) on the other hand.

§ 71. I now end the general account of ethics, and with it the whole development of that one thought which it has been my object to impart; and I by no means desire to conceal here an objection which concerns this last part of my exposition, but rather to point out that it lies in the nature of the question, and that it is quite impossible to remove it. It is this, that after our investigation has brought us to the point at which we have before our eyes perfect holiness, the denial and surrender of all volition, and thus the deliverance from a world whose whole existence we have found to be suffering, this appears to us as a passing away into empty nothingness.

That which is generally received as positive, which we call the real, and the negation of which the concept nothing in its most general significance expresses, is just the world as idea, which I have shown to be the objectivity and mirror of the will. Moreover, we ourselves are just this will and this world, and to them belongs the idea in general, as one aspect of them. The form of the idea is space and time, therefore for this point of view all that is real must be in some place and at some time. Denial, abolition, conversion of the will, is also the abolition and the vanishing of the world, its mirror. If we no longer perceive it in this mirror, we ask in vain where it has gone, and then, because it has no longer any where and when, complain that it has vanished into nothing.

A reversed point of view, if it were possible for us, would reverse the signs and show the real for us as nothing, and that nothing as the real. But as long as we ourselves are the will to live, this last—nothing as the real—can only be known and signified by us negatively, because the old saying of Empedocles, that like can only be known by like, deprives us here of all knowledge, as, conversely, upon it finally rests the possibility of all our actual knowledge, *i.e.*, the world as idea; for the world is the self-knowledge of the will.

If, however, it should be absolutely insisted upon that in some way or other a positive knowledge should be attained of that which philosophy can only express negatively as the denial of the will, there would be nothing for it but to refer to that state which all those who have attained to complete denial of the will have experienced, and which has been variously denoted by the names ecstasy, rapture, *illu-*

mination, union with God, and so forth; a state, however, which cannot properly be called knowledge, because it has not the form of subject and object, and is, moreover, only attainable in one's own experience and cannot be further communicated.

We, however, who consistently occupy the standpoint of philosophy, must be satisfied here with negative knowledge, content to have reached the utmost limit of the positive. We have recognised the inmost nature of the world as will, and all its phenomena as only the objectivity of will; and we have followed this objectivity from the unconscious working of obscure forces of Nature up to the completely conscious action of man. Therefore we shall by no means evade the consequence, that with the free denial, the surrender of the will, all those phenomena are also abolished; that constant strain and effort without end and without rest at all the grades of objectivity, in which and through which the world consists; the multifarious forms succeeding each other in gradation; the whole manifestation of the will; and, finally, also the universal forms of this manifestation, time and space, and also its last fundamental form, subject and object; all are abolished. No will: no idea, no world.

Before us there is certainly only nothingness. But that which resists this passing into nothing, our nature, is indeed just the will to live, which we ourselves are as it is our world. That we abhor annihilation so greatly, is simply another expression of the fact that we so strenuously will life, and are nothing but this will, and know nothing besides it. But if we turn our glance from our own needy and embarrassed condition to those who have overcome the world, in whom the will, having attained to perfect self-knowledge, found itself again in all, and then freely denied itself, and who then merely wait to see the last trace of it vanish with the body which it animates; then, instead of the restless striving and effort, instead of the constant transi-

tion from wish to fruition, and from joy to sorrow, instead
of the never-satisfied and never-dying hope which constitutes the life of the man who wills, we shall see that peace
which is above all reason, that perfect calm of the spirit,
that deep rest, that inviolable confidence and serenity, the
mere reflection of which in the countenance, as Raphael
and Correggio have represented it, is an entire and certain
gospel; only knowledge remains, the will has vanished. We
look with deep and painful longing upon this state, beside
which the misery and wretchedness of our own is brought
out clearly by the contrast. Yet this is the only consideration
which can afford us lasting consolation, when, on the one
hand, we have recognised incurable suffering and endless
misery as essential to the manifestation of will, the world;
and, on the other hand, see the world pass away with the
abolition of will, and retain before us only empty nothingness. Thus, in this way, by contemplation of the life and
conduct of saints, whom it is certainly rarely granted us to
meet with in our own experience, but who are brought before our eyes by their written history, and, with the stamp
of inner truth, by art, we must banish the dark impression
of that nothingness which we discern behind all virtue and
holiness as their final goal, and which we fear as children
fear the dark; we must not even evade it like the Indians,
through myths and meaningless words, such as reabsorption
in Brahma or the Nirvâna of the Buddhists. Rather do we
freely acknowledge that what remains after the entire abolition of will is for all those who are still full of will certainly nothing; but, conversely, to those in whom the will
has turned and has denied itself, this our world, which is so
real, with all its suns and milky-ways—is nothing.

THE METAPHYSICS OF THE LOVE OF THE SEXES

> "Ye wise men, highly, deeply learned,
>   Who think it out and know,
>   How, when, and where do all things pair?
>   Why do they kiss and love?
>   Ye men of lofty wisdom, say
>   What happened to me then;
>   Search out and tell me where, how, when,
>   And why it happened thus."
>   —Burger.

THIS chapter is the last of four whose various reciprocal
relations, by virtue of which, to a certain extent, they constitute a subordinate whole, the attentive reader will recognise without it being needful for me to interrupt my
exposition by recalling them or referring to them.

We are accustomed to see poets principally occupied with
describing the love of the sexes. This is as a rule the chief
theme of all dramatic works, tragical as well as comical,
romantic as well as classical, Indian as well as European.
Not less is it the material of by far the largest part of lyrical
and also of epic poetry, especially if we class with the latter
the enormous piles of romances which for centuries every
year has produced in all the civilised countries of Europe
as regularly as the fruits of the earth. As regards their main
contents, all these works are nothing else than many-sided
brief or lengthy descriptions of the passion we are speaking
of. Moreover, the most successful pictures of it—such, for
example, as Romeo and Juliet, *La Nouvelle Héloïse,* and
Werther—have gained immortal fame. Yet, when Roche-
foucauld imagines that it is the same with passionate love as
with ghosts, of which every one speaks, but which no one
has seen; and Lichtenberg also in his essay, *"Ueber die*

337

Macht der Liebe," disputes and denies the reality and natu-
ralness of that passion, they are greatly in error. For it is impossible that something which is foreign and contrary to
human nature, thus a mere imaginary caricature, could be
unweariedly represented by poetic genius in all ages, and
received by mankind with unaltered interest; for nothing
that is artistically beautiful can be without truth:—

> *"Rein n'est beau que le vrai; le vrai seul est aimable."*
> —Boil.

Certainly, however, it is also confirmed by experience, although not by the experience of every day, that that which
as a rule only appears as a strong yet still controllable inclination may rise under certain circumstances to a passion
which exceeds all others in vehemence, and which then sets
aside all considerations, overcomes all obstacles with incredible strength and perseverance, so that for its satisfaction life is risked without hesitation, nay, if that satisfaction
is still withheld, is given as the price of it. Werthers and
Jacopo Ortis exist not only in romance, but every year can
show at least half a dozen of them in Europe: *Sed ignotis
perierunt mortibus illi;* for their sorrows find no other
chroniclers than the writers of official registers or the re-
porters of the newspapers. Yet the readers of the police
news in English and French journals will attest the correctness of my assertion. Still greater, however, is the number of those whom the same passion brings to the madhouse.
Finally, every year can show cases of the double suicide of a
pair of lovers who are opposed by outward circumstances. In
such cases, however, it is inexplicable to me how those who,
certain of mutual love, expect to find the supremest bliss
in the enjoyment of this, do not withdraw themselves from
all connections by taking the extremest steps, and endure
all hardships, rather than give up with life a pleasure which
is greater than any other they can conceive. As regards

by large presents or other sacrifices, nay, even by cases of rape. That this particular child shall be begotten is, although unknown to the parties concerned, the true end of the whole love story; the manner in which it is attained is a secondary consideration. Now, however loudly persons of lofty and sentimental soul, and especially those who are in love, may cry out here about the gross realism of my view, they are yet in error. For is not the definite determination of the individualities of the next generation a much higher and more worthy end than those exuberant feelings and supersensible soap bubbles of theirs? Nay, among earthly aims, can there be one which is greater or more important? It alone corresponds to the profoundness with which passionate love is felt, to the seriousness with which it appears, and the importance which it attributes even to the trifling details of its sphere and occasion. Only so far as this end is assumed as the true one do the difficulties encountered, the infinite exertions and annoyances made and endured for the attainment of the loved object, appear proportionate to the matter. For it is the future generation, in its whole individual determinateness, that presses into existence by means of those efforts and toils. Nay, it is itself already active in that careful, definite, and arbitrary choice for the satisfaction of the sexual impulse which we call love. The growing inclination of two lovers is really already the will to live of the new individual which they can and desire to produce; nay, even in the meeting of their longing glances its new life breaks out, and announces itself as a future individuality harmoniously and well composed. They feel the longing for an actual union and fusing together into a single being, in order to live on only as this; and this longing receives its fulfilment in the child which is produced by them, as that in which the qualities transmitted by them both, fused and united in one being, live on. Conversely, the mutual, decided, and persistent aversion between a man and a maid is a sign that what they could produce would only be a badly organised, in itself inharmonious and unhappy being. Hence there lies a deeper meaning in the fact that Calderon, though he calls the atrocious Semiramis the daughter of the air, yet introduces her as the daughter of rape followed by the murder of the husband.

But, finally, what draws two individuals of different sex exclusively to each other with such power is the will to live, which exhibits itself in the whole species, and which here anticipates in the individual which these two can produce an objectification of its nature answering to its aims. This individual will have the will, or character, from the father, the intellect from the mother, and the corporisation from both; yet, for the most part, the figure will take more after the father, the size after the mother,—according to the law which comes out in the breeding of hybrids among the brutes, and principally depends upon the fact that the size of the fœtus must conform to the size of the uterus. Just as inexplicable as the quite special individuality of any man, which is exclusively peculiar to him, is also the quite special and individual passion of two lovers; indeed at bottom the two are one and the same: the former is *explicite* what the latter was *implicite*. The moment at which the parents begin to love each other—to fancy each other, as the very happy English expression has it—is really to be regarded as the first appearance of a new individual and the true *punctum saliens* of its life, and, as has been said, in the meeting and fixing of their longing glances there appears the first germ of the new being, which certainly, like all germs, is generally crushed out. This new individual is to a certain extent a new (Platonic) Idea; and now, as all Ideas strive with the greatest vehemence to enter the phenomenal world, eagerly seizing for this end upon the matter which the law of causality divides among them all, so also does this particular Idea of a human individuality strive with the greatest eager-

ness and vehemence towards its realisation in the phenomenon. This eagerness and vehemence is just the passion of
the two future parents for each other. It has innumerable
degrees, the two extremes of which may at any rate be described as Αφροδιτη πανδημος and ουρανια; in its nature,
however, it is everywhere the same. On the other hand, it
will be in degree so much the more powerful the more *in-
dividualised* it is; that is, the more the loved individual is
exclusively suited, by virtue of all his or her parts and qualities, to satisfy the desire of the lover and the need established
by his or her own individuality. What is really in question
here will become clear in the further course of our exposition. Primarily and essentially the inclination of love is
directed to health, strength, and beauty, consequently also to
youth; because the will first of all seeks to exhibit the specific character of the human species as the basis of all individuality: ordinary amorousness (Αφροδιτη πανδημος) does
not go much further. To these, then, more special claims
link themselves on, which we shall investigate in detail further on, and with which, when they see satisfaction before
them, the passion increases. But the highest degrees of this
passion spring from that suitableness of two individualities
to each other on account of which the will, *i.e.*, the character, of the father and the intellect of the mother, in their
connection, make up precisely that individual towards which
the will to live in general which exhibits itself in the whole
species feels a longing proportionate to this its magnitude,
and which therefore exceeds the measure of a mortal heart,
and the motives of which, in the same way, lie beyond the
sphere of the individual intellect. This is thus the soul of a
true and great passion. Now the more perfect is the mutual
adaptation of two individuals to each other in each of the
many respects which have further to be considered, the
stronger will be their mutual passion. Since there do not
exist two individuals exactly alike, there must be for each

particular man a particular woman—always with reference to what is to be produced—who corresponds most perfectly. A really passionate love is as rare as the accident of these two meeting. Since, however, the possibility of such a love is present in every one, the representations of it in the works of the poets are comprehensible to us. Just because the passion of love really turns about that which is to be produced, and its qualities, and because its kernel lies here, a friendship without any admixture of sexual love can exist between two young and good-looking persons of different sex, on account of the agreement of their disposition, character, and mental tendencies; nay, as regards sexual love there may even be a certain aversion between them. The reason of this is to be sought in the fact that a child produced by them would have physical or mental qualities which were inharmonious; in short, its existence and nature would not answer the ends of the will to live as it exhibits itself in the species. On the other hand, in the case of difference of disposition, character, and mental tendency, and the dislike, nay, enmity, proceeding from this, sexual love may yet arise and exist; when it then blinds us to all that; and if it here leads to marriage it will be a very unhappy one.

Let us now set about the more thorough investigation of the matter. Egoism is so deeply rooted a quality of all individuals in general, that in order to rouse the activity of an individual being egoistical ends are the only ones upon which we can count with certainty. Certainly the species has an earlier, closer, and greater claim upon the individual than the perishable individuality itself. Yet when the individual has to act, and even make sacrifices for the continuance and quality of the species, the importance of the matter cannot be made so comprehensible to his intellect, which is calculated merely with regard to individual ends, as to have its proportionate effect. Therefore in such a case nature can only attain its ends by implanting a certain illusion in the individual, on account of which that which is only a good for the species appears to him as a good for himself, so that when he serves the species he imagines he is serving himself; in which process a mere chimera, which vanishes immediately afterwards, floats before him, and takes the place of a real thing as a motive. This illusion is instinct. In the great majority of cases this is to be regarded as the sense of the species, which presents what is of benefit to *it* to the will. Since, however, the will has here become individual, it must be so deluded that it apprehends through the sense of the individual what the sense of the species presents to it, thus imagines it is following individual ends while in truth it is pursuing ends which are merely general (taking this word in its strictest sense). The external phenomenon of instinct we can best observe in the brutes where its rôle is most important; but it is in ourselves alone that we arrive at a knowledge of its internal process, as of everything internal. Now it is certainly supposed that man has almost no instinct; at any rate only this, that the new-born babe seeks for and seizes the breast of its mother. But, in fact, we have a very definite, distinct, and complicated instinct, that of the selection of another individual for the satisfaction of the sexual impulse, a selection which is so fine, so serious, and so arbitrary. With this satisfaction in itself, *i.e.*, so far as it is a sensual pleasure resting upon a pressing want of the individual, the beauty or ugliness of the other individual has nothing to do. Thus the regard for this which is yet pursued with such ardour, together with the careful selection which springs from it, is evidently connected, not with the chooser himself—although he imagines it is so—but with the true end, that which is to be produced, which is to receive the type of the species as purely and correctly as possible. Through a thousand physical accidents and moral aberrations there arise a great variety of deteriorations of the human form; yet its true type, in all its parts, is always again established: and this takes place under the guidance of the sense of beauty, which always directs the sexual impulse, and without which this sinks to the level of a disgusting necessity. Accordingly, in the first place, every one will decidedly prefer and eagerly desire the most beautiful individuals, *i.e.*, those in whom the character of the species is most purely impressed; but, secondly, each one will specially regard as beautiful in another individual those perfections which he himself lacks, nay, even those imperfections which are the opposite of his own. Hence, for example, little men love big women, fair persons like dark, &c. &c. The delusive ecstasy which seizes a man at the sight of a woman whose beauty is suited to him, and pictures to him a union with her as the highest good, is just the *sense of the species*, which, recognising the distinctly expressed stamp of the same, desires to perpetuate it with this individual. Upon this decided inclination to beauty depends the maintenance of the type of the species: hence it acts with such great power. We shall examine specially further on the considerations which it follows. Thus what guides man here is really an instinct which is directed to doing the best for the species, while the man himself imagines that he only seeks the heightening of his own pleasure. In fact, we have in this an instructive lesson concerning the inner nature of all instinct, which, as here, almost always sets the individual in motion for the good of the species. For clearly the pains with which an insect seeks out a particular flower, or fruit, or dung, or flesh, or, as in the case of the ichneumonidæ, the larva of another insect, in order to deposit its eggs there only, and to attain this end shrinks neither from trouble nor danger, is thoroughly analogous to the pains with which for his sexual satisfaction a man carefully chooses a woman with definite qualities which appeal to him individually, and strives so eagerly after her that in order to attain this end he often sacrifices his own happiness in life, contrary to all reason, by a foolish marriage, by love affairs which cost him wealth, honour, and life, even by crimes such as adultery or rape, all merely in order to serve the species in the most efficient way, although at the cost of the individual, in accordance with the will of nature which is everywhere sovereign. Instinct, in fact, is always an act which seems to be in accordance with the conception of an end, and yet is entirely without such a conception. Nature implants it wherever the acting individual is incapable of understanding the end, or would be unwilling to pursue it. Therefore, as a rule, it is given only to the brutes, and indeed especially to the lowest of them which have least understanding; but almost only in the case we are here considering it is also given to man, who certainly could understand the end, but would not pursue it with the necessary ardour, that is, even at the expense of his individual welfare. Thus here, as in the case of all instinct, the truth assumes the form of an illusion, in order to act upon the will. It is a voluptuous illusion which leads the man to believe he will find a greater pleasure in the arms of a woman whose beauty appeals to him than in those of any other; or which indeed, exclusively directed to a single individual, firmly convinces him that the possession of her will ensure him excessive happiness. Therefore he imagines he is taking trouble and making sacrifices for his own pleasure, while he does so merely for the maintenance of the regular type of the species, or else a quite special individuality, which can only come from these parents, is to attain to existence. The character of instinct is here so perfectly present, thus an action which seems to be in accordance with the conception of an end, and yet is entirely without such a conception, that he who is drawn by that illusion often abhors the end which alone guides it, procreation, and would like to hinder it; thus it is in the case of almost all illicit love affairs. In accordance with the character of the matter which has been explained, every lover will experience a marvellous disillusion after the pleasure he has at last attained, and will wonder that what was so longingly desired accomplishes nothing more than every other sexual satisfaction; so that he does not see himself much benefited by it. That wish was related to all his other wishes as the species is related to the individual, thus as the infinite to the finite. The satisfaction, on the other hand, is really only for the benefit of the species, and thus does not come within the consciousness of the individual, who, inspired by the will of the species, here served an end with every kind of sacrifice, which was not his own end at all. Hence, then, every lover, after the ultimate consummation of the great work, finds himself cheated; for the illusion has vanished by means of which the individual was here the dupe of the species. Accordingly Plato very happily says: "ἡδονη ἁπαντων αλαζο-νεοτατον" (voluptas omnium maxime vaniloqua), Phileb. 319.

But all this reflects light on the instincts and mechanical tendencies of the brutes. They also are, without doubt, involved in a kind of illusion, which deceives them with the prospect of their own pleasure, while they work so laboriously and with so much self-denial for the species, the bird builds its nest, the insect seeks the only suitable place for its eggs, or even hunts for prey which, unsuited for its own enjoyment, must be laid beside the eggs as food for the future larvæ, the bees, the wasps, the ants apply themselves to their skilful dwellings and highly complicated economy. They are all guided with certainty by an illusion, which conceals the service of the species under the mask of an egotistical end. This is probably the only way to comprehend the inner or subjective process that lies at the foundation of the manifestations of instinct. Outwardly, however, or objectively, we find in those creatures which are to a large extent governed by instinct, especially in insects, a preponderance of the ganglion system, i.e., the subjective nervous system, over the objective or cerebral system; from which we must conclude that they are moved, not so much by objective, proper apprehension as by subjective ideas exciting desire, which arise from the influence of the ganglion system upon the brain, and accordingly by a kind of illusion; and this will be the *physiological* process in the case of all instinct. For the sake of illustration I will mention as another example of instinct in the human species, although a weak one, the capricious appetite of women who are pregnant. It seems to arise from the fact that the nourishment of the embryo sometimes requires a special or definite modification of the blood which flows to it, upon which the food which produces such a modification at once presents itself to the pregnant woman as an object of ardent longing, thus here also an illusion arises. Accordingly woman has one instinct more than man; and the ganglion system is also much more developed in the woman. That man has fewer instincts than the brutes and that even these few can be easily led astray, may be explained from the great preponderance of the brain in his case. The sense of beauty which instinctively guides the selection for the satisfaction of sexual passion is led astray when it degenerates into the tendency to pederasty; analogous to the fact that the blue-bottle (*Musca vomitoria*), instead of depositing its eggs, according to instinct, in putrefying flesh, lays them in the blossom of the *Arum dracunculus*, deceived by the cadaverous smell of this plant.

Now that an instinct entirely directed to that which is to be produced lies at the foundation of all sexual love will receive complete confirmation from the fuller analysis of it, which we cannot therefore avoid. First of all we have to remark here that by nature man is inclined to inconstancy in love, woman to constancy. The love of the man sinks perceptibly from the moment it has obtained satisfaction; almost every other woman charms him more than the one he already possesses; he longs for variety. The love of the woman, on the other hand, increases just from that moment. This is a consequence of the aim of nature which is directed to the maintenance, and therefore to the greatest possible increase, of the species. The man can easily beget over a hundred children a year; the woman, on the contrary, with however many men, can yet only bring one child a year into the world (leaving twin births out of account). Therefore the man always looks about after other women; the woman, again, sticks firmly to the one man; for nature moves her, instinctively and without reflection, to retain the nourisher and protector of the future offspring. Accordingly faithfulness in marriage is with the man artificial, with the woman it is natural, and thus adultery on the part of the woman is much less pardonable than on the part of the man, both objectively on account of the consequences and also subjectively on account of its unnaturalness.

But in order to be thorough and gain full conviction that the pleasure in the other sex, however objective it may seem to us, is yet merely disguised instinct, i.e., sense of the species, which strives to maintain its type, we must investigate more fully the considerations which guide us in this pleasure, and enter into the details of this, rarely as these details which will have to be mentioned here may have figured in a philosophical work before. These considerations divide themselves into those which directly concern the type of the species, i.e., beauty, those which are concerned with physical qualities, and lastly, those which are merely relative, which arise from the requisite correction or neutralisation of the one-sided qualities and abnormities of the two individuals by each other. We shall go through them one by one.

The first consideration which guides our choice and inclination is age. In general we accept the age from the years when menstruation begins to those when it ceases, yet we give the decided preference to the period from the eighteenth to the twenty-eighth year. Outside of those years, on the other hand, no woman can attract us: an old woman, *i.e.*, one who no longer menstruates, excites our aversion. Youth without beauty has still always attraction; beauty without youth has none. Clearly the unconscious end which guides us here is the possibility of reproduction in general: therefore every individual loses attraction for the opposite sex in proportion as he or she is removed from the fittest period for begetting or conceiving. The second consideration is that of health. Acute diseases, only temporarily disturb us, chronic diseases or cachexia repel us, because they are transmitted to the child. The third consideration is the skeleton, because it is the basis of the type of the species. Next to age and disease nothing repels us so much as a deformed figure; even the most beautiful face cannot atone for it; on the contrary, even the ugliest face when accompanied by a straight figure is unquestionably preferred. Further, we feel every disproportion of the skeleton most strongly; for example, a stunted, dumpy, short-boned figure, and many such; also a halting gait, where it is not the result of an extraneous accident. On the other hand, a strikingly beautiful figure can make up for all defects: it enchants us. Here also comes in the great value which all attach to the smallness of the feet: it depends upon the fact that they are an essential characteristic of the species, for no animal has the tarsus and the metatarsus taken together so small as man, which accords with his upright walk; he is a plantigrade. Accordingly Jesus Sirach also says (xxvi. 23, according to the revised translation by Kraus): "A woman with a straight figure and beautiful feet is like columns of gold in sockets of silver." The teeth also are important; because they are essential for nourishment and quite specially hereditary. The fourth consideration is a certain fulness of flesh; thus a predominance of the vegetative function, of plasticity; because this promises abundant nourishment for the fœtus; hence great leanness repels us in a striking degree. A full female bosom exerts an exceptional charm upon the male sex; because, standing in direct connection with the female functions of propagation, it promises abundant nourishment to the new-born child. On the other hand, excessively fat women excite our disgust: the cause is that this indicates atrophy of the uterus, thus barrenness; which is not known by the head, but by instinct. The last consideration of all is the beauty of the face. Here also before everything else the bones are considered; therefore we look principally for a beautiful nose, and a short turned-up nose spoils everything. A slight inclination of the nose downwards or upwards has decided the happiness in life of innumerable maidens, and rightly so, for it concerns the type of the species. A small mouth, by means of small maxillæ, is very essential as specifically characteristic of the human countenance, as distinguished from the muzzle of the brutes. A receding or, as it were, cut-away chin is especially disagreeable, because *mentum prominulum* is an exclusive characteristic of our species. Finally comes the regard for beautiful eyes and forehead; it is connected with the psychical qualities, especially the intellectual which are inherited from the mother.

The unconscious considerations which, on the other hand, the inclination of women follows naturally cannot be so exactly assigned. In general the following may be asserted: They give the preference to the age from thirty to thirty-five years, especially over that of youths who yet really present the height of human beauty. The reason is that they are not guided by taste but by instinct, which recognises in the age named the acme of reproductive power. In general they look less to beauty, especially of the face. It is as if they took it upon themselves alone to impart this to the child. They are principally won by the strength of the man, and the courage which is connected with this; for these promise the production of stronger children, and also a brave protector for them. Every physical defect of the man, every divergence from the type, may with regard to the child be removed by the woman in reproduction, through the fact that she herself is blameless in these respects, or even exceeds in the opposite direction. Only those qualities of the man have to be excepted which are peculiar to his sex, and which therefore the mother cannot give to the child: such are the manly structure of the skeleton, broad shoulders, slender hips, straight bones, muscular power, courage, beard, &c. Hence it arises that women often love ugly men, but never an unmanly man, because they cannot neutralise his defects.

The second class of the considerations which lie at the foundation of sexual love are those which regard psychical qualities. Here we shall find that the woman is throughout attracted by the qualities of the heart or character in the man, as those which are inherited from the father. The woman is won especially by firmness of will, decision, and courage, and perhaps also by honesty and good-heartedness. On the other hand, intellectual gifts exercise no direct and instinctive power over her, just because they are not inherited from the father. Want of understanding does a man no harm with women; indeed extraordinary mental endowment, or even genius, might sooner influence them unfavourably as an abnormity. Hence one often sees an ugly, stupid, and coarse fellow get the better of a cultured, able, and amiable man with women. Also marriages from love are sometimes consummated between natures which are mentally very different: for example, the man is rough, powerful, and stupid; the woman tenderly sensitive, delicately thoughtful, cultured, æsthetic, &c.; or the man is a genius and learned, the woman a goose:

"Sic visum Veneri; cui placet impares
Formas atque animos sub juga aënea
Sævo mittere cum joco."

The reason is, that here quite other considerations than the intellectual predominate,—those of instinct. In marriage what is looked to is not intellectual entertainment, but the production of children: it is a bond of the heart, not of the head. It is a vain and absurd pretence when women assert that they have fallen in love with the mind of a man, or else it is the over-straining of a degenerate nature. Men, on the other hand, are not determined in their instinctive love by the qualities of character of the woman; hence so many Socrateses have found their Xantippes; for example, Shakespeare, Albrecht Dürer, Byron, &c. The intellectual qualities, however, certainly influence here, because they are inherited from the mother. Yet their influence is easily outweighed by that of physical beauty, which acts directly, as concerning a more essential point. However, it happens, either from the feeling or the experience of that influence, that mothers have their daughters taught the fine arts, languages, and so forth in order to make them attractive to men, whereby they wish to assist the intellect by artificial means, just as, in case of need, they assist the hips and the bosom. Observe that here we are speaking throughout only of that entirely immediate instinctive attraction from which alone love properly so called grows. That a woman of culture and understanding prizes understanding and intellect in a man, that a man from rational reflection should test and have regard to the character of his bride, has nothing to do with the matter with which we are dealing here. Such things lie at the bottom of a rational choice in marriage, but not of the passionate love, which is our theme.

Hitherto I have only taken account of the *absolute* considerations, *i.e.*, those which hold good for every one: I come now to the *relative* considerations, which are indi-

vidual, because in their case what is looked to is the rectifi-
cation of the type of the species, which is already defectively
presented, the correction of the divergences from it which
the chooser's own person already bears in itself, and thus
the return to the pure presentation of the type. Here, then,
each one loves what he lacks. Starting from the individual
constitution, and directed to the individual constitution, the
choice which rests upon such relative considerations is much
more definite, decided, and exclusive than that which proceeds merely from the absolute considerations; therefore
the source of really passionate love will lie, as a rule, in
these relative considerations, and only that of the ordinary
and slighter inclination in the absolute considerations. Accordingly it is not generally precisely correct and perfect
beauties that kindle great passions. For such a truly passionate inclination to arise something is required which can
only be expressed by a chemical metaphor: two persons must
neutralise each other, like acid and alkali, to a neutral salt.
The essential conditions demanded for this are the following. First: all sex is one-sided. This one-sidedness is more
distinctly expressed in one individual than in another; therefore in every individual it can be better supplemented and
neutralised by one than by another individual of the opposite sex, for each one requires a one-sidedness which is the
opposite of his own to complete the type of humanity in the
new individual that is to be produced, the constitution of
which is always the goal towards which all tends. Physiologists know that manhood and womanhood admit of innumerable degrees, through which the former sinks to the
repulsive gynander and hypospadæus, and the latter rises to
the graceful androgyne; from both sides complete hermaph-
rodism can be reached, at which point stand those individuals who, holding the exact mean between the two sexes,
can be attributed to neither, and consequently are unfit to
propagate the species. Accordingly, the neutralisation of

two individualities by each other, of which we are speaking, demands that the definite degree of *his* manhood shall exactly correspond to the definite degree of *her* womanhood; so that the one-sidedness of each exactly annuls that of the other. Accordingly, the most manly man will seek the most womanly woman, and *vice versâ*, and in the same way every individual will seek another corresponding to him or her in degree of sex. Now how far the required relation exists between two individuals is instinctively felt by them, and, together with the other relative considerations, lies at the foundation of the higher degrees of love. While, therefore, the lovers speak pathetically of the harmony of their souls, the heart of the matter is for the most part the agreement or suitableness pointed out here with reference to the being which is to be produced and its perfection, and which is also clearly of much more importance than the harmony of their souls, which often, not long after the marriage, resolves itself into a howling discord. Now, here come in the further relative considerations, which depend upon the fact that every one endeavours to neutralise by means of the other his weaknesses, defects, and deviations from the type, so that they will not perpetuate themselves, or even develop into complete abnormities in the child which is to be produced. The weaker a man is as regards muscular power the more will he seek for strong women; and the woman on her side will do the same. But since now a less degree of muscular power is natural and regular in the woman, women as a rule will give the preference to strong men. Further, the size is an important consideration. Little men have a decided inclination for big women, and *vice versâ*; and indeed in a little man the preference for big women will be so much the more passionate if he himself was begotten by a big father, and only remains little through the influence of his mother; because he has inherited from his father the vascular system and its energy, which was able to supply a large body with blood. If, on the other hand, his father and grandfather were both little, that inclination will make itself less felt. At the foundation of the aversion of a big woman to big men lies the intention of nature to avoid too big a race, if with the strength which *this* woman could impart to them they would be too weak to live long. If, however, such a woman selects a big husband, perhaps for the sake of being more presentable in society, then, as a rule, her offspring will have to atone for her folly. Further, the consideration as to the complexion is very decided. Blondes prefer dark persons, or brunettes; but the latter seldom prefer the former. The reason is, that fair hair and blue eyes are in themselves a variation from the type, almost an abnormity, analogous to white mice, or at least to grey horses. In no part of the world, not even in the vicinity of the pole, are they indigenous, except in Europe, and are clearly of Scandinavian origin. I may here express my opinion in passing that the white colour of the skin is not natural to man, but that by nature he has a black or brown skin, like our forefathers the Hindus; that consequently a white man has never originally sprung from the womb of nature, and that thus there is no such thing as a white race, much as this is talked of, but every white man is a faded or bleached one. Forced into the strange world, where he only exists like an exotic plant, and like this requires in winter the hothouse, in the course of thousands of years man became white. The gipsies, an Indian race which immigrated only about four centuries ago, show the transition from the complexion of the Hindu to our own.[1] Therefore in sexual love nature strives to return to dark hair and brown eyes as the primitive type; but the white colour of the skin has become a second nature, though not so that the brown of the Hindu repels us. Finally, each one also seeks in the particu-

[1] The fuller discussion of this subject will be found in the "Parerga," vol. ii. § 92 of the first edition (second edition, pp. 167-170).

lar parts of the body the corrective of his own defects and aberrations, and does so the more decidedly the more important the part is. Therefore snub-nosed individuals have an inexpressible liking for hook-noses, parrot-faces; and it is the same with regard to all other parts. Men with excessively slim, long bodies and limbs can find beauty in a body which is even beyond measure stumpy and short. The considerations with regard to temperament act in an analogous manner. Each will prefer the temperament opposed to his own; yet only in proportion as his own is decided. Whoever is himself in some respect very perfect does not indeed seek and love imperfection in this respect, but is yet more easily reconciled to it than others; because he himself insures the children against great imperfection of this part. For example, whoever is himself very white will not object to a yellow complexion; but whoever has the latter will find dazzling whiteness divinely beautiful. The rare case in which a man falls in love with a decidedly ugly woman occurs when, besides the exact harmony of the degree of sex explained above, the whole of her abnormities are precisely the opposite, and thus the corrective, of his. The love is then wont to reach a high degree.

The profound seriousness with which we consider and ponder each bodily part of the woman, and she on her part does the same, the critical scrupulosity with which we inspect a woman who begins to please us, the capriciousness of our choice, the keen attention with which the bridegroom observes his betrothed, his carefulness not to be deceived in any part, and the great value which he attaches to every excess or defect in the essential parts, all this is quite in keeping with the importance of the end. For the new being to be produced will have to bear through its whole life a similar part. For example, if the woman is only a little crooked, this may easily impart to her son a hump, and so in all the rest. Consciousness of all this certainly does not exist. On the contrary, every one imagines that he makes that careful selection in the interest of his own pleasure (which at bottom cannot be interested in it at all); but he makes it precisely as, under the presupposition of his own corporisation, is most in keeping with the interest of the species, to maintain the type of which as pure as possible is the secret task. The individual acts here, without knowing it, by order of something higher than itself, the species; hence the importance which it attaches to things which may and indeed must be, indifferent to itself as such. There is something quite peculiar in the profound unconscious seriousness with which two young persons of opposite sex who see each other for the first time regard each other, in the searching and penetrating glance they cast at one another, in the careful review which all the features and parts of their respective persons have to endure. This investigating and examining is the *meditation of the genius of the species* on the individual which is possible through these two and the combination of its qualities. According to the result of this meditation is the degree of their pleasure in each other and this yearning for each other. This yearning, even after it has attained a considerable degree, may be suddenly extinguished again by the discovery of something that had previously remained unobserved. In this way, then, the genius of the species meditates concerning the coming race in all who are capable of reproduction. The nature of this race is the great work with which Cupid is occupied, unceasingly active, speculating, and pondering. In comparison with the importance of his great affair, which concerns the species and all coming races, the affairs of individuals in their whole ephemeral totality are very trifling; therefore he is always ready to sacrifice these regardlessly. For he is related to them as an immortal to mortals, and his interests to theirs as infinite to finite. Thus, in the consciousness of managing affairs of a higher kind than all those which only

concern individual weal or woe, he carries them on su-
blimely, undisturbed in the midst of the tumult of war, or
in the bustle of business life, or during the raging of a
plague, and pursues them even into the seclusion of the
cloister.

We have seen in the above that the intensity of love increases with its individualisation, because we have shown
that the physical qualities of two individuals can be such
that, for the purpose of restoring as far as possible the type
of the species, the one is quite specially and perfectly the
completion or supplement of the other, which therefore desires it exclusively. Already in this case a considerable passion arises, which at once gains a nobler and more sublime
appearance from the fact that it is directed to an individual
object, and to it alone; thus, as it were, arises at the special
order of the species. For the opposite reason, the mere sexual
impulse is ignoble, because without individualisation it is
directed to all, and strives to maintain the species only as
regards quantity, with little respect to quality. But the in-
dividualising, and with it the intensity of the love, can reach
so high a degree that without its satisfaction all the good
things in the world, and even life itself, lose their value. It
is then a wish which attains a vehemence that no other wish
ever reaches, and therefore makes one ready for any sacrifice, and in case its fulfilment remains unalterably denied,
may lead to madness or suicide. At the foundation of such
an excessive passion there must lie, besides the considerations
we have shown above, still others which we have not thus
before our eyes. We must therefore assume that here not
only the corporisation, but the *will* of the man and the *intellect* of the woman are specially suitable to each other, in
consequence of which a perfectly definite individual can be
produced by them alone, whose existence the genius of the
species has here in view, for reasons which are inaccessible
to us, since they lie in the nature of the thing-in-itself. Or,

to speak more exactly, the will to live desires here to objectify itself in a perfectly definite individual, which can only be produced by this father with this mother. This metaphysical desire of the will in itself has primarily no other sphere of action in the series of existences than the hearts of the future parents, which accordingly are seized with this ardent longing, and now imagine themselves to desire on their own account what really for the present has only a purely metaphysical end, i.e., an end which lies outside the series of actually existing things. Thus it is the ardent longing to enter existence of the future individual which has first become possible here, a longing which proceeds from the primary source of all being, and exhibits itself in the phenomenal world as the lofty passion of the future parents for each other, paying little regard to all that is outside itself; in fact, as an unparalleled illusion, on account of which such a lover would give up all the good things of this world to enjoy the possession of this woman, who yet can really give him nothing more than any other. That yet it is just this possession that is kept in view here is seen from the fact that even this lofty passion, like all others, is extinguished in its enjoyment—to the great astonishment of those who are possessed by it. It also becomes extinct when, through the woman turning out barren (which, according to Hufeland, may arise from nineteen accidental constitutional defects), the real metaphysical end is frustrated; just as daily happens in millions of germs trampled under foot, in which yet the same metaphysical life principle strives for existence; for which there is no other consolation than that an infinity of space, time, and matter, and consequently inexhaustible opportunity for return, stands open to the will to live.

The view which is here expounded must once have been present to the mind of Theophrastus Paracelsus, even if only in a fleeting form, though he has not handled this subject, and my whole system of thought was foreign to him; for, in quite a different context and in his desultory manner, he wrote the following remarkable words: "*Hi sunt, quos Deus copulavit, ut eam, quæ fuit Uriæ et David; quamvis ex diametro (sic enim sibi humana mens persuadebat) cum justo et legitimo matrimonio pugnaret hoc. . . . sed propter Salomonem,* QUI ALIUNDE NASCI NON POTUIT, *nisi ex Bathseba, conjuncto David semine, quamvis meretrice, conjunxit eos Deus*" (*De vita longa,* i. 5).

The longing of love, the ἱμερος, which the poets of all ages are unceasingly occupied with expressing in innumerable forms, and do not exhaust the subject, nay, cannot do it justice, this longing, which attaches the idea of endless happiness to the possession of a particular woman, and unutterable pain to the thought that this possession cannot be attained,—this longing and this pain cannot obtain their material from the wants of an ephemeral individual; but they are the signs of the spirit of the species, which sees here, to be won or lost, a means for the attainment of its ends which cannot be replaced, and therefore groans deeply. The species alone has infinite life, and therefore is capable of infinite desires, infinite satisfaction, and infinite pain. But these are here imprisoned in the narrow breast of a mortal. No wonder, then, if such a breast seems like to burst, and can find no expression for the intimations of infinite rapture or infinite misery with which it is filled. This, then, affords the materials for all erotic poetry of a sublime kind, which accordingly rises into transcendent metaphors, soaring above all that is earthly. This is the theme of Petrarch, the material for the St. Preuxs, Werthers, and Jacopo Ortis, who apart from it could not be understood nor explained. For that infinite esteem for the loved one cannot rest upon some spiritual excellences, or in general upon any objective, real qualities of hers; for one thing, because she is often not sufficiently well known to the lover, as was the case with

Petrarch. The spirit of the species alone can see at one glance what *worth* she has for *it*, for its ends. And great passions also arise, as a rule, at the first glance:

> "Who ever loved that loved not at first sight?"
> —SHAKESPEARE, "As You Like It," iii. 5.

In this regard a passage in the romance of *"Guzman de Alfarache,"* by Mateo Aleman, which has been famous for 250 years, is remarkable: *"No es necessario, para que uno ame, que pase distancia de tiempo, que siga discurso, ni haga eleccion, sino que con aquella primera y sola vista, concurran juntamente cierta correspondencia ó consonancia, ó lo que acá solemos vulgarmente decir, una confrontacion de sangre, á que por particular influxo suelen mover las estrellas."* (For one to love it is not necessary that much time should pass, that he should set about reflecting and make a choice; but only that at that first and only glance a certain correspondence and consonance should be encountered on both sides, or that which in common life we are wont to call a *sympathy of the blood*, and to which a special influence of the stars generally impels), P. ii. lib. iii. c. 5. Accordingly the loss of the loved one, through a rival, or through death, is also for the passionate lover a pain that surpasses all others, just because it is of a transcendental kind, since it affects him not merely as an individual, but attacks him in his *essentia æterna*, in the life of the species into whose special will and service he was here called. Hence jealousy is such torment and so grim, and the surrender of the loved one is the greatest of all sacrifices. A hero is ashamed of all lamentations except the lamentation of love, because in this it is not he but the species that laments. In Calderon's "Zenobia the Great" there is in the first act a scene between Zenobia and Decius in which the latter says:

> *"Cielos, luego tu me quieres?*
> *Perdiera cien mil victorias,*
> *Volviérame,"* &c.

(Heaven! then thou lovest me? For this I would lose a thousand victories, would turn about, &c.)

Here, honour, which hitherto outweighed every interest, is beaten out of the field as soon as sexual love, *i.e.*, the interest of the species, comes into play, and sees before it a decided advantage; for this is infinitely superior to every interest of mere individuals, however important it may be. Therefore to this alone honour, duty, and fidelity yield after they have withstood every other temptation, including the threat of death. In the same way we find in private life that conscientiousness is in no point so rare as in this: it is here sometimes set aside even by persons who are otherwise honest and just, and adultery is recklessly committed when passionate love, *i.e.*, the interest of the species, has mastered them. It even seems as if in this they believed themselves to be conscious of a higher right than the interests of individuals can ever confer; just because they act in the interest of the species. In this reference Chamfort's remark is worth noticing: "*Quand un homme et une femme ont l'un pour l'autre une passion violente, il me semble toujours que quelque soient les obstacles qui les séparent, un mari, des parens, etc., les deux amans sont l'un a l'autre, de par la Nature, qu'ils s'appartiennent de droit divin, malgré les lois et les conventions humaines.*" Whoever is inclined to be incensed at this should be referred to the remarkable indulgence which the Saviour shows in the Gospel to the woman taken in adultery, in that He also assumes the same guilt in the case of all present. From this point of view the greater part of the "Decameron" appears as mere mocking and jeering of the genius of the species at the rights and interests of individuals which it tramples under foot. Differences of rank and all similar circumstances, when they oppose the union of passionate lovers, are set aside with the same ease and treated as nothing by the genius of the species, which, pursuing its ends that concern innumerable generations, blows off as spray such human laws and scruples. From the same deep-lying grounds, when the ends of passionate love are concerned, every danger is willingly encountered, and those who are otherwise timorous here become courageous. In plays and novels also we see, with ready sympathy, the young persons who are fighting the battle of their love, *i.e.*, the interest of the species, gain the victory of their elders, who are thinking only of the welfare of the individuals. For the efforts of the lovers appear to us as much more important, sublime, and therefore right, than anything that can be opposed to them, as the species is more important than the individual. Accordingly the fundamental theme of almost all comedies is the appearance of the genius of the species with its aims, which are opposed to the personal interest of the individuals presented, and therefore threaten to undermine their happiness. As a rule it attains its end, which, as in accordance with poetical justice, satisfies the spectator, because he feels that the aims of the species are much to be preferred to those of the individual. Therefore at the conclusion he leaves the victorious lovers quite confidently, because he shares with them the illusion that they have founded their own happiness, while they have rather sacrificed it to the choice of the species, against the will and foresight of their elders. It has been attempted in single, abnormal comedies to reverse the matter and bring about the happiness of the individuals at the cost of the aims of the species; but then the spectator feels the pain which the genius of the species suffers, and is not consoled by the advantages which are thereby assured to the individuals. As examples of this kind two very well-known little pieces occur to me: *"La reine de 16 ans,"* and *"Le mariage de raison."* In tragedies containing love affairs, since the aims of the species are frustrated, the lovers who were its tools, generally perish also; for example, in "Romeo and Juliet," "Tancred,"[2]

"Don Carlos," "Wallenstein," "The Bride of Messina," and many others.

The love of a man often affords comical, and sometimes also tragical phenomena; both because, taken possession of by the spirit of the species, he is now ruled by this, and no longer belongs to himself: his conduct thereby becomes unsuited to the individual. That which in the higher grades of love imparts such a tinge of poetry and sublimeness to his thoughts, which gives them even a transcendental and hyperphysical tendency, on account of which he seems to lose sight altogether of his real, very physical aim, is at bottom this, that he is now inspired by the spirit of the species whose affairs are infinitely more important than all those which concern mere individuals, in order to found under the special directions of this spirit the whole existence of an indefinitely long posterity with this individual and exactly determined nature, which it can receive only from him as father and the woman he loves as mother, and which otherwise could never, *as such*, attain to existence, while the objectification of the will to live expressly demands this existence. It is the feeling that he is acting in affairs of such transcendent importance which raises the lover so high above everything earthly, nay, even above himself, and gives such a hyperphysical clothing to his very physical desires, that love becomes a poetical episode even in the life of the most prosaic man; in which last case the matter sometimes assumes a comical aspect. That mandate of the will which objectifies itself in the species exhibits itself in the consciousness of the lover under the mask of the anticipation of an infinite blessedness which is to be found for him in the union with this female individual. Now, in the highest grade of love this chimera becomes so radiant that if it cannot be attained life itself loses all charm, and now appears so joyless, hollow, and insupportable that the disgust at it even overcomes the fear of death, so that it is then sometimes voluntarily cut short. The will of such a man has been caught in the vortex of the will of the species, or this has obtained such a great predominance over the individual will that if such a man cannot be effective in the first capacity, he disdains to be so in the last. The individual is here too weak a vessel to be capable of enduring the infinite longing of the will of the species concentrated upon a definite object. In this case, therefore, the issue is suicide, sometimes the double suicide of the two lovers, unless, to save life, nature allows madness to intervene, which then covers with its veil the consciousness of that hopeless state. No year passes without proving the reality of what has been expounded by several cases of all these kinds.

Not only, however, has the unsatisfied passion of love sometimes a tragic issue, but the satisfied passion also leads oftener to unhappiness than to happiness. For its demands often conflict so much with the personal welfare of him who is concerned that they undermine it, because they are incompatible with his other circumstances, and disturb the plan of life built upon them. Nay, not only with external circumstances is love often in contradiction, but even with the lover's own individuality, for it flings itself upon persons who, apart from the sexual relation, would be hateful, contemptible, and even abhorrent to the lover. But so much more powerful is the will of the species than that of the individual that the lover shuts his eyes to all those qualities which are repellent to him, overlooks all, ignores all, and binds himself for ever to the object of his passion—so entirely is he blinded by that illusion, which vanishes as soon as the will of the species is satisfied, and leaves behind a detested companion for life. Only from this can it be explained that we often see very reasonable and excellent men bound to termagants and she-devils, and cannot conceive how they could have made such a choice. On this account the ancients represented love as blind. Indeed, a lover may

even know distinctly and feel bitterly the faults of temperament and character of his bride, which promise him a miserable life, and yet not be frightened away:—

> "I ask not, I care not,
> If guilt's in thy heart,
> I know that I love thee
> Whatever thou art."

For ultimately he seeks not his own things, but those of a
third person, who has yet to come into being, although he is
involved in the illusion that what he seeks is his own affair.
But it is just this not seeking of one's own things which is
everywhere the stamp of greatness, that gives to passionate
love also a touch of sublimity, and makes it a worthy subject of poetry. Finally, sexual love is compatible even with
the extremest hatred towards its object: therefore Plato has
compared it to the love of the wolf for the sheep. This case
appears when a passionate lover, in spite of all efforts and
entreaties, cannot obtain a favourable hearing on any condition:—

> "I love and hate her."
> —SHAKESPEARE, Cymb., iii. 5.

The hatred of the loved one which then is kindled sometimes goes so far that the lover murders her, and then himself. One or two examples of this generally happen every
year; they will be found in the newspapers. Therefore
Goethe's lines are quite correct:—

> "By all despised love! By hellish element!
> Would that I knew a worse, that I might swear by!"

It is really no hyperbole if a lover describes the coldness of
his beloved and the delight of her vanity, which feeds on his
sufferings, as cruelty; for he is under the influence of an
impulse which, akin to the instinct of insects, compels him,
in spite of all grounds of reason, to pursue his end uncon-

ditionally, and to undervalue everything else: he cannot give it up. Not one but many a Petrarch has there been who was compelled to drag through life the unsatisfied ardour of love, like a fetter, an iron weight at his foot, and breathe his sighs in lonely woods; but only in the one Petrarch dwelt also the gift of poetry; so that Goethe's beautiful lines hold good of him:—

> "And when in misery the man was dumb
> A god gave me the power to tell my sorrow."

In fact, the genius of the species wages war throughout with the guardian geniuses of individuals, is their pursuer and enemy, always ready relentlessly to destroy personal happiness in order to carry out its ends; nay, the welfare of whole nations has sometimes been sacrificed to its humours. An example of this is given us by Shakespeare in "Henry VI.," pt. iii., act 3, sc. 2 and 3. All this depends upon the fact that the species, as that in which the root of our being lies, has a closer and earlier right to us than the individual; hence its affairs take precedence. From the feeling of this the ancients personified the genius of the species in Cupid, a malevolent, cruel, and therefore ill-reputed god, in spite of his childish appearance; a capricious, despotic demon, but yet lord of gods and men:

> "Συ δ'ω θεων τυραννε κ'ανθρωπων, Ερως!"
> (*Tu, deorum hominumque tyranne, Amor!*)

A deadly shot, blindness, and wings are his attributes. The latter signify inconstancy; and this appears, as a rule, only with the disillusion which is the consequence of satisfaction.

Because the passion depended upon an illusion, which represented that which has only value for the species as valuable for the individual, the deception must vanish after the attainment of the end of the species. The spirit of the species which took possession of the individual sets it free again

Forsaken by this spirit, the individual falls back into its original limitation and narrowness, and sees with wonder that after such a high, heroic, and infinite effort nothing has resulted for its pleasure but what every sexual gratification affords. Contrary to expectation, it finds itself no happier than before. It observes that it has been the dupe of the will of the species. Therefore, as a rule, a Theseus who has been made happy will forsake his Ariadne. If Petrarch's passion had been satisfied, his song would have been silenced from that time forth, like that of the bird as soon as the eggs are laid.

Here let me remark in passing that however much my metaphysics of love will displease the very persons who are entangled in this passion, yet if rational considerations in general could avail anything against it, the fundamental truth disclosed by me would necessarily fit one more than anything else to subdue it. But the saying of the old comedian will, no doubt, remain true: "*Quæ res in se neque consilium, neque modum habet ullum, eam consilio regere non potes.*"

Marriages from love are made in the interest of the species, not of the individuals. Certainly the persons concerned imagine they are advancing their own happiness; but their real end is one which is foreign to themselves, for it lies in the production of an individual which is only possible through them. Brought together by this aim, they ought henceforth to try to get on together as well as possible. But very often the pair brought together by that instinctive illusion, which is the essence of passionate love, will, in other respects, be of very different natures. This comes to light when the illusion vanishes, as it necessarily must. Accordingly love marriages, as a rule, turn out unhappy; for through them the coming generation is cared for at the expense of the present. "*Quien se casa por amores, ha de vivir con dolores*" (Who marries from love must live in sorrow), says the Spanish proverb. The opposite is the case with mar-

riages contracted for purposes of convenience, generally in
accordance with the choice of the parents. The considerations prevailing here, of whatever kind they may be, are at
least real, and cannot vanish of themselves. Through them,
however, the happiness of the present generation is certainly
cared for, to the disadvantage of the coming generation, and
notwithstanding this it remains problematical. The man
who in his marriage looks to money more than to the satisfaction of his inclination lives more in the individual than in
the species; which is directly opposed to the truth; hence it
appears unnatural, and excites a certain contempt. A girl
who, against the advice of her parents, rejects the offer of a
rich and not yet old man, in order, setting aside all considerations of convenience, to choose according to her instinctive inclination alone, sacrifices her individual welfare to
the species. But just on this account one cannot withhold
from her a certain approbation; for she has preferred what
is of most importance, and has acted in the spirit of nature
(more exactly, of the species), while the parents advised in
the spirit of individual egoism. In accordance with all this,
it appears as if in making a marriage either the individual or
the interests of the species must come off a loser. And this is
generally the case; for that convenience and passionate love
should go hand in hand is the rarest of lucky accidents. The
physical, moral, or intellectual deficiency of the nature of
most men may to some extent have its ground in the fact
that marriages are ordinarily entered into not from pure
choice and inclination, but from all kinds of external considerations, and on account of accidental circumstances. If,
however, besides convenience, inclination is also to a certain
extent regarded, this is, as it were, an agreement with the
genius of the species. Happy marriages are well known to
be rare; just because it lies in the nature of marriage that its
chief end is not the present but the coming generation.
However, let me add, for the consolation of tender, loving

natures, that sometimes passionate sexual love associates it-self with a feeling of an entirely different origin—real friendship based upon agreement of disposition, which yet for the most part only appears when sexual love proper is extinguished in its satisfaction. This friendship will then generally spring from the fact that the supplementing and corresponding physical, moral, and intellectual qualities of the two individuals, from which sexual love arose, with reference to the child to be produced, are, with reference also to the individuals themselves, related to each other in a supplementary manner as opposite qualities of tempera-ment and mental gifts, and thereby form the basis of a har-mony of disposition.

The whole metaphysics of love here dealt with stands in close connection with my metaphysics in general, and the light which it throws upon this may be summed up as follows.

We have seen that the careful selection for the satisfac-tion of the sexual impulse, a selection which rises through innumerable degrees up to that of passionate love, depends upon the highly serious interest which man takes in the special personal constitution of the next generation. Now this exceedingly remarkable interest confirms two truths which have been set forth in the preceding chapters. (1.) The indestructibility of the true nature of man, which lives on in that coming generation. For that interest which is so lively and eager, and does not spring from reflection and in-tention, but from the inmost characteristics and tendencies of our nature, could not be so indelibly present and exer-cise such great power over man if he were absolutely perish-able, and were merely followed in time by a race actually and entirely different from him. (2.) That his true nature lies more in the species than in the individual. For that in-terest in the special nature of the species, which is the root of all love, from the passing inclination to the serious passion, is for every one really the highest concern, the success or failure of which touches him most sensibly; therefore it is called *par excellence* the affair of the heart. Moreover, when this interest has expressed itself strongly and decidedly, everything which merely concerns one's own person is postponed and necessarily sacrificed to it. Through this, then, man shows that the species lies closer to him than the individual, and he lives more immediately in the former than in the latter. Why does the lover hang with complete abandonment on the eyes of his chosen one, and is ready to make every sacrifice for her? Because it is his immortal part that longs after her; while it is only his mortal part that desires everything else. That vehement or intense longing directed to a particular woman is accordingly an immediate pledge of the indestructibility of the kernel of our being, and of its continued existence in the species. But to regard this continued existence as something trifling and insufficient is an error which arises from the fact that under the conception of the continued life of the species one thinks nothing more than the future existence of beings similar to us but in no regard identical with us; and this again because, starting from knowledge directed towards without, one takes into consideration only the external form of the species as we apprehend it in perception, and not its inner nature. But it is just this inner nature which lies at the foundation of our own consciousness as its kernel, and hence indeed is more immediate than this itself, and, as thing-in-itself, free from the *principium individuationis*, is really the same and identical in all individuals, whether they exist together or after each other. Now this is the will to live, thus just that which desires life and continuance so vehemently. This accordingly is spared and unaffected by death. It can attain to no better state than its present one; and consequently for it, with life, the constant suffering and striving of the individuals is certain. To free it from this is reserved for the denial of the will to live, as the means by which the individual will breaks away from the stem of the species, and surrenders that existence in it. We lack conceptions for that which it now is; indeed all data for such conceptions are wanting. We can only describe it as that which is free to be will to live or not. Buddhism denotes the latter case by the word Nirvâna. It is the point which remains for ever unattainable to all human knowledge, just as such.

If now, from the standpoint of this last consideration, we contemplate the turmoil of life, we behold all occupied with its want and misery, straining all their powers to satisfy its infinite needs and to ward off its multifarious sorrows, yet without daring to hope anything else than simply the preservation of this tormented existence for a short span of time. In between, however, in the midst of the tumult, we see the glances of two lovers meet longingly: yet why so secretly, fearfully, and stealthily? Because these lovers are the traitors who seek to perpetuate the whole want and drudgery, which would otherwise speedily reach an end; this they wish to frustrate, as others like them have frustrated it before.

THE END

The Best of the World's Best Books
COMPLETE LIST OF TITLES IN

THE MODERN LIBRARY

For convenience in ordering use number at right of title

MISCELLANEOUS

MODERN LIBRARY GIANTS

*A series of full-sized library editions of books that formerly
were available only in cumbersome and expensive sets.*
THE MODERN LIBRARY GIANTS REPRESENT A
SELECTION OF THE WORLD'S GREATEST BOOKS

These volumes contain from 600 to 1,400 pages each
